LEADING A SOFTWARE
DEVELOPMENT TEAM //

LEADING A SOFTWARE DEVELOPMENT TEAM //
A DEVELOPER'S GUIDE TO SUCCESSFULLY LEADING PEOPLE AND PROJECTS
RICHARD WHITEHEAD

Addison-Wesley

An imprint of PEARSON EDUCATION

Harlow, England ■ London ■ New York ■ Reading, Massachusetts ■ San Francisco ■
Toronto ■ Don Mills, Ontario ■ Sydney Tokyo ■ Singapore ■ Hong Kong ■ Seoul ■
Taipei ■ Cape Town ■ Madrid ■ Mexico City ■ Amsterdam ■ Munich ■ Paris ■ Milan

PEARSON EDUCATION LIMITED

Head Office:
Edinburgh Gate
Harlow CM20 2JE
Tel: +44 (0)1279 623623
Fax: +44 (0)1279 431059

London Office:
128 Long Acre
London WC2E 9AN
Tel: +44 (0)20 7447 2000
Fax: +44 (0)20 7240 5771
Website: www.informit.uk.com
www.aw.com/cseng/

First published in Great Britain in 2001

© Pearson Education Ltd 2001

The right of Richard Whitehead to be identified as Author of this Work has been
asserted by him in accordance with the Copyright, Designs and Patents Act 1988.

ISBN 0-201-67526-9

British Library Cataloguing in Publication Data
A CIP catalogue record for this book can be obtained from the British Library

Library of Congress Cataloging in Publication Data
Applied for.

Many of the designations used by manufacturers and sellers to distinguish their products are
claimed as trademarks. Pearson Education Limited has made every attempt to supply trademark
information about manufacturers and their products mentioned in this book.

10 9 8 7 6 5 4 3 2 1

Designed by Sue Lamble
Typeset by Pantek Arts Ltd, Maidstone, Kent
Printed and bound in Great Britain by Biddles Ltd.

The publishers' policy is to use paper manufactured from sustainable forests.

For my family

ABOUT THE AUTHOR

RICHARD WHITEHEAD has led a number of software development teams over recent years, ranging from a multinational project to take a medical scanner from research in Silicon Valley into production in England, to a short project to deliver up-to-the-minute traffic information over the web.

He has had a wide and varied experience in industries as diverse as diamond prospecting, medicine, communications, transport and digital mapping, and in companies of many sizes and cultures from a high-tech start-up to a multi-billion dollar multinational.

If you wish to comment on anything in this book, you can do so by visiting his website, www.richardwhitehead.com

CONTENTS

REQUIREMENTS CAPTURE

STRESS AND CONFLICT MANAGEMENT

RELATIONSHIP WITH MANAGEMENT

MAKING DECISIONS

ANALYSIS AND DESIGN

TESTING AND PROJECT RELEASE

CONCLUSIONS

BIBLIOGRAPHY

APPENDICES

INDEX

FOREWORD

Congratulations! You have been promoted! You loved being a developer, and your company thought you were doing a great job. Your reward is that you have been named a team leader, heading a group of developers in creating or maintaining a software-related system. Why then do you feel uncomfortable with your new title and responsibilities? For two reasons. First, you have never before been a team leader, so you feel a bit like a fish out of water. Second, suddenly you have shifted from the technical to the management ladder. In other words, because you did software development well, you are now being asked to oversee others doing software development – so the company has taken away the tasks you were so good at and were most familiar with.

Fear not. This book will help you become an effective and respected team leader. Organized by the kinds of questions you are likely to ask, 'Leading a Software Development Team' suggests strategies for finding the right balance between technology and management. With this book, you can avoid the Peter Principle (rising to your level of incompetence) and instead lead your team in producing quality products enjoyably and successfully.

Richard Whitehead's advice derives from his own experiences as developer, team leader and manager. His many practical suggestions tell you how to balance technical needs with business needs, and how to make tough choices about human resources as well as technology. What you read here is sometimes unorthodox; he's not a fan of practices that have little or no clear benefit other than to check off an activity on a list. But his view from the trenches will help guide you in making your own decisions in the context of your own organization and its values. So read on. With Whitehead as your mentor, you can anticipate and diffuse problems. Soon you will be as effective as a team leader as you were a developer.

Shari Lawrence Pfleeger
President, Systems/Software, Inc.
January 2001

PREFACE

WHY THIS BOOK WAS WRITTEN

As software engineering matures as a profession, the position of team leader
– the person responsible for the technical direction of the project and the
work of the other engineers on the team – is becoming increasingly recognized as crucial to the success of a software development project.

This book provides the help needed by team leaders to enable them to
rise to the responsibility of leading a project. It is a practical book, containing tried and tested advice and techniques to help leaders overcome
common problems, lead other people, make good decisions, and get
projects out on time.

WHO THIS BOOK IS FOR

This book is for anyone whose work involves *both* of the following:

▶ making detailed decisions concerning the architecture, design or coding
of software products, or performing hands-on software development;

▶ leading, managing or mentoring other people who are developing software.

This book is especially relevant for someone who finds themselves leading
a software development team for the first time, or who feels that their
skills with people are not as good as their skills with technology, and
wants some help and direction.

This book is most relevant for someone leading a medium-sized team, say 4
to 8 people. It should also prove useful, to a lesser extent, to the leader of a
single-person project, or to a leader of a larger team or of a team of teams.

This is a practical book for practising engineers. It is not intended to teach management theory, nor to contain the very latest thinking in every field. It promotes those practices that have been shown to work in the real world.

ABOUT BEING A SOFTWARE TEAM LEADER

A really good software team leader needs to be totally competent with technology, and also very good at getting the best out of other people. It's a unique position, combining detailed hands-on software knowledge and skill, and yet requiring the leader to be able to step back from the details and see the broader picture.

The way that a team is led has a critical impact on the success of a software project. The team leader makes a vital contribution to the quality of the software, the appropriateness of the technical decisions made, and the quality of team-spirit and motivation that the team members enjoy.

Becoming a team leader forces you to have a different perspective on software development. As a developer, you know that you will be judged mostly by the quality of the designs and the code that you produce. But as a leader, you will be judged in two different ways:

▶ By your bosses, you will be judged on how quickly and cheaply your project is completed and by how satisfied the customers or end-users are.

▶ By your team, you will be judged on the soundness of your judgement and on the way you work with people.

This book aims to help you be better at these things and so to earn more respect both from your bosses and from other team members.

Leading a software development team can be stressful, and it can be risky. It might not be as stressful or as risky as, say, managing a football team; but it does share some of the same stresses and pressures of trying to satisfy many people who are hungry for success, with there being no prospect of getting a second chance if things go wrong.

Not surprisingly, it's a job that not many people can do well. The difficulty of the task makes it all the more rewarding when you know you are doing it well. Once you have led a successful project, you will want to keep doing it and you will want to keep getting better at it. I hope that you find this book useful in helping you to achieve and to build on success.

HOW THIS BOOK IS ORGANIZED

The book is organized around real-world problems faced by leaders in their everyday work, such as 'how do I draw up a project plan?' and 'how do I earn the respect of my team?'. Many real problems have both people aspects and technical aspects, and the book approaches these together, as different dimensions of a given situation, rather than as completely separate issues.

However, as can be seen from the contents page, the sections have been collected into groupings according to the major aspect of each, so you can start reading about a particular aspect of the job if you feel the need to do so.

The individual sections are quite self-contained, and include references to other relevant sections and to the bibliography where relevant, so they can be read in any order.

ABOUT JOB TITLES SUCH AS 'TEAM LEADER' AND 'PROJECT MANAGER' IN THIS BOOK

The software industry does not have a universally recognized set of job titles; they tend to vary from one organization to another. In this book, I have used the following job titles:

▶ **Developer** Someone who does the hands-on job of making software. Making detailed technical decisions, designing, coding, testing, documenting. May be responsible for their own area of development but not for the project as a whole.

▶ **Team leader** Someone who makes technical decisions concerning the architecture, design or code of a software project. Responsible for the technical success of the project as a whole, and for directing and reviewing the work of other team members. Critically responsible for the quality of the software produced. Has extensive and current development experience. May do hands-on development. On a small project, may act as Project Manager as well.

▶ **Project manager** A person who is responsible for planning, budgeting, liaising with management and negotiating with customers. May have technical training, but does not do development. In a larger project, or a multidisciplinary project, would direct the work of several Team Leaders. Critically responsible for the delivery of the project on time and within budget.

▶ **Software manager** The line manager for the developers. Responsible for hiring and firing, training and developing staff, also for procedures and working practices. Sets the strategic technical direction for the organization. Part of the management team.

If your work (or part of your work) includes the role of Team Leader as defined above, this book is for you. It doesn't matter whether you have been given responsibility 'officially', or you just find yourself leading other technical people because that seems the best way to organize things. It doesn't matter what your job title is.

The boundary between these jobs is not very distinct. Most team leaders do some development, and every team leader has to do some planning and other 'project management' activities. In this book I haven't distinguished between tasks on the basis of who should do them. I've just tried to give the best help with a task that I can, for those people who need it.

CONTACTING THE AUTHOR

If you wish to comment on any aspect of this book, you can do so by visiting my website, www.richardwhitehead.com.

ACKNOWLEDGEMENTS

I would like to thank Robert Sander, Oemer Karacan and Donald Matthews, the reviewers of this book, for all their hard work and words of wisdom.

Thanks to Mark Birdseye for giving me a copy of 'Why the Neanderthals Became Extinct'.

I am very grateful for the helpfulness and encouragement shown to me by everyone at the publishers, Pearson Education, who have kept me going and helped me to get it right.

Thanks also to my friend David Krause for his detailed reviewing, helpful criticism and late-night e-mails.

I must also thank my sons, Thomas and James, for tolerating all the times that Daddy spent 'scribbling' when he should have been playing.

Last but not least, I thank my wife Susan, without whose love and support I would never have completed this book.

PERMISSION ACKNOWLEDGEMENTS

The author and the publishers wish to thank the following for permission to reproduce material within this book:

Figure on page 133 from *Work Redesign* by Hackman and Oldham, ©1980. Reprinted by permission of Prentice-Hall, Inc., Upper Saddle River, NJ.

Quotation on page 54 from *The Saga of Erik the Viking* by Terry Jones. Reprinted with kind permission from Pavilion Books.

 **THE NEW LEADER**

1

I'VE JUST BEEN MADE TEAM LEADER OF A NEW PROJECT // WHERE DO I START?

GETTING INTO THE ROLE

Being given the leadership of a new project is an exciting experience, and is recognition of your professional standing. It is also a scary experience. You are suddenly responsible for delivering something that you may not at first understand. It can be rather bewildering.

There will be all sorts of pressures on you to make progress in several different areas, and you may not be sure where to start. *This section sets out the series of steps to go through to get started*. This sequence is applicable to almost all projects.

It is important to keep a cool head and avoid missing out any steps. It can be tempting to try to justify skipping out a step – for instance, 'we all understand what is required, it's a small project, there's no time to write a requirements document for it'. This is a mistake, and that time you apparently save will be wasted later on in the project. It's important to understand that being effective (doing the right thing) is much more important than being efficient (doing things quickly). If you skip out a stage of requirements capture or design, for instance, you may seem to be making fast progress, but you will probably find later that you've been doing the wrong thing and that your apparent efficiency will have been illusory.

I'll assume for the purpose of this section that your team starts off small – yourself and maybe one other – and grows to full strength as you get into the coding stage. This is actually a very convenient and efficient resource shape. For political reasons a few managers like to allocate the entire team to a project right from the beginning, and if this is the case you are going to have to find ways of keeping people busy doing prototypes or technology investigations, or you could make use of the opportunity to let them learn new skills. Don't feel too bad if some of the work they do is not 100% useful at the beginning – this is a consequence of having too many people at the start, and there's little you can do about it.

Right from the start, you should be sure to act the part of team leader. Make sure you do all the things that a team leader is supposed to do. Be proactive about the project, make things happen and get other people to do things for you (including your boss). Be ready to make decisions and to make them stick – that is part of your job. This does not involve being pompous. You are a part of the team, not its superior, but you do have roles and duties to fulfil that others on the team do not – make sure you fulfil them.

At first, the leadership position is bound to feel alien, and you will find yourself putting on an act, until you become comfortable with leading the team. Make sure when you're acting that you portray a confident and capable leader, neither apologetic nor autocratic.

THE PROLOGUE

Let's get started then. The first thing to do is get a handle on the issues by reading up about the project and, just as importantly, talking to people about it. As well as an understanding of the technical issues, you need to understand the reason that the project exists – the business case for it – which includes the customer's needs, market position, and your organization's priorities that resulted in this project being started now. Make a point of going to talk to the customers of the project – these may be real end-users, or your marketing department. It is very easy to get involved in the technical issues and fail to get a balanced understanding of what is really important to the customer and what is merely nice to have.

What does marketing want? What does the customer want? What does the actual end-user want? Sometimes there is a very long chain from engineer to actual user – try to get to meet all the stakeholders in the project if possible. As well as informing your requirements capture activity (see below), these investigations and discussions help to mould your own opinions and priorities concerning the project and are very important in gaining confidence about how to proceed.

It may be that at this stage you can identify skills or aptitudes that you will need on the project, and so be able to influence the choice of people

At the start of a project it is sometimes unclear exactly how far your role goes, and people may feel that you are overstepping your position. This will be resolved officially in the project plan documentation soon to be written (see below), but in the meantime you should tread carefully, and if you feel that your position is weak or unclear you should ask your management to clarify it, so that there is no contention and you can do your job effectively.

who will be made available to the team. The earlier you can make some justifiable claim for the people you want the better, and getting the right people on your team is crucial to its outcome. It may be that people will be recruited specifically for your project. If so, spend some time specifying exactly what sort of people you are looking for, so that the recruitment process can get under way as soon as possible.

You should also take a critical look at any legally binding documents, such as bids or contracts. You need to know about these to make sure that you comply with them. You also need to be aware of what is in them in case it turns out, when you get into the project, that you will not be doing things the way the bid assumes, or that you won't be able to fulfil the contract. If you've read the contract you will be aware of the implications and be able to do something about it.

Before you start writing up the requirements of the project, take the time to create a project plan document (or to give input into one if a project manager or someone else will prepare it). This document is the sort of thing that engineers usually hate writing – it sets out roles and responsibilities, methods of working and so on (see SECTION 9: HOW DO I DRAW UP A PROJECT PLAN? for more details about project plans) – but it is worth the hours that it takes, because it clarifies the way the project will run and gives you a framework to think about the bigger picture of the project. It also grants formal approval to your role and leads to a smooth running of the team.

You may be under some pressure very early on in the project to produce estimates of costs and time-scales, and maybe to produce a Gantt chart (see SECTION 9: HOW DO I DRAW UP A PROJECT PLAN?). It's really much too early to do this, before the architecture of the solution is apparent, but you might be required to do it anyway. In this case the best you can do is to produce an outline plan that includes several 're-planning' tasks built into it, to make it clear that the plan will be revised at certain key points in the project. Also, build lots of contingency into the first plan. As plans become more detailed, they almost always become longer, so the less detail you are sure of, the more time you should add.

REQUIREMENTS CAPTURE

The real work starts with the requirements capture. This is where you clarify and document your understanding of what needs to be done, typically by writing a document based on some marketing specification or bid/tender document, but being much more precise and technical about what will be done. Sometimes a database is used to record requirements. See SECTION 25: REQUIREMENTS CAPTURE.

If you write the requirements document alone, ask the rest of the team to review it before circulating it. This provides a good introduction to the project as it concentrates on the project from the customer's point of view. It also gets people used to the fact that reviews are going to happen on the project (and getting them to review your work is a friendly way to start this off). And last but not least it gets them to actually bother to read it.

Writing the requirements document usually involves several iterations – usually you propose something and send it out for review. **Frequent and detailed review by the customers of the document is essential** in order for it to be useful. If you are not getting review feedback from the right people (especially the most important people, such as customers or marketing), then try to find out why and get it to happen. It may be that they don't realize that the document is important. Or perhaps it is too technical for them, in which case you could create a non-technical explanation, and put all the really technical stuff in an appendix.

The requirements document is probably the most important thing that you as team leader will be responsible for. Get as many relevant people to review your document as possible, as this will increase its quality. Make sure it is clear enough and also complete enough that someone new joining your team can read the requirements document and know what needs to be done.

Do not rush the requirements through, and do not fudge the issues in order to get the document approved. If there are difficult or contentious issues, bring them out into the open and get them settled before the project goes any further.

If you have several people on the project you must keep them busy during this phase. Personally I think that requirements capture is a one-person, or at most two-person, task. It can't be done by a big team, although you can delegate specific areas that require analysis. So keep the other team members busy doing analysis, investigating technical issues, creating user interface prototypes or learning new skills, and keep them involved in the main requirements capture process only as reviewers.

Writing the requirements document may benefit from some formal **analysis** (see SECTION 34: ANALYSIS).

ARCHITECTURE

The time when the team first starts to come together and work as a team (and when the first friction and arguments appear, see SECTION 28: ARGUMENTS) is when the architecture of the solution is being defined.

This should involve the whole of the technical team. Junior people should come to the design meetings to see how it is done and to feel part of the team. Senior managers and project managers should not come to the meetings if they are not directly involved, as they may stifle the work of the team; instead they should be given a chance to review the results if they need to do so.

This is the time when the **block-diagram-level structure** of the solution is decided upon – how the software will be split into clients and servers, libraries and components, and what operating systems, databases, third-party libraries and so on will be used. Some of these basic technology choices may have been dictated in the requirements, or may be constrained by organizational policies, whilst others will be free for you and your team to choose. See SECTION 35: ARCHITECTURE AND DESIGN for more details on architecture design.

The architecture should be broken down into modules and libraries that represent significant areas of work that rely on each other to form a system, but which are sufficiently self-contained to be independently designed, implemented and tested.

Architectural decisions are not just about technology, they are also about people. Make sure that you consider how each component will be developed and who will work on it, or at least what sort of skills will be needed to work on it. It is surprising how often architectural decisions are constrained more by the skills of the available people, or by the existing arrangement of teams in an organization, than by pure design choices. These constraints can be challenged if they represent a barrier to success, but in general they simply reduce the number of available options without preventing a solution.

This is the time when you step through some of the requirements and make sure that you have a solution, in outline, that will implement them. This is also the time when the crucial interfaces in the system are specified.

Do not miss the opportunity to reuse the work of other teams or to get them to do work for you. Look for modules developed in-house, or available from websites or other sources, that can be reused. If you can get work done outside your team, with high confidence that it will be delivered on time and with good quality, then put pressure on management to make that happen. Reduce the work of your team if possible. Be prepared to pay money for commercial libraries or tools if these save time and money on your project.

The architecture will have a critical impact on the success or otherwise of the project, both technically and interpersonally, as it affects not only the technical solution, but also the way the project will be organized, the tasks that will get allocated to people, and possibly the training and recruitment needs of the project.

A good architecture also helps to reduce stress and tension in the team, see SECTION 27: STRESS

FRAMEWORK

Once the architecture is complete, you should create the framework of the code. This means designing and coding the empty building blocks that you have decided upon in the architecture, including the main internal and external interfaces. At this stage, a crude user interface might be created, just to give some entry point into the code. Code this, all the way down to the interface methods, and get the structure right – make all those libraries and executables that were identified in the architecture, even if they do nothing at present. You might set up the framework for fundamental issues like threading or national language support. Get it to compile and to run, even if it does very little.

At this stage you can decide which of the internal interfaces will require their own unit test bench code, and you can create those test benches as well, again providing a crude user interface that calls the code under test (see SECTION 39: UNIT TESTING OR FINAL TESTING?).

I think that this framework creation is another one-person or two-person task. If possible (that is, if you have the skills and the time), then again I suggest you complete it yourself, letting others review the code (the team's first code reviews!). This framework creation means that everyone has a skeleton of code to fill in, reducing the scope of work that each person has to think about and reducing the potential for chaos. It also lets you demonstrate, by example, the style of code that you expect – so show that you are a good developer, by writing code that is well structured, clear, thoroughly commented, and has lots of error checking. And make sure you subject yourself to a genuine review, where you accept suggestions and criticism graciously. If you don't do these things, you can't expect the rest of the team to bother later. If you don't write the framework yourself, delegate it to someone very experienced, and be very particular about checking what they have done before letting the team start to work with it.

At the same time, you can organize the project structure on your IT system – creating a project directory, setting up version control, intranet pages and the like, again creating a framework for everyone to work within.

Create embryonic directories and documents, even if there is nothing in them. For example, create a final test document now, at the start of the project. It can be used throughout the project to note things that need to be remembered in the testing, so that they don't get forgotten.

DETAILED PLANNING

At this stage you should be able to put together the detailed project plan and Gantt chart, with meaningful estimates of time-scales (see SECTION 9: DRAWING UP A PROJECT PLAN for help on Gantt charts and some hints on estimating time-scales). You should be able to make some initial allocation of people to tasks, based on the architecture of the project and on your knowledge of the abilities and interests of the people on the team.

If your estimates show that the project will not be delivered on time or within budget, then you must *present your plan to management* and explain that you either need more time or more resources, or you need features to be cut or pushed into future releases. Your plan is the proof you need to justify these demands. Do not give in to pressure to trim down your plan. If you believe it to be correct then defend it robustly and demand the changes that are needed. This can be very difficult, indeed it is probably the first really hard and stressful thing that the new leader may be faced with. It is worth remembering that if you give in to pressure and commit to an unrealistic plan, you are sentencing yourself and your team to a prolonged period of stress fighting a losing battle to get your project out impossibly quickly. See also SECTION 10: I'VE BEEN TOLD WHEN I MUST DELIVER MY PROJECT concerning unrealistic plans.

THE DESIGN–CODE–TEST PLATEAU

At long last it is time to for the team to start implementing the features required by filling in the detailed design of the project, doing the coding and day-to-day testing and documentation.

At the beginning of this stage, you need to review what has been done already. It is quite likely that you will have a few prototypes or technology testers that have been created. It is important that these do not just become part of the deliverable code, because most likely they do not conform to the structure of the project, or meet the quality that you would expect. So you need to look at these projects and decide how to pull code from them into the framework that you have created, and how to make sure that the quality is adequate. Most likely, the people who made the prototypes can transfer code from them into the main code, but you should be certain to review the code after this as prototype code will need to be tidied up and have commenting and error checking added, before it is up to production standard. Never try to build on a prototype and turn it into something final. Always start again with a new project for the final code, and use what has been learnt from the prototype, without reusing the prototype as a whole.

It is at this stage, with the requirements fairly stable, the team working together around a framework of the architecture and a plan in place, that you enter the 'plateau' region of team leadership, when the demands of leadership fall off somewhat and you are able to relax a little, and maybe do some of the coding yourself if you have time (see the infobar // HOW MUCH CODING SHOULD I BE DOING? below). However, you must always remember that *your leadership duties come first*, because nobody else on the team should be doing those (whereas other people can do the coding). *Your main tasks during the plateau region are:*

► **Clear away obstacles.** Think forward to problems that might be approaching and try to solve them before they hold up the rest of the team. You should be well placed to do this, armed as you should be with a detailed plan showing the tasks to be done, the interdependencies between them and likely risks.

One factor to be especially aware of is the need for training – you may need to think weeks or months in advance to get people the training they will need in time for it to be useful.

► **Keep everyone usefully occupied** and moving forwards together. Assign areas of responsibility and detailed tasks to people. Keep developers busy developing and as free as possible from other tasks.

► **Defend the design.** Prevent anyone taking shortcuts in the design that would damage the architecture or reduce encapsulation. People often do this just because it would save a little time in the coding, or because they haven't bothered to consult the design before coding.

▶ **Represent the project to management and to the customer.** Make sure you announce successes as well as making people aware of problems. Champion the project and also defend your people.

▶ **Liaise and negotiate** with other projects, departments and organizations to get the help and the resources that you need and to keep people aware of the project.

▶ **Call in experts or consultants**, from inside the organization or from outside, if you think the project will benefit from their help. If you bring in outside experts, take charge of the relationship with them to ensure that you get the most from them without paying excessive charges.

▶ **Make, or delegate, the small day-to-day technical decisions** that are needed on the project.

▶ **Keep the project organized and tidy.** Manage the project folder, intranet area and IT directories. Archive old work and organize configuration management.

▶ **Steer the project in the right direction.** If necessary, make sure that mistakes are corrected, rather than letting the project drift off course.

▶ **Decide when to make releases** to the customer or to marketing, including interim internal releases for more formal testing, and decide what should be in the releases.

▶ **Hold reviews** of design, code and documentation as you feel fit (see SECTION 4: WHEN SHOULD I REVIEW OTHER PEOPLE'S WORK, AND HOW? about reviews). Early on you need to use these to set the quality level you expect.

▶ **Update** requirements documents, test specs, designs and so on, keeping them up to date by making small changes as they become apparent.

▶ **Handle requirements changes**, resource problems, and other disturbances that knock the project off its planned route.

▶ **Call meetings** when necessary (see SECTION 5: CALLING AND CHAIRING MEETINGS).

▶ **Mentor** and keep an eye on the other team members, especially the junior ones. Keep an eye on the way people are working. If necessary spell out how tools should be used, and what processes and procedures must be followed.

▶ **Develop people** by delegating areas of responsibility, and encouraging people to take training if needed. Keep your own knowledge up to date (see the infobar // KEEPING UP TO DATE).

▶ **Take charge of personnel issues** and recruitment.

▶ **Keep the project functioning in a social sense.** Act as the social 'glue' holding the team together.

▶ **Make sure that testing and documentation are adequate.** Plan how the work will be tested, and work on the details of the testing if appropriate.

Independently test other people's work in order to get a feel for what they are doing and to spot any quality problems that may be appearing in the code.

▶ **Keep the plans up to date.** Be aware of the progress of the project towards the agreed delivery dates, and if necessary adjust features, resources or time-scales in co-operation with the customer and your management. Get people to work overtime if necessary (see SECTION 20: HOW MANY HOURS TO WORK?).

▶ **Make sure the company's procedures are applied correctly.** Define working practices for the team either by example, or more formally by writing them down.

▶ **Perform tasks that are not getting done by others.** For example, if you cannot get anyone on your team to make a good job of writing the user manual, then you may have to write it yourself. Teams are not usually completely balanced and there may be nobody who has the right aptitude for certain tasks. In this situation it falls to you as leader to be very flexible and pick up the tasks that need doing. This lets the developers get on with developing. This does not apply to fixing bugs, doing detailed testing, design or design documentation – developers must fix their own bugs, and do their own detailed design, their own routine testing, and must do their own design documentation (see SECTION 18: THEY JUST WANT TO CODE).

▶ **Manage your own time.** Prioritize and spend your time wisely to avoid becoming overloaded. More about this in SECTION 27: STRESS.

▶ **Coding, possibly.** See the infobar // HOW MUCH CODING SHOULD I BE DOING? below.

Although this sounds like an awful lot do do, most of these things will take place routinely and you will hardly notice that they are happening, so long as you remember to see the big picture of the project as a whole,

Infobar // **KEEPING UP TO DATE**

Software is an unusual business because it changes so fast, and skills that are mainstream one year can be obsolete a year later. It is important therefore to maintain your own skills, so that you can continue to be effective. This does not mean that you must become an expert in every new technology that comes along, but you do need to be aware of them, and understand when they are appropriate and what they are for.

If your team is using a technology that you have not used in anger yourself, then you need to learn enough to detect when someone is trying to pull the wool over your eyes. For a team leader, reading 'white papers', doing tutorials, and looking at other people's code is often enough to keep you informed.

Whilst developers should be gaining a deep and detailed understanding of the languages and technologies that they are using, it is more appropriate for a team leader to keep aware of a broader spectrum of technologies, achieving a wide but not necessarily deep understanding of the options available.

and don't allow yourself to get engrossed in some detailed technical issue that takes your attention off things.

LATER STAGES

As you near the time for a release, whether a formal release to the customer or just an internal release for formal testing, you will again be under more pressure and have to **take firmer control** of the project to make sure that testing, documentation and release procedures are as thorough as they should be. See SECTION 40: PRODUCT RELEASE.

CONCLUSIONS

Getting a project moving and keeping it going in the right direction can be very hard work. But once it gets moving it gains a momentum of its own, your job becomes easier and you only need to make light adjustments to the helm and keep an eye on the charts. Things get more frantic again towards the end of the trip.

infobar // HOW MUCH CODING SHOULD I BE DOING?

Most routine coding is of course quite low down on the list of priorities for a team leader. This means that the larger the team you have, the more likely it is that there will be something more important for you to get on with. With a team of more than five or six people, you will probably not have much time to do any serious coding at all.

There are three situations where it is appropriate and high priority for you, the leader, to do the detailed coding, providing you have the skill, or to take very close control and review of the process if you don't have the skill:

1 When you are creating the framework code for the project. I believe that this is best done by the leader with perhaps one other person helping, and should be taken all the way down to the smallest detail of the interface code before implementation starts.

2 Just before a release, or when you have promised something, and it's 'all hands to the pumps'.

3 Where there are code sections that are of critical importance or where you have unique expertise, **if** there is no time to help someone else to do this. But it is not healthy for the leader to be the only one with such key skills or knowledge, and you should try to transfer your knowledge to others when there is time.

It is certainly *not* appropriate for a team leader to delegate some leadership tasks to developers simply in order to gain himself or herself time to do some coding. The leader should aim to keep everyone on the project busy and doing the work to which they are best suited, and that usually means that the leader has to take on the overhead, routine and planning tasks, so that other people can keep developing. It can be very tempting to allocate little (interesting) coding tasks to yourself, but this often backfires, as these tasks get delayed by your other priorities and other people get held up waiting on them.

If you see your career path as leading into project management or departmental management, and consider it a blessed relief to leave coding behind, then you will probably find it easy to identify priorities that mean you never have to do any coding. However, for those who see their careers as very much centred on the ability to write software, rather than managing others, and yet who find themselves leading a fairly large team, there is a tricky compromise to be made between that personal goal of maintaining the ability to code, and the immediate needs of the project. In an extreme case you may have to abandon all coding for the duration of a particular project, and hope to catch up on the next one, or keep coding in your own time.

For all this hard work there are many rewards, but most important is the knowledge that you made a significant personal contribution to the project, and that your team, your customer and your organization have all benefited from your judgement and hard work.

2

I'M TAKING OVER THE LEADERSHIP OF AN EXISTING PROJECT // WHERE DO I START?

If you find yourself taking over the leadership of a project that is already up and running, you may want to dive in and take charge as quickly as possible. You may feel that the project had previously been run badly and is in need of a good shake-up, and you may even have been told this by management. It is tempting therefore to start making changes straight away. **This is usually a big mistake.**

There is a great deal to learn when you take over any project, usually much more than is apparent at first. Even if you have been part of the project team you may have had quite a restricted view of the project, and been insulated from some of the external pressures driving it.

You may see things that you consider to be blatantly wrong or stupid. Beware commenting on these, let alone doing anything about them, until you are really sure of the full background and of the consequences if you change things.

So initially, you should remain quite passive, taking things in and keeping your own counsel. Make small day-to-day decisions as they crop up, but defer all major decisions until you are in full possession of the facts. Give priority to clearing obstacles out of the way of the team and preventing interruptions, letting them concentrate on development. If you are being pressed to make large decisions, by team members or by management, tell them that you will decide later – or better still that the whole team will decide later – and maybe give an indication of when you think this can happen.

It is especially important to avoid acting on personnel issues too soon. **Do nothing on personnel issues until the technical issues are clear.** Initial impressions can be very misleading, especially in projects that have had an unhappy history, where a culture of blame can build up, from which you should try to remain detached. People may try to get you 'on their side' by criticizing other team members – this is not something to encourage. Never take a bad impression of an individual, even if it appears to be universally held, at face value. You must always look at their work, their background and training, and the directions they were given, before you can judge the quality of what they have done.

For example, you may be told that 'Fred is very slow, he always holds everything up', and first impressions may seem to confirm this; everyone may be waiting for Fred so that they can finish their release. But does this mean that Fred is the problem? Not necessarily, although someone obviously wants you to think so. Just as likely is that Fred is doing the hardest work that takes the most time – someone may be jealous of this hard, and probably interesting, work. Or it's possible that Fred is testing his work more thoroughly than other people and so taking longer, but making a better job. Or that Fred is taking on work that other people should be doing, but he knows it won't get done if he leaves it to them. Beware taking accusations at face value and don't propagate impressions from anyone – including the previous leader – but wait until you have enough evidence to make up your own mind.

So much for what *not* to do. The first thing that you *should* start to do is to review the situation. This involves more than just absorbing impressions; you need to organize these impressions into a framework. Try to organize your thoughts into the following areas, and in each area try to separate technical issues from personnel ones:

▶ **Where is the team now?** What has it achieved? What has it learnt? What is working and what is failing? How good is the work? How do people feel? What processes are being followed?

▶ **Where is it supposed to be getting to?** What are the requirements of the project? What do management and the customer expect? What is the least that needs to be done, and what things should be done really well?

▶ How does the team currently intend to continue (**i.e. how does it expect to get from where it is now to where it needs to be**)? What's the current plan of action? What options have been chosen?

Do not miss out the first of these three points. You need to know what has been done and by whom, and you need to make your own estimation of the quality of the work that has been done. You also need to understand the different abilities and aspirations of the people on the team. Finding out where you are can be surprisingly difficult, and can involve lots of frustrating and sometimes ill-tempered meetings with team members, managers and people from other groups. Try not to be judgemental, just record facts as you see them. It is vital that you make up your own opinions on the issues, basing these opinions on objective facts. You will probably be handed opinions from all quarters – listen and understand them all, but make up your own mind. Don't be afraid to be a minority of one.

As far as the requirements go, don't be afraid to question them as well as to clarify them. Does the user really need the functions listed? Are they going to pay for them? It's surprising how often engineers make up their own requirements – either in an attempt to prove something with the technology, to enhance their CVs, or in an honest attempt to give the customer something better – which when investigated turn out to be unwanted or even undesirable for either the company or the customer. When thinking about the requirements, always keep an outward-looking view, thinking about the needs of the customer and the end-user, and the marketing stance of the organization, and giving less importance to issues that are internal to the project team.

Only when you have a good idea of where the team is and where it needs to be can you make a valid appraisal of the current plan. You need to know whether you can commit yourself to the plans as currently formulated, or whether fundamental changes are needed. The way to approach this is to start again at the beginning of the project and work through it. So you should review and propose changes to things roughly in the following order:

▶ The requirements.

▶ The architecture of the solution.

▶ The resources (people and equipment) available, and the way they are allocated.

▶ The practices and procedures adopted – how the team approaches configuration management, reviews, design, testing and other processes.

▶ The existing code base.

Team members will probably resist changes to the architecture of the software on the basis that it will take too long. Often this is not true. Moving elements of a design around often takes less time than people fear, whereas a poor architecture usually wastes much more time than people realize, as every change that must be made is hampered by architectural weaknesses. If the project really has an architecture that is so fragile and complex that it cannot realistically be altered, then there really is a serious problem to solve. See SECTION 38: RESTRUCTURING.

Of course, you need to be pragmatic. The later you start into the project, the less it will be possible to make fundamental changes to the project's organization, architecture or staffing. Even if you can make big changes, you need to choose your timing carefully – just before a major release is not a good time to do anything except try to get that release out.

Personnel issues are the most problematic when taking over a project. To a large extent it is easier to take over a project that was perceived to be failing, than to take the place of a popular and respected leader who has left behind a successful team.

When coming into a *failing project* you may be faced with a barrage of anger, resentment and hostility, as team members may not accept blame for the failure, or may deny that there is any failure at all. There is a positive side to this situation, however, as it should be fairly easy to persuade management of the need for changes, including personnel changes, in a project that is perceived to be failing.

When taking over a project that is apparently *doing well*, the personnel issues are more subtle and this can make them all the more difficult. If you are new to the team you will be coming into a well-knit team, as an outsider, and you will be resented for interfering. If you are an existing team member who has been given the leadership role, others may be suspicious or resentful. Any changes you try to make will be resisted, and you might even be told by management not to 'rock the boat'. Even knowing that it is normal, inevitable and even healthy for a team to act this way will do little to reduce your misery. You can only wait for it to pass, as it will eventually, by staying calm and objective.

When you believe you know the current state of the project, and understand the requirements, you can put together your own plan of action. A good way to do this is to write a new project plan, covering all the issues that a project plan should address – see SECTION 9: HOW DO I DRAW UP A PROJECT PLAN?. Everything you propose should be based on facts that you can verify, and all the consequences of your proposals must be thoroughly thought through. Base your estimates of what needs to be done, and of the time this will take, both on your own experience and on the history of the project so far. If things have always taken a long time on this project, don't assume that they will suddenly speed up. When you estimate, use appropriate historical information to help you.

Present this plan to your team. Listen to what they tell you and decide whether to change your plan. This meeting is a crucial point in your new leadership. It is a time when grievances may be aired, issues hotly debated. Be as open as you can with the team, and where you disagree with something say so, but keep to the issues and avoid personal remarks. Of course there may be some issues you cannot discuss with the team, such as personnel issues.

This meeting is also a clear indication to the team that you are now fully in place as the team leader – it marks the end of your introduction to the team and the beginning of your leadership. Presenting your plan to the team before presenting it to management not only gives it a review, it also says something to the team – if people see this as a game of sides, it shows that you're on the team's side.

It's now time to present your plan to management. Some of your proposals might be unwelcome to the management and they might not be willing to listen. This is especially true if you propose any sort of rework such as reworking parts of the software, requiring more time or people. Stand your ground, defend your position using the facts as you see them. You will have to accept the decisions that management make, but do not back down. Let them tell you that you are wrong if they want to, but do not be beaten down into saying so yourself.

See SECTION 22: SOMEONE WHO'S A PROBLEM.

If there are personnel changes to be made, such as difficult people to be removed from the team, it is often best to make all such changes simultaneously. Include this in your plan for management review, allowing for the disruption it will cause.

Taking over an existing team is much harder than starting to lead a new project. In the first few weeks of a project, important decisions are made and the team starts to knit together. If you were not present or had little influence during that time, there may be some decisions that you hate but cannot reverse, some difficult issues that you just have to live with, and you may never get to feel completely part of the team. All you can do is to make up your mind as objectively as possible about the issues, making decisions that you honestly believe to be in the best interest of the project and of the team members. Taking over an existing project is a bit like wandering into a minefield; it pays to take things slowly and very carefully.

3

I AM THE MOST EXPERIENCED ENGINEER ON THE TEAM // IF I LET OTHERS DO THE DESIGN AND CODING, THEY WILL NOT DO IT AS WELL AS I WOULD // HOW CAN I DO THE IMPORTANT DESIGN AND CODING, IF I AM EXPECTED TO WRITE DOCUMENTS AND PLANS ALL THE TIME?

You were probably given the job of team leader because of your ability to design and write solid software code. So it can be frustrating to find that, as leader, you cannot directly apply these abilities to the project at hand, and have to spend time on planning, documentation, organization and so on.

It is important to realize that the most valuable part of your experience is not your detailed knowledge of design tools, coding syntax or APIs. Of far greater value is your approach to solving problems – the understanding of how to break down a problem into parts, knowing which parts to tackle first and knowing when you are on the right track – when to persevere and when to admit defeat. This sort of sound judgement – *software wisdom* if you like – is only learnt the hard way.

If you have a detailed knowledge of coding, that will still be of great value to your team. Even if you do little coding yourself, you will still be a source of help to other people when they need it, and you should still be attending reviews. Through helping other people and through these reviews you get the opportunity to coach others, transferring some of your knowledge to others. As team leader your skills are used indirectly, through other people.

You are *responsible* for the project. That does not mean you have to do all the work yourself. You have to delegate to others, and that should include delegation of the interesting and difficult parts of the job, not just the boring bits.

Your primary *technical* responsibility is for the architecture and design of the project. A poor, ill-considered design will hamper the efforts of the whole team. It will lead to either bodging or backtracking, usually in a short-term panic as the structural problems come out near the end of the project. Therefore it is a very good use of your time to be involved in design meetings and reviews, and to make, or be involved with, top-level design decisions. Like many issues in a development project, the architecture should stem from the project requirements, and these should be constantly in your mind when you make technical decisions.

See SECTION 35: ARCHITECTURE AND DESIGN

Of course, less skilled people will not do the design or coding at the same speed or to the same quality as you might. This is another reason to control the architecture and top level design of the project, which acts as a framework for others to work within. Poor detailed design can be spotted during reviews. Detailed coding bugs can be found by reviews and by unit testing. If you have broken down the work into independent modules and provided a framework, these issues will matter little. In the extreme, a piece of work might need to be discarded and rewritten. With a solid, well-encapsulated design, this will be possible with the minimum of disruption to the rest of the team. But with a hacked-together spaghetti-like piece of code, making large changes to any piece of code might be so disruptive that it could not be done.

Letting go of details and letting other people make their own mistakes is an important part of leadership. You should aim to provide an environment where people can learn from each other, and can safely make mistakes that can be found and rectified quickly. Letting people make mistakes, or 'reinvent the wheel', is an important part of letting them develop and become more useful (see SECTION 19: WHEN TO LET PEOPLE DO THINGS THEIR OWN WAY).

Another way to put your detailed knowledge to use is to coach people on your team explicitly, teaching them skills that you have acquired. This is a difficult thing to do, and is probably only best attempted if you know that it will be appreciated. But the time spent sitting with someone and working through an issue can be repaid many times over by better quality and increased motivation in future. Coaching is not the same as leading. When you take the leading role, you are expected to make decisions. As a coach, you are merely providing options, and helping people to think through the consequences of these options. It is all too easy to slip back into the lead role and start making the decisions, thus denying others the opportunity to think through the issues themselves. When you coach people, you hand them skills, but you don't dictate how they should use them. You can also hand out attitudes, but you can't force people to share them.

Coaching is often a frustrating business, as people often seem to disbelieve what you say until they have tried to prove you wrong, and failed to do so. Don't let this get you annoyed. Within reason, it is very healthy for someone to 'test' what they have been told, and it will result in them having a greater respect for what they have learnt. When it works, coaching is one of the most rewarding aspects of leadership.

So what about all those documents you have to write? Well, if they really are unimportant and could be done by someone else, perhaps you should let someone else do them. But not so that you can do some coding – only delegate them to someone else if there is something else more important that you need to do, which only you can do well.

As leader, your job is to clear away obstacles from the rest of the team so that they can be productive. It may seem frustrating that they are being productive by using skills that you have and would like to use, but can't because you have to write documents. However, if you are the best person to write the documents (as you often will be), then by doing so you are doing your team a double favour – you are doing something that only you can do best, and you are relieving the rest of the team of the task so they can get on and do development.

Your reward for this selflessness will come as you see your project progress towards its goals, and know that you made a major contribution to its direction and success – something you can't do if you have your head down, coding.

4 WHEN SHOULD I REVIEW OTHER PEOPLE'S WORK, AND HOW?

Most software development departments have a defined process by which people's work is reviewed, either by the team leader or by other members of the team. Reviews can be very helpful in improving quality and in getting the team to work together more closely, provided that they are handled properly. If reviews are handled badly, they can engender such conflict and stress that they cause more problems than they solve.

Many software departments have procedures that make a distinction between the everyday informal work of a team leader keeping himself or herself aware of progress and quality, and a much more formal process for identifying deficiencies and ensuring that they are rectified. I believe that this distinction is artificial and too strict, and that the everyday process and the formal process should be almost the same, as I set out below. If reviews are very formal then the sudden change of atmosphere and increase in formality immediately put people on the defensive.

I want to make it clear that reviews are vitally important. Nothing in this chapter should be read as an excuse to not hold reviews – quite the opposite. I believe that by keeping reviews informal and relaxed for the most part, you can have more of them, and that they will be more effective in finding problems and in helping people to learn from each other.

It's for you to decide *what* to review (or get reviewed), and *when*. There are not many occasions where it's worth reviewing every single line of code written, or every word in a document. Normally, you need to skim over what has been done to get a feel for how the problem has been approached, and dive into the detail where you think it necessary.

If you have someone on your team who is quite new to development, or who you're worried about, it might be worth reviewing more of their work, to try to find and correct basic mistakes. It's important that the person doesn't feel picked-on, and you should treat this more as mentoring than reviewing, helping the person to understand issues rather than trying to find fault.

With people who are quite experienced and whom you know well, you may decide not to review their work at all, except perhaps when something is critically important (and in this case, most experienced people will probably ask for their work to be checked rather than having to have it forced on them). However, people are generally good at one thing and not so good at another, and also we all make mistakes – so it's usually worth reviewing a package of work, even in overview, as a final 'sanity check'. It's not uncommon for the reviewer to get more out of the review than the person who's work is being reviewed – if someone really is good, reviewing their work is a good way to learn from them.

It's up to you *who* reviews the work. You may do it yourself, or get other people on the team to review each other's work. Reviews may be one-to-one, or you may have two or more reviewers. Remember that you remain responsible for the work on your team – even work that you personally neither wrote nor reviewed. If you delegate the review to someone else, make sure it's delegated to someone who will be careful and conscientious in the task, without being officious.

Make sure that your own work is reviewed as thoroughly as everyone else's, both to improve its quality, and to let others get their own back!

Informal reviews usually just 'happen' – you get talking to someone about how they're doing, they show you problems they are fighting, you talk it over. You may have been doing this without thinking of it as 'reviewing'. If so, I'm not trying to encourage you to be more formal about this everyday process; quite the opposite, I'm trying to encourage you to think of reviews as informal, everyday affairs that are just part of normal work, not something that necessarily has an agenda or written actions. More formal reviews, which *do* produce records of discrepancies and so forth, are usually appropriate when a section of work has been completed, such as an important document written, a design finished, or a set of features coded, and it's time to polish it and check it before moving on to the next stage.

It should never be the case that a final, formal review to close down some work is the first time that that work has been reviewed. It's your job as team leader to be aware of what people are doing and how well they are doing it; you should know this while the work is in progress, you shouldn't find out for the first time when it's 'finished'.

Even when reviews are informal, you should still make sure that any discrepancies are acted upon. With a formal review you have a written record to work from, but with an informal review you should remember to check up later that necessary changes have been made. This is one reason why there should always be a more formal review just before any important work is accepted as finished. With informal reviews you are just providing the extra brain to help get things right, but with the more formal review you have written evidence of the review points made, and can prevent the work being finalized until these points have been addressed to your satisfaction.

If you find something really serious in an informal review, or it degenerates into heated arguement, then it may be best to call a formal review, perhaps inviting along someone independent as well, so that things don't go too far without careful checking.

As I said in the introduction to this section, I believe that formal reviews should not be very different from informal reviews – in effect, I think that formal reviews within a development team should not, usually, be very formal. Here are some examples:

Documents:

▶ Informal review: You send someone a document. They scribble on a hard-copy, or make changes to the soft-copy, and send it back.

▶ Formal review: Same as an informal review, except that once you are happy with the document, its revision number will be increased, and it will be signed off as approved.

Note that I don't see any value in keeping review minutes, or of keeping copies of draft versions of documents, or of maintaining a detailed history of changes, even for formal reviews. What matters is the quality of the final document, and the formal authorization.

Documents with change-marks are often useful so people can see what has been changed, and don't have to review the whole document next time it comes round, but I don't think this should be mandatory.

Designs:

▶ Informal review: You sit together around the design, which is on the screen, on paper, or sketched on a board. You think it through together, making sure it can do everything that's required of it, and change it when you agree ways in which it can be improved.

▶ Formal review: Same as informal review, but you make a note of the design decisions made and the reasons for them as you go along, so that you can later remind yourself why you did something and consider whether it still makes sense.

Code:

▶ Informal review: You sit next to someone at their machine and they show you the most important bits of what they did. You mention things you like and also suggest ways it could be improved, such as 'I think a comment would be useful there', 'don't forget to check for errors from that function', or 'the way you've laid out the code doesn't comply with the coding standards'.

▶ Formal review: Same as informal review, but you work on a version of code that has been given a version number so that it can be identified, and any changes that you agree to make are recorded so they don't get forgotten.

You may also find a checklist helpful for checking that the coding standards have been applied.

With code reviews, unlike design reviews, try to discourage people from making changes during the review, as it's very distracting. If you think that something may get forgotten, make notes about what to change, even in an informal review.

To a large extent these are my personal preferences and I'm not suggesting this is the 'only right way'. I happen to prefer to read a document at my own speed, whereas I think designs should be reviewed in a group, but that's just me. The point I'm trying to get over is that formal reviews are just informal reviews, with some notes kept. There should be no sudden change in your attitude or behaviour when you start a formal review.

You might decide that the best way to review work is just to look at it yourself without involving the author of the work, and only mention something if you find a problem. This has its place, but it also has its drawbacks. For one thing, it seems like spying, and trying to find fault. For another, reviews are part of the social process at work, and you should be reviewing people's work (*i.e. talking to your team about their work*) several times a day. But it can often be useful to look through someone's work on your own, to decide which parts you want to review with them in detail.

The review notes should be in a form that is useful to the person making the changes, not designed for audit checking. It's useful if you take a copy of the notes yourself and keep them as a reminder of work that needs finishing, but don't make a big issue about it. You may keep the notes afterwards to comply with your procedures, but that should not be in your mind when you write them. The focus should be on improving the quality of the work, not on satisfying an auditor.

If your procedures dictate a format for reviews that is much more onerous than the ones I've described, then I suggest you are careful about how you apply the procedures. For instance, I have attended a meeting of 15 people to review a document, where the document was totally irrelevant to 12 of them, because the procedures dictated that every department must review such a document. It's not so much that the procedure was stupid, it's also crazy for people to follow such a procedure slavishly, and have 12 people sit for two hours listening to three other people discuss a document paragraph by paragraph. In such a case, it is perfectly acceptable to send the document round for review before the meeting, incorporate everyone's comments, and then call the meeting just to 'rubber stamp' the document. This meets the procedures, not just for the sake of it, but it also still achieves the function that the procedure was intended to provide, in that it gives every department the opportunity to review the document and to block its approval if it is unacceptable. Similar logic can be applied to other situations where procedures dictate actions that are not appropriate – do the right thing, and then do anything else that's needed to satisfy the procedures as quickly as possible.

Try to make reviews relaxed, everyday affairs, even the 'formal' ones. Make it clear that the reviewer is spending his or her time to make the author's work even better – which will be to the benefit of the person who did the work, in the long run. If reviews become an accepted part of working life, and you handle them properly, then most people can accept their work being scrutinized, without too much stress. To 'handle a review properly':

▶ Concentrate on actions that could be taken to improve the work, not on the personality who did it.

▶ Say what needs to be said, don't be apologetic for holding the review, but refrain from raising petty issues or trying to score points. Equally, don't give praise except when it is genuine.

▶ If the standard of quality is too low, refer to examples of other work that can be used as a benchmark for the required quality level, rather than just criticizing the work under review.

▶ LISTEN. Understand what is being said to you. Accept that your ideas might be just preconceptions and that someone else's ideas may be as good as yours or better. Don't force people onto the defensive.

▶ Differentiate fact from opinion. For example, 'this code doesn't comply with the coding standards' is a fact, whereas 'the code could be laid out more clearly' is an opinion. It's not that opinions are less valuable than facts, but you have to be careful not to present your opinions as if they are indisputable facts.

This is one place where tools such as code-metrics generators and static code analysers can be very valuable, as they provide an automated and objective 'opinion' of code quality. Using such tools has other benefits, in that code authors can run the code through the tool themselves and sort out any warnings it throws up, rather than have them come up in a review. These tools cannot replace manual code inspection because they cannot comment on the structure, naming conventions, clarity of comments and so on, but they can provide a very useful pre-filtering of code before it even gets to the stage of inspection.

▶ Be constructive; look forward to the way the work will be when it is finished.

The aim is to work together to improve the quality, not for you to impose rigid control, nor to impose your own preferred style on others or to demonstrate your superiority. It's a shared effort to make the product better – reviewers are giving their time to help someone (whom they trust) to improve their work, not to pick fault.

It can be very hard to decide whether a given point really is important, or is merely a matter of style. For instance, different people lay out their code differently, and one person's code can look messy to another. No matter how much you find it unpleasant, if it falls within the coding standards, then you should say nothing. If you keep seeing code that you think should not be allowed, then you should try to change the coding standards, or make your own ruling for your project! That's not to say that you shouldn't comment on things that do matter, but you must only comment when the problem really makes it difficult to understand what is being said, rather than simply irritating you. For example, names of variables and other things in code do matter – if a variable has a stupid name then it's misleading and leads to errors in maintenance. But I wouldn't make a huge fuss if someone doesn't leave many blank lines in their code. While the code might be more readable with some white space, the lack of it is not going to prevent anyone maintaining it. Deciding what matters and what doesn't is one of the hardest parts of reviewing someone else's work. One approach is to comment on everything, but state that some things are 'low priority' and some higher priority. Personally I don't like this in practice – if something's low priority then it would be better simply left unsaid, because people have always got higher priority work to get on with. Commenting on it and marking it as low priority is a cop-out. Perhaps you should ask yourself, for a given issue, *'is this so important that I want this fixed before the person does any more new work?'*. Only raise review points for those where the answer is 'definitely yes'.

There are some people who just can't stand having their work reviewed. Often, this stems from having an ego the size of the Horsehead Nebula. Such people cannot accept any criticism, even if it is intended to improve their work, because they believe that it cannot be improved, and certainly not by you. They may refuse to co-operate, or constantly put you off, or keep 'forgetting' about the review. You must not give in to this attitude. Everyone must be treated equally. If everyone has their work reviewed, that must mean everyone – including yourself, and including this Mr Fantastic. If you give in to petulance you'll find that it only grows stronger.

My own opinion, expressed in this section, is that reviews are vital but that formality rarely increases the quality of what is done. I reserve formality for a final approval of a document or design or for accepting code into a product. Even then, the only formality I add is to make sure that discrepancies are recorded and that they are fixed, and that an approval signature is obtained if necessary.

However, not everyone would agree with me. It's only fair to point out that many experts on software development processes might consider my opinions as degenerate. Most documented software processes make a distinction between different types of reviews, such as 'review', 'walk-through' and 'inspection', and often these each have prescribed activities, roles, checklists and record sheets. If you want to be more formal about reviews, or you find that your reviews are not working effectively and you want to follow a defined process in order to improve them, then such processes are probably for you. See the 'process and procedures' section of the bibliography (SECTION 42) for some excellent books covering this area.

Reviews are worth the pain. They spread knowledge among the team, they improve quality, and they give you control. It's for you to decide what gets reviewed, how it is reviewed and by whom. Make informal reviews a regular, everyday part of life on your team, but don't make a big deal about reviews, whether formal or informal.

5

WHEN SHOULD I CALL A MEETING AND HOW SHOULD I CHAIR IT?

Meetings can be a very effective way of communicating with people and getting decisions made. Unfortunately, they can also be a very effective way of simultaneously wasting lots of people's time.

Valid reasons to call a meeting include:

▶ To get several people together who should all talk about a specific topic, rather than having lots of individual conversations.

▶ To get a decision made that should be made by consensus, not by decree.

▶ To discuss something that is contentious. Always have face-to-face meetings about contentious issues if possible, rather than using telephone, e-mail or whatever.

Video conferencing is better than telephone or text-based communication, but it's nowhere near as good as actually meeting face to face.

▶ When people have not met before. When people first start working together it is good to get them to meet, as this helps them work more effectively together afterwards and reduces the chance of conflicts arising. In addition, if people work in different environments it can be very helpful if they experience each other's situations (especially in a customer–supplier relationship, it helps if the supplier has experienced something of the way the customer works).

If a meeting isn't necessary, don't call one. Equally, if someone isn't needed, don't invite them (sometimes it's appropriate to send them an invitation but say that their presence is not mandatory). Sounds obvious, but how many hours have you sat in meetings where you weren't needed? If you set up a meeting that happens regularly, but on one occasion the meeting is unnecessary, then cancel it. Even if your procedures stipulate that you must have a certain sort of meeting (e.g. a project progress meeting), you should still be able to cancel it if you are able to justify why it is not needed.

If a meeting has more than about eight people in it, it's unlikely that everyone will contribute. That's fine if it's a 'get everyone together to tell them all something' type of meeting, but if a discussion is needed, you need fewer people, to enable it to work. Split the meeting into multiple meetings, or invite people for only part of the meeting if they don't need to attend all of it.

Remember to reserve a location for your meeting and arrange a time when people are available. If you're going to have a long meeting (say, two hours or more) and senior people are involved, it may be worth arranging to meet off-site. This gets people away from interruptions. Getting out of the office also helps to clear the mind of day-to-day concerns, so an off-site meeting is good for discussing forward-thinking strategy or radical proposals.

If you need a meeting, call it. Encourage those on your team to call meetings if they need to do so. Sounds obvious again, but it's amazing how often you hear people say things like 'I don't know how to do that because nobody has called a meeting about it yet'. Nobody including them! Make it clear that anyone can call a meeting if they need one and can decide whom to invite. Normally, the person who calls a meeting will chair it; see the >skills box CHAIRMANSHIP.

If you intend to invite senior people to a meeting it might be an idea to clear it with your boss first.

Remember that meetings cost a great deal of money. People's time is expensive, not just because of their pay, but because when they're in your meeting they can't be doing their normal jobs, which presumably make money or otherwise benefit your organization in some way. Meetings need to be large enough and long enough to achieve their purpose, but no larger and no longer.

Don't be one of those people who call meetings for no reason except they seem to think this is what leadership is about. Equally, don't be afraid of calling on people's time if you need it.

Chairmen can be men or women.

> skills box

CHAIRMANSHIP

The sort of meeting I'm talking about in this section is the sort of day-to-day meeting that happens informally as part of getting a job done, or the slightly more formal meeting where senior management are involved or specific procedures must be followed. There are some types of meeting that are very formal, with written procedures, moderators and secretaries and so on and where 'the chair' is a very formal position. I'm not going to talk about that sort of meeting here. If you have to go to one, make sure you know the rules before you attend.

Before the meeting is held, make sure everyone who will come has the *background information* they will need, in plenty of time to look at it before the meeting. Also, always send round an agenda. This doesn't have to be very grand, it could be just one point for discussion, but make sure people arrive at the meeting having had a chance to think about the issues to be discussed.

Normally, the person who calls a meeting will chair it. For most meetings this is not a formal position and often it's not even apparent that someone is chairing a meeting, but people will always look for someone to lead a meeting, so if you want the meeting to happen in a certain way then make sure you take charge of it at the beginning, otherwise someone else will. At the start of a meeting, wait for everyone to arrive and then welcome people to the meeting and remind them what it is about. How long you wait for people to arrive depends on your organization's culture. In some places it is intolerable to be a minute late for a meeting, in others, the published time is just a guideline for people to wander together. Fit in with your organization's norms even if you don't fully agree with them. Give out any new information and make sure people have copies of any papers you have distributed (have some spare).

If minutes are going to be circulated then make sure someone takes notes – you may have to do this yourself.

Once the meeting starts it is the chairman's job to keep the meeting on course, which means keeping it to the agenda and preventing it going over time.

It can be hard to maintain an objective view about whether the meeting has wandered off its agenda, when you are yourself involved in the discussions. A simple trick is to keep the agenda open in front of you, and to ask yourself periodically whether what is being said fits in with the point that is supposed to be being discussed. If not, say so. This becomes natural after a while.

Equally, it can be hard to bring a discussion to a close if it is going over time, if it is in full swing. Sometimes the only thing to do is to call another meeting to discuss a point. If the discussion is supposed to be leading to a decision, and the discussions have gone round in circles over and over the same points, you (or the most senior person present) may have to make a decision without there being a consensus, and just tell people what it is. This is usually far better than letting the meeting break up with no decision made.

Towards the end of the meeting, draw discussions to a close, perhaps by summarizing what has been said and what is to be done. If you feel comfortable about it, informally thank people for coming.

If people are going to have to do things as a result of the meeting, always send out minutes afterwards, and include clear 'actions' for specific people to do, by specific times. Agree these in the meeting, don't make them up yourself afterwards. If you need to raise an action on someone who is not present in the meeting, go to talk to them immediately after the meeting so that they hear about it very soon and have a chance to raise objections.

If you are going to distribute minutes, write up the minutes and send them out as soon as possible after the meeting. They should be sent to everyone present, everyone with actions and everyone affected by any decisions made.

6

I HAVE TO INTERVIEW A JOB APPLICANT //
HOW DO I GO ABOUT IT?

Recruiting the right people – people who bring in the right *skills, experience and attitudes* to an organization – is one of the single key ways that you can make it a more productive and more pleasant place to work.

If you are lucky enough to be recruiting people to your own team then of course you will have a big incentive to get it right. You will also have nobody to blame if you recruit someone who fails to perform or whom you can't stand working with after the first week.

Whether for your own team or not, recruiting people is a *very good use of a team leader's time*. If you find that you are not involved in recruiting people, I suggest that you try to muscle in on the process. Tell those that matter that you want to be involved. The time you put into recruiting people will be repaid many times over in the future.

Interviews and tests are usually the part of the recruitment process that team leaders get involved in, but it's worth being aware of how this fits into the rest of the recruitment process in your organization. If you understand the background to the process, such as the wording that is being put into advertisements, what brief the recruitment agency has been given, how candidates' CVs have been filtered and so on, then you will be able to give a better impression to candidates and to judge them more fairly. See if you can find out about these things from your boss or Human Resources department.

If you have not been involved in interviewing before, it can be quite a daunting prospect. But it's quite easy if you **stick to a formula**, going through the same process for each candidate. This makes for a fairer comparison of the candidates and helps to give the impression that you know what you are doing.

▶ Always **read the CV before the interview**, and take it with you to the interview. It is rude and unprofessional not to do this.

▶ If more than one person will be interviewing the candidate, then make sure you **know who will be covering what**, to avoid duplication.

▶ The interview will need **space, time and privacy**. Make sure you make any necessary arrangements before the candidate arrives. Get the phone diverted if you are using an office that receives a lot of calls.

▶ Preferably, go to collect candidates rather than having them 'delivered' to an office or meeting room. This gives you a less formal situation where you can greet them and **put them at ease** by chatting about trivialities such as the weather or their journey to find you. If you do go into an interview where the candidate has already arrived, you could offer a drink or a 'comfort break'. If the candidate declines then it's probably better just to press on with the formal interview.

▶ **Always play the part.** You don't have to act like a stuffed jacket, but, for a candidate's first interview at least, you do need to keep things quite formal and under your control. This is what candidates will be expecting, and they will be more confused than pleased if you don't act like their preconception of an interviewer. Think how you expect to be treated in an interview, and act that way.

▶ **Remember that candidates will be judging you as much as you are judging them.** You represent the organization, and candidates may extrapolate anything you say or do as applying to the whole organization. For example, if you forget to book a room for the interview and then have trouble finding one that is free, the candidate may have decided that your organization is 'totally disorganized', before the interview even starts. Impressions are as important as facts.

▶ Start off by making sure that the candidate knows a little about the organization and what it does, and **explain what the job is** and why there is a vacancy now. Encourage the candidate to ask questions.

▶ Go through the CV, starting with the most recent work. This helps put people at ease and gets them talking, as most people can talk quite readily about what they are doing at the present. Go back to previous work as well, but only ask about work that seems relevant; there is no need to cover everything.

▶ Ask in general terms about the content of the work and how much the person enjoyed it, and then home in on more specific issues of skills and knowledge.

It's best to start off with some 'open' questions that allow candidates an opportunity to demonstrate their interests and experience. Examples of 'open' questions would be 'That must have involved some tricky algorithm development?', 'Do you enjoy doing that kind of thing?', or 'What was your part in the project team?'. This sort of question gives candidates a chance to express themselves and tell you about things they are proud of. When you ask an open question, give the candidate lots of time to answer and avoid interrupting; the more the candidate talks the better, within reason.

Then from these open questions you can ask a few 'closed' questions on specific skills and experiences that are relevant. Examples of 'closed' questions might be 'Can you remember what tool you used for that?', 'Did you create the user interface yourself?', or 'Are you familiar with the TIFF file format?'. Closed questions are the sort with a short answer that delivers specific information. Don't use too many of these sorts of questions as they are very specific and don't tell you much about the person's motivation and personality. It's best to reserve them for probing into specialist skills, or to detect whether candidates really know what they are talking about.

▶ You need to **control the flow** of the interview. If you want to hear more, it's often enough just to nod and make eye contact and perhaps make some encouraging remark. If you've heard enough then you can also convey this by your body language – if you reduce eye contact and give little encouragement, most people will realize that they have said enough. If this doesn't work and you feel that the candidate has answered the question, then you can simply interrupt, thank the candidate and move on to another question.

You should find yourself talking for much less of the time than the candidate; you can't learn anything if you do all the talking.

▶ Having gone through the CV, you should set the candidate some tests. It's a good idea to write out a set of tests that you can give to every candidate, to help you compare one candidate with another.

It is vitally important to set tests that are **as similar as possible to the work that you want the person to do**. If you are trying to find someone that can

Each interviewer should use the same set of test questions on each candidate they see. They may not set every test to every candidate. It's not so important for all interviewers to work from the same set of questions, people should be able to use their own sets that work for them, although building up a standard set of questions for interviewers to choose from can be useful in improving interview practice.

design, then don't just ask them coding questions, get them to do some design for goodness' sake! Be clear about *what* each test is testing. If you want to find someone who can design then make sure the test determines whether they can design, and does not simply test their skill with a given methodology or tool. You can write other tests for those things if they are important. If you want to find someone who can write code then get them to *write* some code, not just to read some code and talk about it.

▶ Tests don't have to involve written or spoken answers. A very good test for programmers is to *sit them in front of a computer and make them write a program*. You can watch how they use the tools, how well they can use the help systems, how much commenting they do, how much error checking they put in, how they test their own work and so on. If you are interviewing people who may not have used a given tool before, then you could write the shell of the problem for them, so that they only have to complete a small part.

Personally I never get people to look through code on paper, trying to spot syntax errors. This is not a realistic test because in real life they have compilers and debuggers to help them.

People rarely write comments if you ask them to write code on paper but you would expect to see some if you ask them to write it for real.

▶ **Start off with simple tests and work up to harder ones.** This helps to let people relax and it also saves you time as you can stop when you reach the candidate's level of knowledge. Sort the tests into areas, for instance start with an easy coding question and move on to harder coding questions, and then start again at the easy end of the scale for design questions (or whatever categories of question make sense to you).

Don't be scared to ask questions that are hard. Better people like being asked harder questions, because it gives them a chance to stand out from the crowd.

▶ **Never over-sell the job.** The single most common reason given by technical people for leaving their job is that it did not live up to the expectations they had following the interview. Be honest. You can talk up the positive points of the job, but don't hide the negative side. Don't pretend it's more exciting or more senior than it really is. If everyone works 10 hours a week overtime then say so. It's better to talk about this with a job candidate, than find yourself talking about it to a very upset employee a week after he or she arrives.

▶ Towards the end of the interview, make it clear that you're finished, invite candidates to **ask any questions** they may have, and allow plenty of time for answering them. Also make sure that **candidates know what will happen next** – when and how your decision will reach them, and whether they might have to come back for another interview.

▶ You may also like to **show candidates around** the place where they would be working – this makes it much easier for them to imagine themselves doing the job, which improves the chance of them accepting. It also gives another more informal situation, where questions can be asked with less pressure. It is a good time to talk about the person's life outside work, such as their hobbies, to try to get a more rounded picture of the candidate as a human being.

▶ With many candidates, there comes a point during the interview where you are certain that you would not want to offer them a job. A common reason is that you realize the candidate has over-stated their knowledge to a huge extent, claiming years of experience when they have merely read a book – such people must not be hired. There is little point continuing after this point, you might as well draw the interview to a close, as you are wasting each other's time. In particular I would only give tours of the facilities to those candidates that you are really impressed by – these tours take time and often cause distraction to other people.

▶ Following the interview, make sure your impressions are given as soon as possible to whoever will make the decision. The three questions you should ask yourself are:

1 Can they do the job?
Have they got the skills, knowledge and experience that it requires?

2 Will they do the job?
Are they interested in this type of work? Are they enthusiastic? Would they work hard and work smart or do they just want an easy ride?

3 Would they fit in?
Do you think you would enjoy working with the person? Were they easy to talk to, easy to communicate with? Would they be accepted into the organization?

The answer to all three questions has to be 'definitely yes' for you to consider hiring someone. It is no good, for instance, taking someone who knows their stuff and is enthusiastic, but whom you can't work with.

The question that often causes the most soul-searching on the part of the interviewer is the last one. You must not reject competent people merely because they are 'not like one of us', but you cannot accept someone who is technically skilled but will be unable to work with other people.

It's very healthy to bring in people who have different outlooks and experiences. People with interests outside software, or who came to software through a roundabout route, often have the broadest interests and can apply ideas from other areas.

The fundamental question is, 'is this person a team player?' You can take someone with just a little arrogance (*only* a litle), a little timidity, a reasonable amount of ambition, or quite strong personal or political opinions, as long as you believe that the person will not let these things get in the way of working with others.

▶ It is good practice to write notes immediately after an interview, while it is fresh in your mind, as things can get muddled later.

▶ Never see more than three or four candidates in a day, otherwise you will be very tired and confused by the end of it.

▶ It used to be standard practice to ask candidates back for a second interview, although this is becoming less common. If you do this, it is worth considering how you could ensure that you cover as much *new ground* as possible, perhaps by involving new people, setting different tests, or making the second interview a more informal affair.

▶ It should go without saying that you should avoid discriminating against candidates on the basis of factors that have no bearing on their work, such as gender, race or religion. Finding good people is hard enough without rejecting people for no good reason. This is another good reason to keep notes about candidates, in case a rejected candidate complains of discrimination.

In the case of disabled candidates, don't assume that their disabilities will make it impossible for them to do the job, or that they will require expensive equipment. Find out the facts. Find out how competent disabled candidates are and how productive they can be by testing them, as you would anyone else. Note specifically that typing speed actually makes very little difference to a software engineer's productivity; competence is much more important than speed.

Remember that while recruitment is expensive and time-consuming, BAD recruitment is VERY expensive and VERY time-consuming. Bringing someone in who does poor work or who disrupts the rest of the team can have a lasting negative effect on the organization.

If you've been recruiting for some time, and getting desperate to find someone, you may start to doubt that you will find the right person. You

An expert on image processing who I once knew was previously a bricklayer. I often wondered if this experience of making a big object from thousands of tiny ones helped him in his image processing!

Some organizations routinely photograph all candidates – it helps people remember them later.

I would like to encourage the recruitment method usually found in France, where the candidate is taken out for a really good meal if they get through the first round!

The importance of hiring good people applies as much to contract staff as to permanent staff – it is a mistake to think that contractors can be hired with a less thorough interview process. Although contractors can be got rid of quickly, it is a mistake to reduce the selection process with this in mind. Poor people make a mess of your project very quickly, and a succession of poor people is a disaster. Be as choosy with contractors as you would be with permanent staff.

Eventually, if the job is not filled the organization may have to go back and reconsider why it is recruiting for this position, and might have to split the job into two roles, arrange for existing staff to be retrained, reorganize departments or take other larger decisions. It is not your job to make these kinds of decisions; you should just try to recruit a good person to the job as currently described.

might worry that you are setting the standard too high. You will be tempted to bring in someone who is not really all you wanted. DON'T DO IT. Never accept a mediocre candidate because you have not yet seen anyone good enough; keep looking. Having a vacancy is better than having it filled by someone who is a waste of space.

When someone has accepted a job offer, it's still not the end of the process. Eventually that person will arrive for their first day of work. If they work on your team, then you should be prepared to **spend a great deal of time with them to start with**. Write off all your time on their first day at least. The way people are treated on their first day has a lasting effect on them. Spend time introducing them to the team and to other people in the organization, telling them about the project and what they will be working on, explaining the company's procedures and its IT set-up and so on. Recruiting someone is not just about getting someone in, it's about getting someone who will do a good job and stay for some time, and the first day is an important part of that process.

7

HOW DO I MAKE A PRESENTATION?

In this section I'm going to talk about the sort of presentation where you speak to an audience, with a set of slides or overhead projection images. Most of this section will apply equally well to other types of presentation such as demonstrations or lectures.

Even when you've done it a few times, standing up in front of people and talking for some time can be a daunting prospect. The key to delivering a presentation that has the desired impact, and to reducing your nerves, is *preparation*.

Before you do anything else, **consider the audience**. Who will be in the audience, and what impact do you want your presentation to have on them? Are you there to entertain, to inform, to sell, or what? Are the audience knowledgeable about your subject or ignorant of it? Are they really interested or are they attending out of duty or by coercion? Are there important decision-makers in the audience, or people who will influence the decision-makers? You need to be clear on these points in order to pitch your presentation at the right level and pace, and to select the appropriate content and style.

Content is vital. You can't achieve much by jazzing up poor content with fancy presentation. Put together the key points that must be said and that you would like to be remembered. Leave out anything that is peripheral, unimportant or obvious to your audience. Together, your points should form a presentation that is:

▶ **Complete**
Decide what your presentation will contain and what it will leave out. The points that you cover should form a whole picture, from introductory

explanations to filling in the relevant details. Don't allude to points that you won't be covering. You want your audience to be left with the impression of an issue well covered, not with heads full of unanswered questions.

▶ Balanced

If you're trying to make the case for a decision or a change to be made, then don't be entirely one-sided. You should be honest right from the outset about which side of the argument you favour, but you should include an honest assessment of the points in favour and against.

▶ Interesting

Nobody will remember what you say, no matter how earth-shattering the implications, if they are asleep when you say it. This starts with the content – include information that you know your audience will find interesting, or controversial, even if it takes you off the main point just a little. Good presentation can stop the eyes glazing over, but it doesn't help people remember the facts afterwards.

▶ Relevant

Keep in mind what the purpose of your presentation is, and don't allow yourself to be side-tracked into lengthy discussions of related but irrelevant material. Leave out things that you find interesting but the audience will not find interesting or relevant.

▶ Structured

Your content has to be arranged into a structure, and this should be done before you start creating slides. At the very minimum, every presentation should have three sections: introduction, body and conclusions. Or, as I was taught, 'Tell them what you're going to say. Say it. Then tell them what you just said'. Usually, the body of your presentation will need a structure as well, just like a document would, reflecting the nature of your content.

Whilst most of the rest of this section is devoted to presentation and delivery, you should actually spend more time thinking about your content than about those things.

Nowadays, most presentations are multimedia affairs using overhead projectors, slide projectors or video screens, and because this is the expectation, your presentation will seem appallingly dull if you just stand and talk or draw on a board. Even if you feel that your subject doesn't really need it, if you are going to make a presentation then make a good job of the visual side of it – don't aim for clever and fancy, just presentable

Don't go overboard on controversy. It is dangerous to slip a huge bombshell of a controversy into a talk unless the talk is about that issue, as the audience may forget everything else you say.

and legible will do. If you're really convinced that you don't need visual aids (maybe you're lecturing on mathematics?), then in a business context it might well be best not to make a presentation at all, and just circulate a document. Your content has got to be riveting, and your abilities as a presenter superb, for a business presentation to be successful without visual aids.

Do what you can to keep your audience awake and listening to you:

▶ **Use colour in your visuals.** Monochrome photocopied overheads look just pathetic. Don't go overboard on effects, sounds and so forth – a clear, consistent style is ideal. Colour is important because it helps people distinguish types of items such as headings, important information, and background points. You can also use colour to distinguish the different sections of your content. The aim is to make the presentation style *enliven and clarify* your content, not take over as an experience in itself.

▶ **Don't put too much on a slide.** Make one important point per slide, clarified by up to five or six bullet-points.

▶ Do not simply read the slide. **What you say should not be the same as what is written.** You should explain, clarify or justify what is printed on the slide – typically, you should say about three or four times more than is written on the slide (as a very crude rule of thumb).

▶ Have some notes so you don't forget something important, but don't hide yourself away in them. See the `infobar //` SPEAKER NOTES.

▶ **Face the audience and keep eye contact with them.** Every time you look up, make eye contact with one or two people, scanning the audience so everyone gets noticed eventually.

▶ **Your voice needs to rise and fall in order to punctuate the presentation.** Stress things that are important, let some enthusiasm creep in when you talk about something you care about. Above all, avoid the dull monotone that puts everyone to sleep. You should also use silence in order to separate sections – between sections, pause for a count of three. This will seem like a long time to you, especially if you're nervous, but for the audience it will be barely noticeable. After the pause, announce the title of the next section in a bold tone, before talking about the content.

▶ Try to adopt a relaxed pose; don't stand rigidly in front of the audience. **Use gestures** if you would normally use them when speaking.

There is little excuse nowadays for 'kitchen-worktop' overheads drawn by hand. You almost certainly have some computer software that can put together a simple set of overheads. If you don't have access to a good colour printer, for a very small fee you should be able to get your overheads printed by a local printing firm.

If you have a list of important items, put the *least* important at the top of the list. Otherwise, people will tend to read the first one or two and then mentally dismiss the rest as 'minor'. See also the 'three out of four trick' in SECTION 29: I WANT TO TACKLE THE PROJECT IN A PARTICULAR WAY.

▶ If the structure of your content is complex and you want people to be sure where you are in the talk, write out the content separately. You could keep showing a slide containing the structure of your talk at the start of each section, and pointing to where you are, or you could display the structure separately on a board or flip-chart.

▶ Avoid distractions. If you don't need the visuals for a while, turn the projector off. If you keep getting interrupted, ask people to save their questions for the end. Avoid passing around objects or handouts during the presentation.

Always practise your presentation. The most important part is the first three or four sentences; if you can get those out smoothly then the rest tend to follow, as long as you've practised out loud a couple of times.

If you can arrange it, practise your presentation to the room where you will give it – the empty room. You may feel a bit of a fool but it's great preparation, and when you get a real audience it feels more of a relief than anything.

If you tend to mumble, try practising with someone sitting at the back of the room. Another method that works well is to practise at home, standing at the top of the stairs and talking to someone at the bottom.

Time your presentation. Even if you don't have to fit into a tight schedule, it's useful to be able to tell people how long it will take. If you do have to meet some time limit, don't forget to include a couple of minutes for questions.

Speaking in front of an audience is something that you get used to quite quickly after a few times. A few nerves remain, even for the most experienced presenter, and the key to overcoming these is to put together content that you can be proud of, and to gain confidence through preparation.

infobar // **SPEAKER NOTES**

It's useful, though by no means essential, to have some notes to remind you what you want to say. The trouble is that in the midst of the presentation you won't find much time to read them, and if you get them mixed up you may not have time to sort them out. So:

- Make the text of your notes very large and very brief. Just putting down a list of key words may well be enough to remind you to mention a subject. Only write complete sentences if you are going to pick up the notes and read something from them out loud to the audience. The larger the text the better, because you want to be able to see the notes without holding them to your face.

- Make sure you can access your notes and find your place easily. Number the slides and the notes that go with them, in case you drop the lot on the floor. For printed overhead projector slides it works well if you interleave your notes between the slides, so that as you put a slide onto the projector, your notes for that slide are revealed to you. In other situations, it's useful to print pages that include a small image of the relevant slide on each note page. Most presentation packages can do this for you.

8

HOW DO I EARN THE RESPECT OF MY TEAM?

Being respected, being taken seriously, is something that new leaders often worry about. Sometimes they worry about it too much.

The thing people *most* respect in a leader is *good judgement.* Good judgement comes:

▶ **From experience.** When you know what works and what doesn't, put that knowledge to work. Be willing to do a thing differently if your experience shows that the 'accepted' way of doing it doesn't work very well. Extract generalizations from your experiences to guide you in new situations.

▶ **From being flexible.** The right action to take in any situation is determined by the situation and by the people involved. Don't be dogmatic about the 'right' way to do things, but think instead about the appropriate way to do things.

▶ **From listening.** Listen to what people have to say, don't dismiss their opinions out of hand, and equally don't accept them without question no matter how good the person's credentials may be. This applies to the opinions of team members, of your customers, of managers, of suppliers and of authors of books.

If you're not sure whose point of view is the most appropriate, try looking at things from your customer's point of view.

You will earn the respect of your team by being part of the team and by doing your job well. One of the easiest ways to lose respect is to demand it. Remember that the other people on your team work *with* you, they don't work *for* you. You are just a team member, who happens to have some non-developmental responsibilities. You lead a team from within,

not from on top. Nobody will respect you if you become pompous and overbearing, so don't put people down or try to protect your own situation by stifling disagreement. **Take your project seriously, don't take yourself too seriously.**

People find it hard to respect someone who can't organize themselves. Make sure that *you* are the one who does the timesheets on time, that *you* can find your desk under all the paper, that *you* don't lose important information, that *you* don't forget tasks that need doing, and that *you* don't procrastinate.

Give highest priority to doing those things that need to be done by the leader, like making decisions (which might sometimes be unpopular decisions), representing the project to management, liasing with the customer, or doing the planning. Give yourself tasks that are important for the team, especially in looking forward, avoiding obstacles and **enabling the rest of the team to make progress.** Be willing to do dull or menial work if this lets the rest of the team progress. Never give yourself a task just because you find it interesting.

Be the person who has all the information about the project. Be the collecting point and the distribution point for information relating to your project. Don't hang on to information to try to control it, but be willing to share it with anyone who needs it. Make sure that you have access to information about the project from all angles, and that you receive new information that comes in, for instance from sales or marketing departments. Be proactive about gathering information and impressions, for instance take it on yourself to stay in touch with your customers.

Be positive about the project. It never does the leader any credit to moan or to be negative about the project or its chances of success. Treat problems as challenges to be overcome by the team, and be proactive about finding solutions and making things happen. Don't pretend everything is OK when it isn't, but always be the one that looks for solutions, not excuses.

Have high expectations. Don't let people get away with work that is not good enough. Though you can't afford to achieve perfection in everything, you can and should expect people to do the best that they can achieve within the constraints of time and money available, and not try always to get away with the minimum effort. Never let inferior work get through to the product, get it changed, and if necessary get it done again by someone else. Every task should be done adequately. What is 'adequate' varies from task to task. Sometimes you may want only the bare minimum done; at other times, only the best will do.

If you make a mistake, be honest about it, and then do what you can to put it right. Don't try to cover it up or to pretend, even to yourself, that you still think you were right, and certainly don't try to find excuses or blame other people. We all make mistakes; be brave enough to admit it when you realize you have made one.

Lead by example. Do your job well and be thorough and organized, and take on responsibility. Deliver work of high quality. Let others review your work, and accept the review points in good humour.

Respect has to be earned. Don't expect to be given respect just because you're the leader. In fact, the leader has to do more to earn respect than any other team member does. Try not to be too uptight, over-serious or intense about being a leader, but equally don't deny your role. Just like the rest of the team, aim to be relaxed, but productive.

     I am not your leader because I have the strongest arm for the bow, or the mightiest sword, or even the bravest heart, but because you have learned to trust my judgement, and know that even when I am wrong I speak for the good of us all and not for pride

(from '*Eric the Viking*' by Terry Jones)

>> PROJECT MANAGEMENT

9

HOW DO I DRAW UP A PROJECT PLAN? WHAT USE IS IT?

In this discussion, I am going to consider that planning includes both of the following:

▶ Writing the *project plan documentation* that you might have to help produce, which might be one document, or might be several (such as a Quality Plan, Development Plan or whatever they are called in your organization).

▶ Creating the *task plan*, consisting of tables or charts (such as 'Gantt charts', see below) that show tasks, with their estimated times (and possibly costs).

'WHY SHOULD I GET INVOLVED IN PLANNING?'

As an experienced software engineer, you may feel that there are better things to do with your time than write project plans, which never seem to become reality in any case. After all, there is never time to do everything perfectly, so you have to prioritize, and you might feel that spending your time designing and coding would contribute more towards a positive outcome for the project than writing a plan. You may feel that planning is something that can be left to someone else, such as a Project Manager, while you concentrate on the more technical aspects of the project.

So why should you, the technical team leader, spend hours, or days, drawing up and maintaining plans?

Firstly, here's why planning needs doing at all:

▶ **To give you and your team a framework to think within.** Just as a drawing of the technical architecture of the project lets you think about the technical solution, so the project plan lets you think about the organization of the project. Work needs organizing and structuring, every bit as much as software code does. You need to think about the people you have, their skills and abilities, and how these match up against the tasks to be performed. Just letting events unfold is not a wise way to organize anything!

By thinking about such issues as risks, training, tools, dependencies, responsibilities and so on, you get to see problems ahead of time, and think about ways to avoid them. The documentation that results is not the thing of value. It's the mental effort, forced on you by having to confront the issues, that is valuable.

▶ **It helps you defend your decisions.** The project plan lets you justify your position. It gives you ammunition to fight battles for the people, time, resources and support that you need. If you go to management with a 'feeling' that you need more staff on your project, you are likely to be given short shrift. After all, senior people in the organization may have committed to delivering the project within the estimated time and cost, and they will not want to hear that they were wrong. But if you set out realistic estimates of progress, both with and without the extra resources, then you are giving the management the input they need to make a decision, and if your arguments are well founded then that decision is much more likely to go in your favour.

▶ **It is a communication tool.** By setting out a plan you generate a focus for discussion. For example, you may realize that it will be necessary for a certain team member to do a particularly undesirable task, because he or she is the only person with the skills available at that time, and the job has to be done at a certain time or the project will suffer. All of this should be visible on the plan. If this necessity can be seen from the plan, and especially if the person concerned has been given a chance to review the plan and feel some 'ownership' of it, then that individual is far less likely to resent having to do the job.

Talking through the plan, especially the Gantt chart, lets you explain the logic of the project to your team. Even if the plan does not turn out exactly as predicted at the beginning, the logic of the dependencies and priorities should stay valid.

It may be that you have project managers and administrative staff who can do some of the planning work. So how much of the planning activity do you **personally** need to do?

On a small project it is easy for the team leader to prepare the documents and charts. On a larger project there may be a complex structure of interdependent plans and document trees, which the project manager would normally maintain. The team leader would prepare sections of documents and tentative charts, to be incorporated into the main system.

Unfortunately, the answer is 'quite a bit'. Only the technical staff, not the project managers or departmental managers, can provide valid estimates of the tasks to be performed and the time these will take, and only the technical staff can determine which work is dependent on other work. Only the technical staff can make the fundamental choices of direction and technology for the project, which directly affect the time-scales and the risk. Project managers are essentially good at organizing, co-ordinating and negotiating – but they are not in charge of the technology and it is not their job to estimate times, risks or costs.

The team leader is responsible for the planning and it will normally fall upon him or her to put the plans together. When the project is up and running, it will be the team leader's job to decide 'who does what, with what, and when'. So it makes sense that the same person tries to predict these things in the project plan. The leader may not need actually to prepare the documents and charts, but only he or she can take responsibility for what is in them.

Of course, experience shows that projects rarely run the way the plan said they would. Often this is because the plans were unrealistically optimistic to start with, and also events usually conspire to upset things. Unexpected problems crop up – risks happen. It's rather like going on a long journey – diversions and delays crop up to make your itinerary obsolete.

Certainly, planning takes time – but not as much time as going the wrong way and having to backtrack. Many technical people moan that they 'haven't got time' to do the planning – they just want to get on with the design and code – 'that's what really matters'. This is like arguing that there is no time to consult a map before setting off on a journey – 'let's forget that and just drive as fast as we can' is not the smartest way to get somewhere quickly.

As with all other activities in the real world of software development, there is no time to do everything perfectly. Planning, like everything else, needs doing well enough to give you most of the answers, but no better. Better to do a plan that lets you see as far ahead as you can reasonably see, and revisit it some time further down the road. Nobody can expect your vision to be perfect, but everyone can rightly attack you if you do not bother to look, or if you looked but didn't take notice of what you saw. Even a crude outline plan that identifies critical activities, resulting in these activities being started early and being well resourced, will contribute a great deal to the smooth running of the project.

'WHAT NEEDS TO BE IN THE PLAN?'

The project planning usually consists of the two parts noted in the introduction to this section: project plan documentation, which is written very early in the project and remains fairly static for the rest of the project duration, and the time charts that are written as soon as the architecture of the project becomes clear and are constantly updated as the project progresses.

The **project plan documentation** should contain some or all of the following – skip out sections that are inappropriate to your project (if you are allowed to do so by your formal procedures):

▶ Identification: What is the project's name, code number and so on?

▶ References: What other documents such as bids, marketing papers, minutes of relevant meetings or other sources of input are relevant?

▶ Background: What is the project for? Why is it needed? Why does the customer want it? Why it is being done now?

▶ Roles and responsibilities: Who are the people on the project? What are their responsibilities? Who is ultimately responsible for technical decisions, marketing decisions and commercial decisions? Who will be the primary point of contact for the customer? Who approves documents, gives permission for deliveries and checks that testing has been adequate? Who allocates tasks to individuals on a day-to-day basis?

▶ Methodologies for design: Will you be using object-oriented methods, formal methods, rapid prototyping? Will code be automatically generated from design tools? What level of detail will be included in the designs?

▶ Technologies: What languages, platforms or protocols will you be using?

▶ Tools needed: What tools will you use for design, coding, testing, documentation and planning?

▶ Staffing: The time chart will indicate how many people are needed during the life of the project. What skills, knowledge and experience are required? Will the right people be available at the right times? Will permanent or contract staff need to be recruited, and if so when will they be needed?

▶ Training needs: What training, either external or in-house, will be needed and when? When and how can it be provided? How much will it cost?

▶ External relationships and dependencies: Who are you depending on? Who is depending on you? What is the nature of the relationships? What will your deliverables be? Will the source code be released externally?

▶ Risks: What could happen that would grossly upset your plans? What would be the consequences to the project? How much time and money would it cost? What would the customer make of it? How could you reduce the likelihood of these risks occurring? How could you reduce the consequences of them occurring if they did?

▶ Hazards: If something you deliver is faulty, will people be hurt? How likely is this to happen? How badly would people be hurt? What will you do to mitigate these hazards?

▶ Procedures and quality: What procedures will you follow? Are you going to have any special working practices for this project? How will the quality of the design, code, documentation and deliverables be ensured? What sort of reviews will you hold? What level of change control is appropriate?

▶ Configuration management: How will you keep your work safe against accidental loss? How will you prevent more than one person working on a file at the same time? At what stages in the project will safe copies be taken so that you can roll back to them if necessary? Will data (such as test data) be included in configuration management? Will documents be included? If not, how will you match document revisions against release versions? Will you keep old versions of documents? Will you need to take branched copies of work and then merge it later?

▶ Documentation: What documents need to be produced for this project? How will they be reviewed and approved?

▶ Progress monitoring and reporting: How will time and costs be monitored against the predicted plan? What regular management meetings or reports are required? How will the time that people spend on the project be booked to it?

▶ Testing: How much unit testing will be applied? How will final testing be performed? How will the tests be documented and the results recorded? Will there be beta releases to customers? How will feedback be collected from customers? Will you need to set up a test environment or create test data? Will you need to replicate your customer's environment for testing purposes?

▶ Bugs and issues: How will you track bugs and other problem issues? Who will decide the seriousness of problems?

▶ Release procedures: What will a release consist of? What documentation (internal and external) is needed? How will it be delivered to the customer? Who will approve it? How will a release be archived?

▶ Acceptance: How will the customer indicate whether they accept the software as fit for purpose? Who will decide how to respond if the customer rejects the product?

▶ Warranty and support: When does the warranty period start, and how long does it last? What types of problem will be fixed for free during the warranty period, and what counts as an enhancement request to be covered by a support contract?

▶ Licensing: What licences do you require for development? What licences must your customer purchase? How will your licences be enforced?

▶ Security: How will you protect the intellectual property created by the project? How will you protect secrets to which you have been given access? How will you prevent illegal copying of your products?

▶ Requirements change procedure: If the customer wants something changed, how should they communicate this to you? How will you respond? Who will decide what is a change request and what is a bug report? How will decisions be made on whether to accept change requests?

▶ Organization: How will information be held on the IT system? What will the project folder look like on your servers? Where will electronic copies of documents be archived? How will you organize hard-copy such as letters or documents sent to you? Will you retain documents that have been given approval signatures, and if so, how?

The project plan documentation is normally quite static. It is written at the very start of a project and then usually it needs little maintenance. Remember, the value of this document is *not* in the paperwork that is produced, it is in the *thinking and decision-making that goes into it*. It also gives you approval for decisions that have been made.

For example, the issue of allocating people to tasks can sometimes be contentious. Sometimes there is both a team leader and a project manager who both think this is their job. The project plan should make it clear on what occasions each can allocate people to tasks.

It is vital that this plan does not avoid issues or plaster over problems. Its main purpose is to clarify issues and give authority to people. If known problems are avoided in this document then it really will be a waste of paper.

You may not have to write the entire contents of this document. Much of it will be similar to previous documents of the same type, and if you have a project manager, he or she may write much of it. But you should provide input to it, and review it.

Make sure that this document gets approved by senior management, because it is this document that gives people on the project the authority to make project decisions.

The task plan is used to estimate how long the project will last, when major deliveries will happen, how much the project will cost, and how many people are required.

Typically, a Gantt chart is used. If you are not familiar with these, see the >skills box GANTT CHARTS. Gantt charts show the tasks that must be performed, when they are predicted to happen, and who is expected to do them, in an easily accessible visual form. They also show the dependencies between tasks, dependencies on external inputs, and the outputs being produced.

Typically, the plan is created early in the project, and then updated constantly as the project progresses. The plan is updated to reflect how long tasks actually took, new tasks that are uncovered, revised estimates, and requirements changes.

I would recommend that you always use some sort of software tool, even for your own rough ideas, when putting together plans. They save time, and let you see things from several different views. But beware getting carried away with the technology – remember to use the tool to produce the sort of output that you want, and don't spend non-productive time fine-tuning the software to produce beautiful reports when this is not necessary.

It doesn't matter too much whether the plan shows an accurate history of what has already happened. What does matter is that it accurately reflects what is happening now, and shows an accurate estimation of what will happen in the future.

Gantt charts are not always appropriate. If you have a small amount of work to do, that just needs to be finished, and you don't need to worry about dependencies, then simply estimating the time for each task and adding up the total produces a perfectly adequate task plan. This could be done in a spreadsheet, for example.

'HOW DO I COME UP WITH REALISTIC ESTIMATES?'

Estimation is mostly a matter of applying your experience, and a knowledge of what has happened previously on projects similar to yours. Here are a few notes concerning estimation of time-scales:

▶ When estimating time-scales, be clear what you are estimating. Is it just the coding you are thinking of, or are you allowing for the design, documentation, testing, debugging and so on? If you ask most engineers how long something will take, they think only about the coding. Worse than that, they often think only about the 'essential' code, and don't allow for all the error handling, sanity-checking and user-comforting code that is needed. When you think up an estimate, or someone gives you an estimate, you need to know how much of the total effort this estimate represents.

▶ Estimates tend to get longer as you break them down into more detail. If your plan consists of tasks that are several weeks long, try breaking one of them down into individual elements. For example, if you have a task for implementing a module, break it down into parts such as design, code, making the test bench, documentation, unit test, reviews, rework and so on. Or alternatively, into implementation sections such as user interface and embedded code. I find that when I do this, the total time increases – usually becoming more realistic.

However, you can go too far, breaking the tasks down to microscopic levels and allocating a nominal time such as 'half a day' for each, resulting in a plan that is overcrowded with meaningless little tasks.

Combining the two points above: if you find that someone has made estimates based only on coding, get them to do it again with more detail, including the other aspects of the work. Add up the total and compare this to the original 'coding-only' estimate. It is not unusual to find that the detailed estimate comes to significantly more – a factor of 2.5 times longer would not be unusual. If so, you could break down all the other tasks in your plan, or you could go through and find all other tasks that are of the same type as the one you've examined, and make them all longer by the factor (2.5 times for example).

▶ Most engineers are optimistic when estimating. They tend to assume that things will go well. The degree to which this is true varies from person to person. Also, people tend to estimate longer times for tasks that they are not looking forward to, and less time for tasks they expect to enjoy. Use your knowledge of the people on your team to modify their estimates as necessary – more often than not, this means giving *more* time than they asked for.

▶ **Don't forget holidays**, including people's annual leave. If you pretend that people don't have holidays then your plan will be unrealistic before you even start. If you know when people have vacations booked then put these into the plan. Otherwise, add a proportion of the annual leave, spread over the life of the project. Similarly, estimate time for sick leave.

▶ **Structure the plan around tasks, not requirements.** For example, don't take the requirements document and list the requirements in the task plan. Some requirements will produce single tasks, others will produce many, and there will be many tasks that need doing to make other things possible. **The best way to structure the plan is to base it on the architecture of your design.**

As explained in SECTION 1: I'VE JUST BEEN MADE TEAM LEADER OF A NEW PROJECT, the project plan cannot be considered to be realistic and useful until the architecture of your design is complete. See SECTION 35: HOW DO I DECIDE ON THE BEST ARCHITECTURE AND DESIGN FOR MY PROJECT?.

▶ **Include a realistic allowance for contingency** (see the infobar // CONTINGENCY).

▶ Don't forget to **include time in the plan for ongoing team leadership effort.** As well as keeping the plan up to date there will also be meetings, reporting, reviews and co-ordination tasks that you as leader must attend to. The percentage of your time to book to this overhead depends on how your organization works and how much help you get from project managers or your boss, as well as the size of the team. It's very easy to underestimate the call that leadership effort will have on your time. For example, if you're leading a team of five people it wouldn't be unreasonable to expect three-quarters of your time to be taken up in reviews and liaison efforts, leaving just a quarter for design, coding, testing and documentation.

▶ **Allow time for recruitment of new people.** And don't pretend that they will be fully productive from day 1.

▶ On larger projects, **estimate how many people may leave and have to be replaced during the project.** This is a major reason why some projects are late.

▶ If your project depends on some other project or activity, build in that dependency. You may like to play safe and assume that it will be late.

▶ Never give in to management pressure to 'cut the time-scales'. This can only be done if you also cut features or have significantly more people or better people. Just giving in and reducing the plan will not make the project come in any sooner, it will just make your plan unrealistic.

▶ Base your plan on what has happened before. For example, after you deliver your product to your customer, is it usually accepted first time, or is there usually a bug-fix phase and a re-release? Be honest. If it happens every time, can you honestly say that it won't happen on your project? If it is realistically likely to happen, then show this bug fixing and re-release on your plan.

▶ Try to find out how long things really take so you can improve your estimates in future. If your organization has a system that allows people to book time to individual tasks, use it to give yourself, and the other team members, feedback on the quality of the estimations. If your organization hasn't got such a system, make notes yourself so that you can compare prediction to reality. This is the only way to learn to make better estimates in future.

'WHAT DO I DO IF THE PLAN SHOWS THAT THE PROJECT WILL BE LATE?'

Having made the estimates, you will need to arrange your project plan so that people are kept busy and the time-scale is as short as possible. The planning software can be a big help with this – with most packages, for example, things can be arranged so that you can indicate all the people that *could* do a given task, allowing the software to choose those that are free, to keep the overall time-scale as short as possible.

If your estimates show that your project will complete too late, then you will probably want to put together another version of your plan, based on the assumption that more people are available. This is a perfectly sensible thing to do so that you can calculate the effect. The effect is not a linear one – the time-scales do not reduce in proportion to the people available:

▶ If your project is grossly under-resourced, then adding more people will be a real help. You need a certain 'critical mass' of people to produce a sense of progress. There are certain aspects of a project – for example, progress reporting – that are fairly fixed and do not take much longer if there are more people. With more people, the effect of these fixed tasks is reduced, and the project becomes more efficient. With more people, more work can be done at once, and a sense of progress ensues.

▶ **Once the 'critical mass' is exceeded, adding extra people to the project starts to have less benefit.** People tend to get in the way of each other and get stuck waiting for other people to release shared files and resources. There is an extra burden of communication that increases enormously as more people are involved. The leader will start to become overloaded with co-ordination tasks and reviews. If you *greatly* exceed the critical mass, then the project will start to 'thrash' so badly that adding extra people may actually slow the project down. **If your plan shows that you are going to deliver late, you can't just 'throw people' at the problem.**

It's usually quite easy to get an idea of what the critical mass for a project is, from the plan. It's usually obvious if you try to arrange your plan so that an unrealistic number of things are happening at the same time. If you find yourself thinking 'how can I do more things in parallel to keep everyone busy?' then you've probably exceeded the critical mass and your plan is becoming over-resourced. If on the other hand you look at a task on the plan and think 'why is that getting done so late, it could have been done long before that?' and on examination you find that the only reason is lack of people, then probably your plan is under-resourced.

If you find that more people will be useful, then you will need to present your plan to management and use it to justify your needs. As well as planning for more people, you may also want to consider reducing the functionality, or delaying deliveries. These things need to be done in agreement both with management and with your customers or marketing department.

No matter what gets agreed with management, always keep your plan updated and realistic. For example, if you don't get the people you need, take them out of the plan. If this means that you expect to deliver late, then you need to communicate this to management. Don't get in the trap of being expected to deliver to time-scales that you know to be impossible – challenge this situation as early as possible. See also SECTION 10: BEING GIVEN AN UNREALISTIC TIMESCALE.

'HOW DO I USE THE PLANS?'

Once the plan is written, use it as a basis for negotiating with management and your customers. Use the plan to justify any demands you need to make for more people, more time, reduced or delayed features, or mitigation of risks.

infobar // **CONTINGENCY**

Contingency is time and money that is added to the project estimates and plans to cover unexpected eventualities. It is NOT added simply to cover individual tasks over-running – you should be confident of the time-scales you've estimated and not need to add extra time for this reason. The contingency basically covers these things:

- Risks that happen. As part of the planning process you should have considered what risks there are, how likely they are to occur, and what effect they would have if they did. How do you add these to your time and cost estimates? You can't assume that no risks will happen, and you can't assume that they all will. The correct way to handle risks is to calculate the 'likely' outcome, which is a sort of weighted average of the risks – see SECTION 33: TAKING A RISK. This 'likely risk' is added to the plan as contingency.

- Unexpected tasks that crop up. These may be things that you simply missed when drawing up the plan, small parcels of extra work added by minor 'feature creep', or work to undo mistakes made as the project progresses. These things happen and a realistic plan must include them.

In many cases, it is very difficult to calculate meaningful estimates for any of these elements of contingency, and a heuristic ('rule of thumb') approach is appropriate. Typically, the contingency is calculated as a percentage of the total time and cost. The percentage to use depends on how confident you are in your estimates. For example,

- For a project that is to implement something quite straightforward and very similar to something that has been done before (for example, an internet house producing a new, simple, non-interactive website), 10% might be appropriate.

- For a development project where most of the code will be new, but using entirely known technologies and suppliers and where the requirements are well documented, 20% would be reasonable.

- For a development project where the team is to adopt a language, platform or technology that is new to it, or where the requirements are intrinsically unclear and will be discovered as the project progresses, then 40% is sensible.

- If there are risks that might justify a higher factor than this then the likely-outcome approach described in SECTION 33: TAKING A RISK should be adopted.

cont >>

>>

Contingency is not for things that will definitely happen. For instance, the adoption of a new technology will definitely incur a 'learning curve' and early tasks should be estimated on the long side to allow for this. This is not contingency – contingency is for risks beyond the expected.

Make sure you don't count the risks twice. Don't add a factor to every task to cover the risks, and then add it again as explicit contingency.

Contingency is included in the plan and will add time and money to the estimated cost of the project. This cost may be used to estimate a price for the customer, and so the contingency will increase the cost your customer will be charged. That is correct – the customer should bear the brunt of the cost of risks that you take on their behalf. If none of those risks happen then your project will come in under-budget, but if more risks happen than predicted then it will come in over-budget. That is the way it should work.

However, many organizations don't like to see an explicit task called 'contingency' on the project plan, especially if it takes up 40% of the time. You may be asked to remove it. If so, then you need to include the time and money some other way – by adding invisible delays into the project and adding hidden 'fixed costs' for example, or by increasing all the time-scales by the contingency factor. I think that increasing all the estimated times is wrong, because it makes a farce of you learning from your actual performance in future. Contingency is there for unexpected things that really happen – for instance, suppose a major supplier goes bankrupt and you have to find a new one. What task code are you going to book that work to? The answer should be 'contingency'. To my mind, contingency should be visible on the plan and people should be able to book their time to it.

However you add contingency to the plan, it should be placed where it affects delivery dates according to the nature of the risks being covered. It is **not** automatically correct to spread the contingency evenly over the project lifetime, so that half the contingency happens in the first half of the time, nor to add it all at the end. The contingency should be shown on the plan in the place where it makes sense. For example, contingency to cover the adoption of a new technology should probably appear *near the start of the project*, when the technology is first being adopted and risks (beyond simple learning time), such as 'the new technology is a disaster and has to be abandoned', will take effect, if you are unlucky enough for them to materialize. The effect of such a risk happening would be to delay all tasks on the project, pushing out all the work and all the deliverables. Therefore, the contingency included for this risk should be at the start of the project, where it has exactly that effect.

Note that there are other ways to handle both risks and uncertainty of estimation, such as the 'PERT' method. This is beyond the scope of this book. See the Project Management section of the bibliography (SECTION 42) for a suitable reference.

Keep the plan up to date. That doesn't mean you have to look at it every day, although you might need to towards the end of a project, if you're following a tight schedule to deliver. Typically you will need to work on it every couple of weeks or so.

Firstly you need to make any rearrangements to the plan that are needed, such as moving tasks around or including new tasks that have come to light, or taking account of increases or decreases in resources.

You also need to record progress that has happened so far. You can do this by using the time that people have booked to the project, or you can estimate how complete you think each task is – more on this in the >skills box GANTT CHARTS below.

Use the plan to:

▶ Predict problems before they arise and take action to avoid them. Give priority to those tasks that must be done urgently to avoid holding other things up. Look at where the plan shows you are going to be held up by dependencies on external events, and rearrange your own work or put pressure on other teams if necessary.

▶ Allocate tasks to people appropriately, making the best use of the skills and aptitudes of the team members.

▶ Help the project run smoothly and avoid people 'thrashing' from one task to another.

▶ Check that the delivery dates currently predicted by the plan are acceptable. If they are not, use the plan to help decide on the best action to correct this (see also SECTION 10: BEING GIVEN AN UNREALISTIC TIMESCALE and SECTION 13: MY LAST PROJECT NEVER SEEMS TO GO AWAY).

Project plans are usually the basis for reporting progress to management. Managers may not want to see the detailed plan, but they probably will want to know whether you are still expecting to fulfil your original delivery and cost predictions. An up-to-date plan is essential for providing accurate information to management.

'WHAT DO I NEED TO REMEMBER?'

Planning is about balancing time, resources, features and risk. The point is not to produce wonderful documentation, but to apply the mental effort of confronting the issues and of looking as far ahead as possible. Once written, the plan gives you a basis on which to negotiate with management, and it remains useful throughout the project as a way of avoiding problems before they occur and making sure that the project is going to complete on time.

> skills box

GANTT CHARTS

Gantt charts show tasks against time, forming a visual representation of the work to be done on the project. This sort of chart is easy to understand and relate to the real world, and it is possible to use the chart to derive all sorts of useful information – such as how busy people are expected to be, or what the project will cost – and to compare what was planned against what actually happened, to track progress and costs.

The following picture shows a typical Gantt chart:

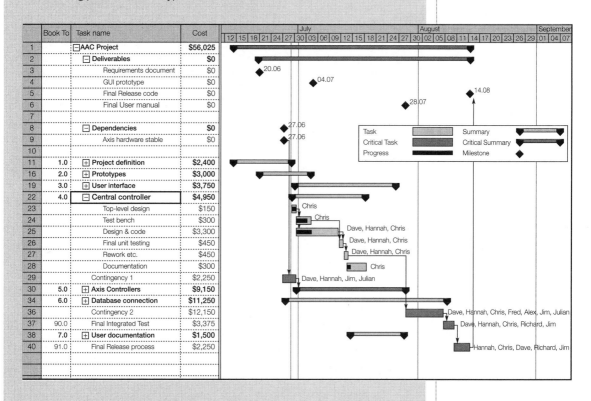

Most of the tasks that you can see in this example are 'rolled up' overviews – the details below this level have been closed up for simplicity. Only one level has been opened up, the 'Central Controller'. In this level you can see the tasks to be performed. Where one task must come before another (for example, development has to come before final test), these are linked – the arrows show these dependencies. Where there is no dependency, the software has moved tasks around to make best use of people's time, so if three things need to be done at the same time but the same person must do them all, the software will automatically sequence them one after another so that the person is not overworked.

See also the infobar // **CRITICAL PATH ANALYSIS**.

cont >>

>>

At the top of the chart there are 'deliverables' – this provides a quick indication of when the important products from the project will be finished. These represent the outputs to customers and to the rest of the organization.

Below the deliverables there are 'dependencies' – things from outside the project on which we are relying. If these dependencies are not delivered on time, our project will be impacted.

Some tasks in the Central Controller are already in progress, and this has been entered into the software. The progress is shown by the horizontal black line across part of the task bars. There are basically two ways to enter progress into the chart:

1   You can estimate how complete each task is. For instance, the test bench is about 75% complete. This is the method used in the above example.

2   You can enter actual hours booked to each task, day by day, to make a true history of 'what happened when'. You can also update the amount of time that you think will be needed to complete each task to reflect what you've learnt about it. If you do this, the software will update the chart to show what really happened up to this point, and will rearrange future tasks to take account of what happened so far.

The second method produces a chart which more realistically shows what is going on and provides a more accurate finishing date, but it takes more effort to enter the information, and the software can rapidly lose the original structure that you put into the plan.

The plan includes contingency. I have provided this contingency in two places because this makes sense for the project in question:

■   Some of the contingency (about 10% of the project time) is near the start, after 'axis hardware stable', to provide a mitigation for risk – there is a reasonable risk that the hardware will be 'flaky' to start with and slow the team down.

■   The second block (about 20% of the project time) is near the end of the project and represents risks in the software development itself, such as the risk of feature-creep, and of rework due to requirements that cannot be pinned down entirely. There is only one delivery in this short project, so putting the contingency at the end is acceptable. If there were several deliveries, the contingency would have to be apportioned so that it delayed each delivery by the appropriate amount.

You can see how these contingency tasks look like very large blocks of time and invite management to attack them – this is why many team leaders find ways to hide the contingency.

The plan makes some allowance for people to take leave. This is a very short plan and I knew that nobody had booked any leave during it, but it is summer, so I allowed for one day's unplanned leave per person. This was achieved by marking one day (17 July) as 'non-working' in the software's calendar.

This example plan also shows how you can incorporate other information into your plan, or derive information from it. In the example, booking codes have been assigned to the top-level tasks, so that people can use the codes on their timesheets. This allows the team to receive feedback on actual effort against what was estimated. There is also a Cost column, which the software automatically computes, using the daily cost of each person. This is useful if you need to report costs in management reports.

Gantt charts can be extended in all sorts of ways to provide different views on the project, its people, costs and management; for example, you can look at the plan from one person's point of view, listing the tasks assigned to that person. This has been an overview only. See the Project Management section of the bibliography (SECTION 42) for books providing a more detailed and more advanced treatment of Gantt charts and of other types of chart useful in leading a project.

infobar // **CRITICAL PATH ANALYSIS**

Project planning software can be made to show automatically which tasks are on the 'critical path'. A critical task is one that cannot be late without affecting the final delivery date. You can see, for instance, that 'final integrated test' is on the critical path (not surprisingly).

However, the **critical path does not tend to be very useful for managing the work of a single team**. The reason is that most teams are limited by the people available. Although a task may not be shown as critical, **in fact all tasks are really critical because the project is limited by available effort**. In the example, the Central Controller tasks are not critical, because all the tasks finish before the Axis Controllers. But this is very misleading. What the critical path analysis does not take into account is that David and Hannah are needed to work on the Axis Controllers once they have finished on the Central Controller. If the Central Controller work over-runs, their move onto the Axis Controllers work will be delayed and the whole project will be late. So in fact the Central Controller work, like most other work on the project, is in effect critical or very nearly critical.

The critical path is most useful where you have resources that cannot be flexibly moved from one task to another. For instance if you have a multidisciplinary team, or have experts in certain areas, or you are co-ordinating multiple teams – in these cases the critical path can be very useful indeed for prioritizing effort and for identifying any specialist skills shortages that might critically delay the whole project.

In a project that has a pool of people with similar skills who *can* be allocated freely between tasks, the main use of the critical path is to show whether the project delivery date is primarily constrained by available effort or due to external dependencies. In the example above, the plan shows that the project is dependent on the delivery of axis hardware. It would therefore make sense for the team leader to try to concentrate on liaising with the team who will deliver this hardware, to get early releases or phased releases of it so that work can start as early as possible.

10

I'VE BEEN TOLD WHEN I MUST DELIVER MY PROJECT, BUT THE TIME-SCALE DOESN'T SEEM REALISTIC TO ME // WHAT SHOULD I DO?

There may be very good reasons why a project must be finished by a particular date – it may be needed for an event or show, or may have been promised to an important customer who must not be let down. But that doesn't mean that the date is achievable with the resources you've been allocated, or indeed that it is achievable at all. It may be that you're being expected to work miracles.

There are four variables that need to be balanced to make a realistic, achievable plan:

▶ **The time-scales.** Not just the amount of time available, but the number and nature of deliveries and milestones along the way. Interim deliveries keep the customer happy but have a significant overhead in time and money.

▶ **The features.** The number of features and their detailed capabilities. The degree to which these features are interconnected and complex.

▶ **The resources.** The number of people, and their skills, knowledge, experience and attitudes. The equipment available for development and testing. The budget.

▶ **The risk elements of the project.** New technologies. Partnerships or dependencies with other organizations. Dependencies on suppliers of equipment. The need to recruit new people.

I'm going to draw this as follows. The features need to be balanced by sufficient time and resource. Meanwhile, risk hangs over the project:

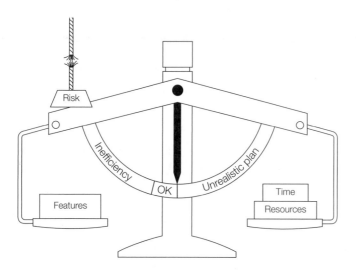

The diagram is intended to show that if the right balance is struck, with enough time and resources to implement the features, and just a little spare 'contingency', then things are looking good. If you have much more time and resources than you need, your chances of delivering on time will be high, but people are likely to spin out the work to fill the available time, and the project will be inefficient and not cost-effective. If you don't have enough time and resources – *both of them* – to implement the features, then you have an unrealistic plan, a project that is doomed to failure. Meanwhile, risk factors hang over the project, ready to throw it off balance. If you have incorporated enough contingency into your plan, you will still have a workable project if a risk 'drops' on you.

It's not at all unusual to be given a project where all four variables are fixed for you right from the start. It is by no means unusual to feel that these don't make up a realistic combination, and you are being 'set up to fail'.

If you feel right from the start of a project that the time-scales are unrealistic, avoid saying anything about this until your plan is ready. You need to put together your own detailed estimates and plans, and this will take some time. You will need to understand the requirements, and the business pressures behind the requirements, which may itself require meetings, documents to be written and reviewed and so on. You will need to get to know the people on the project, to understand the technologies involved, and to get a feel for the risks being taken. This all takes time, and during this time it is important to appear optimistic but to avoid

committing yourself to the constraints you were given. During meetings with customers and your managers, take the tone that 'things are going well, but I can't be confident that all the requirements can be met within the time-scale until I've put together a detailed plan'. Senior people may find this rather exasperating but that's a problem you will have to make them live with at this stage.

When you do finally put together your detailed plan (SEE SECTION 9: DRAWING UP A PROJECT PLAN?), it may well show that the time-scale is not realistic. This is when you need to go back to your customers or your management and talk through the options. Of course, it could be quite tricky. Promises will have been made, budgets allocated, and people committed to other projects. It may appear that nothing can budge. But you need to stand by your plan. **Never allow yourself to be 'bargained down'**, accepting that a task 'might not take as long as I've estimated' – this makes a very poor impression and **it doesn't do anything towards making the project get delivered any sooner**. It just makes your plan less realistic.

You need to include some contingency – time and money to allow for the risks that will happen on your project. If you have considered the risks and their likely probabilities and effects (see SECTION 9: DRAWING UP A PROJECT PLAN and also SECTION 33: TAKING A RISK) then you should have included quite a reasonable allowance for risk in the form of contingency. It would not be unreasonable for this to be a very significant period of time – months rather than weeks on a one-year project, for example. You may come under heavy pressure to reduce this. Again, giving in to this pressure will do nothing for your chances of delivering on time.

Usually there are options, although they may be unwelcome ones. Features may be dropped or deferred. People may be released from other projects or hired or contracted in. Delivery dates may be moved. Your attitude throughout the negotiations to obtain a more realistic plan should always be **positive and imaginative, but never weak**. Be willing to discuss any ideas, consider all options, promote any compromise, but don't accept a combination of factors that does not form a realistic plan.

The reason that managers try to pressure you to reduce time and resource estimates is that every day the project is lengthened by, and every resource that is added to it, greatly reduces your organization's profits and has knock-on effects on other projects. It is understandable and correct for managers to put pressure on you to counteract this. I'm not suggesting that you resist this pressure simply in order to have an easy life or even to

Keep referring to your plan and any associated documents during negotiations. Don't just say that the time-scales 'feel tight'. Say that your plan shows them to be *unrealistic*.

get the best for your customer. Whilst you should want the best for your customer, you should give only what your organization can afford to give and has agreed to give, and you should not fight your management to let you go further than this. Sometimes engineers get carried away by what is possible and start to exceed what is required; in organizations where this has happened, management may assume that you are doing the same, and will try to knock this out of the plan by a process of bashing every item to see what can be removed. It is essential that your plan represents what needs to be done, no more and no less, and that you can defend it from this position.

Often, interim deliveries may be proposed, as a way of delivering at least something early on, with more to follow later. This is a perfectly sensible strategy, which can greatly improve your relationship with your customer. But remember that every release has an overhead in time and money. As well as the cost of the release process, there is quite often some 'dead-end' work done for an interim release, to be thrown away afterwards. You can't just drop in an interim delivery without delaying the final delivery and increasing the final cost. Also, beware being pressured into making a very early first release, because this is likely to result in the requirements capture, analysis and design being rushed, which will cause great damage to the quality of the project. If an early release is essential in order to gain confidence from your customer, try to make it a release of documents for review only, with perhaps a small prototype, but no 'final' code.

The issue of risk is often ignored when negotiating a project plan, possibly because risk does not appear directly on a Gantt chart (see SECTION 9: HOW DO I DRAW UP A PROJECT PLAN?). This is a shame because it is an important issue that often makes the difference between a realistic and an unrealistic plan. For example, quite often the requirements will state that a certain technology must be used, and this will be accepted by the team without challenge – but many times the customer will have included mention of a particular technology more by way of example, or to make it look as if they know what they are talking about, than because of a concrete need to use it. Often, a customer will quite gladly accept a recommendation to do things a different way if you can show that it is more appropriate or has lower risk.

Some managers will assume that if you say you need 10 more weeks then you must really need 5. They will try to reduce your estimates in the honest belief that everyone always tries to grab as much resources as they can. That's how some managers work and they assume that other people play the same game. Don't join in this game – don't overestimate in the first place to allow for being knocked down later; this is the start of a slippery slope into politicking, which is best avoided (at the bottom of that slippery slope is something very smelly).

If your plan shows that your project will cost much more than expected, this is a problem for your organization. If it shows that it will take much longer than expected then this is a problem for the customer as well. For commercial and marketing reasons many management teams would like to keep the time-scales down and so would rather add resources to a project than extend the time-scales. Remember to trust your estimates of what is realistic, and don't allow your project to be over-resourced in an attempt to stop slippage. If time-scales have to slip then your organization will have to renegotiate with the customer, and this could result in commercial penalties or other severe problems. Never let this swerve you from presenting a realistic plan. You can work only with the facts as you see them at the time, and cannot undo poor estimates or other mistakes made in the past.

It's easy to get angry when people make estimates for you and then expect you to fit in with them. There's no point in getting angry, because people usually make these decisions in good faith. Estimates and budgets have to be drawn up by managers early on, in order to decide whether even to go ahead with a project, long before the detail becomes clear. Someone has to pull some numbers out of the air to allow a decision to be made. The problem is that once concrete numbers have been used, it's very difficult for people to accept them as wrong, even if they were based on only the scantiest information. Equally, it's no good taking an 'I know it won't work but I'll do my best, there's nothing I can do, I'll just do what I'm told' kind of attitude – usually there is something you can do if you try, and as leader you are required to try.

It is your responsibility to estimate times and resources for your project. Nobody can blame you for doing that, but they certainly will blame you if you don't. People may not want to hear that you disagree with estimates and plans that they made, but that has to be faced up to. You are the person nearest the action and that makes your estimates the most reliable available.

It is good commercial practice to include clauses in a quotation for work, which acknowledge that time-scales and costs must be renegotiated after requirements capture is complete.

Your management may accept your estimates but may want you to present a 'modified' version to the customer. Avoid this if possible. If your bosses want to make pretences or play politics then that is their business, but try to avoid doing their dirty work for them.

11

HOW CAN I STOP MY PROJECT FROM COMING IN LATE?

The six-million-dollar question!

Many software projects come in late, but that doesn't mean it's inevitable, or acceptable. The fact that it is a common problem is no excuse for complacency. Your customers, both inside your organization and outside, can reasonably expect you to deliver on your promises. If you constantly deliver late you will be regarded as unreliable, and that will not do you, your team, or your organization any good at all.

Let's just be clear about what is meant by being 'late'. Just because your product finishes after the date you initially planned, it is not necessarily late. It could be that the requirements have changed along the way, for example, and a new date has been agreed – but often the original date has been communicated around so much that you will be told you are late because you missed the original date, not the revised one. As well as trying not to be late, it's also important to challenge the perception of lateness that other people may have of your project.

When I've been part of a project that's over-run and I've looked for the reasons, they are nearly always things that went wrong at the *start* of the project. Looking back, I realize that if I'd spent more time at the beginning, I would have saved much more at the end. But at the start there's always a strong desire to get stuck in. If a project over-runs, or has a heavy maintenance burden, is fragile in use, doesn't satisfy the customer, or is just plain unpopular, the problem is not usually in the coding (if your team is reasonably competent), but nearly always with fundamental things that were not done properly at the start, such as contracts that were poorly negotiated, requirements that were unclear, responsibilities that were not defined, plans that were unrealistic, analysis that was skipped, or architecture and designs that were not thought through.

So if you take nothing else from this section, in fact if you take nothing else from this *whole book*, take this: **Don't start coding too early.** Not one line of production code should be written until the requirements are clear, there is a design that can demonstrably deliver, you understand who is on the team and what their roles are, and the project is working to a realistic plan. Any coding that happens before these criteria are met should be 'dirty' prototyping to answer technical questions, to help design user interfaces, or as part of training and development. Never let this dirty prototyping become the basis of your production code! Remember that it's just dirty prototyping, and will need significant rework later if it is to be used in the final production code. Frequently, prototypes answer questions about user interfaces, algorithms and technologies, not about how to code solutions. Take the answers that a prototype gives and use them in the production code, without taking the prototype code that yielded those answers.

Leading a team is a matter of balancing time-scales, resources, features and risks, but in today's world it's often the time-scales that are most important, as part of the offensive to get features to market before competitors. This does not imply that you should concentrate only on time issues, ignoring issues of cost or feature-creep. On the contrary, it implies that in order to keep the time aspect on target, the other aspects must be carefully managed and balanced.

The only way to have any hope of justifying your resource needs, or of arguing for more time or reduced functionality if you need to, is if you are armed with a *credible plan*. Up-front planning is therefore essential. And you can't make your plan credible unless it's based on a proper understanding of what packages of work the project involves, which in turn can only happen once you have captured the requirements and produced an architecture for the solution.

▶ **Do thorough requirement capture.** This is something that is often tempting to skip. You've got some blurb from marketing, you've spoken to the customer, you know what to do, what's the point in writing it up? Experience shows that, even on the smallest project, it is worth spending time on requirements capture. Especially on a very small project it's often tempting to think that you simply haven't got time – 'this has got to be done in four weeks, I can't afford to spend days writing specs'. This argument doesn't hold water. Requirements capture takes time in proportion to the size of the project – let's say it takes 5% of the time – so on a four-week project you might expect it to take a day. Experience shows that if you skip out that day you will pay for it later by spending several stressful days trying to fix or patch over fundamental problems you didn't see coming.

I find that I always need to write a requirements document. The way requirements come from marketing departments and customers is not the way you need them. You need to be more specific, and you need to pin down issues that others would rather gloss over. For more information, see SECTION 25: REQUIREMENTS CAPTURE.

▶ With all issues at the start of a project, you need to tackle problems and contentious issues head-on and not avoid them. That's not to say that you should get confrontational or negative. But you should not accept that your project is on a firm basis until any contentious issues have been sorted out. Often, people would rather gloss over and ignore issues that cause friction, but if you allow this to happen you add risk to your project. You may need to approach the issues sensitively and carefully, taking account of politics and personal feelings. If you don't try to resolve these kinds of problems then the tensions will be there throughout your project and may be a constant source of arguments and irritations.

▶ Choose the right technologies. The right technology is the one that has the highest chance of getting the job done to adequate quality in the shortest time with the available people. It's no good choosing a brilliant new technology if you're not sure it will work, or you can't find anyone with the skills to use it. More about this in SECTION 37: SHOULD WE USE A NEW TECHNOLOGY?.

▶ Design an architecture that is well modularized and straightforward. Spend the time that it takes to design the modules and interfaces, encapsulating and organizing the work. Hacking the design, even more than hacking code, results in a late project. See SECTION 35: ARCHITECTURE AND DESIGN.

Throughout the project it will be one of your responsibilities to defend the architecture – to keep the design clean, to stop people bypassing the design by hacking. Keeping the architecture clean helps new features to go in smoothly without breaking other things and so helps you get those features in more quickly and reduces the testing burden. If you keep the design clean, poor code can always be reworked, replaced or at least put through thorough unit testing to get the bugs out. You can't do this with a hacked design.

▶ Once you know what you've got to do, you can prepare a project plan. See SECTION 9: DRAWING UP A PROJECT PLAN? for more details of estimating and drawing up project plans. A realistic plan is essential if you want to get your project out on time.

▶ Review any bid documents, contracts and other top-level documents pertaining to the project. If you're not going to do things the way the bid assumed, or your plan shows that the contract will not be fulfilled as written, then some renegotiation will be needed to avoid serious problems later on.

▶ Have reviews of both design and code. This is the only way to know whether the design is clean and whether the code adheres to it. If a review reveals that the design has been compromised or code has been hacked, then make sure that the person responsible puts these things right before doing any new work.

▶ Prioritize. This is one of the key aspects of any leadership role. This means:

1 Make sure that effort is applied to the most urgent things first, and then to the most important things after, with less important things being done when there's time. People should be spending their time in the most useful way possible. It's important to look at the priorities from your customer's point of view – do what *they* consider highest priority – not from the point of view of what is most convenient for the project team.

2 Make sure that problems are solved adequately, but that people don't do too much in search of excellence where excellence is not required. The priorities determine what is 'adequate'. For some issues, only the best is good enough, while for others, your customer may not care too much and a solution that is acceptable, but not brilliant, is perfectly OK. It's up to you to decide what level of quality and ease of use is adequate on any given feature and issue. To do this, you need to be very familiar with the requirements of the project, not just as written down but in a more intimate way, by really understanding what your customers want and how they will use the product you deliver.

infobar // **PERFECTIONIST?**

I am a perfectionist by nature. I like to keep going until a job is done as well as I can do it. But this attitude can be a killer to getting a project out on time – customers far prefer to receive a product where everything works adequately, than one where some things work brilliantly and some work not at all.

To help me overcome my perfectionism, I came up with the concept of the 'perfect compromise'. I realized that there needs to be a compromise between the quality and functionality of the result, and the amount of time spent on it. By concentrating on this compromise I was able to take a more balanced view.

I still am a perfectionist, but now I try to achieve perfection of the compromise, **optimizing the compromise** between time, functionality and quality as much as possible.

▶ **Handle requirements changes**, no matter how small, by feeding back the consequences of the change to your customer or marketing department. Projects are often late – or rather, perceived to be late – because of many small requirements changes that were accepted along the way, all adding up to significantly more work than was originally planned. It is not unreasonable for people to want requirements changes, just make sure that you are not expected to do more work with no more time or resources. Often, the reason teams don't get the extra time or people they need to do extra work is that they don't ask.

▶ It's essential to **keep people working hard and smart**. If you push people too hard, then they will start to get stressed, quality will suffer and you will start spending time fire-fighting problems that could have been foreseen. People need to be under some pressure, but not too much. Different people respond to pressure in different ways and some will get stressed earlier than others as pressure builds. Some people will simply not work until the pressure is at a certain level. Similarly, some people require constant encouragement to give them confidence and make them feel appreciated, but others would regard this as condescending. As you work with people you will soon get a feel for what helps to keep each individual motivated. See SECTION 27: I'M VERY STRESSED AT THE MOMENT, AND SO ARE SOME OF MY TEAM.

The project plan gives a guide to what people should be doing at any given time, but don't get manic about making sure that every task happens precisely to the plan, as if the project is some sort of machine that should play out the plan like a set of instructions. It doesn't usually work out that way. As long as the work is getting done and the plan is being roughly followed without any major slips, then don't panic about what each person should be doing at each individual minute. Trust your people to be aware of what is required and to be doing their best to work towards it.

One way of keeping people focused without concentrating too much on individual tasks is to emphasize deliveries. Make sure everyone knows when the next delivery is due, and what it should contain. In general, it helps to name deliveries by time and/or function rather than just a number; for instance, if everyone knows that they are working on the 'Mid April Major Control Upgrade' release, they may prioritize and organize their work more appropriately than if the release is called 'version 2.7' and you have to keep reminding people what it should contain. Remember that effectiveness is more important than efficiency. It's no good working very hard on something if you are working on the wrong thing. If you press people too hard then they start to panic and don't spend time considering what they should be doing before they start doing it.

▶ Reduce risk. For example:

- Don't use new technologies, languages or methodologies for the sake of it. Choose new technologies, new methodologies or new working methods only when they are directly appropriate to your project. Do not use them just because you or the other team members want to try them out.

- Avoid mixing languages or technologies if at all possible. If you are forced to mix languages or technologies, then try to isolate areas of complexity so that you don't have a closely linked complex system implemented in a mix of languages or technologies. For example, suppose that the requirements of your project force you to write code with a Java front-end driving a C++ component. Ideally, all the complexity should be in one of the languages or the other – either you should have a complex C++ object being wrapped by a very thin piece of Java, or else you should have a complex piece of Java driving a simple and dumb C++ object. What you want to avoid is having some Java that does quite a lot of stuff working intimately with some C++ that also does quite a lot of stuff. Similar logic applies in a system involving multiple technologies, such as a database being driven by a user interface written in a high-level language: complex functionality such as data integrity checking should be done all in the database or all in the client, but not partly in each, if at all possible. If you must split functionality across languages or technologies, design it very thoroughly and make sure that each part is independently testable.

- **Reduce dependencies on other teams and on other organizations.** For instance, by agreeing detailed interfaces early on, you can create stub code to simulate modules being developed elsewhere that you have not received yet.

  In this way your team can continue to work effectively, even if the other teams do not deliver on time. By agreeing the interfaces, you are able to design and code final production software that will work with the output of the other teams when it arrives, without significant rework and integration.

- **Include adequate contingency in your project plan.** Projects often come in late because some major risk happened, such as a failure of a new technology or because a supplier failed to deliver. Often, an estimate can be made of these risks at the start of the project, and included into the contingency of the plan (see SECTION 9: HOW DO I DRAW UP A PROJECT PLAN?). Contingency is a form of insurance against risk. If you fail to account for risks then you are exposing your project completely to those risks and making it very likely that the project will be late.

  As well as allowing for the major risks, you need to include some contingency for the minor things that go wrong, such as minor feature-creep, people leaving, other projects having knock-on effects on yours, and so forth. See SECTION 9: HOW DO I DRAW UP A PROJECT PLAN?.

▶ **Don't reinvent the wheel.** If you can buy in, or copy in, some useful functionality then do so. Encourage people to search popular programmers' websites for code if they are getting stuck. Do not be swayed by arguments that 'we could do it better ourselves'. Do you need to do it much better? Can you afford the time? There is no excuse for not even looking to see if someone has already solved a problem.

If you do download some code off the internet and later fix a bug in it, it is polite to upload the corrected version so that future engineers don't have to fix it again – not so much reinventing the wheel as re-mending the puncture.

When you do download some code off the internet you often find that it 'looks' horrible – but it usually works anyway. Rather than spending time tidying it up, the only sensible thing to do is to package it up and treat it as a black box, fixing bugs in the code if you find them, but otherwise leaving it alone.

Your team should spend its time doing the things that only it can do. Buy in supporting libraries and tools that others can provide. If there's a sensible choice between spending money and spending time, spend the money.

▶ Adopt a solid coding style, enforced through reviews if necessary. For example,

- Use the maximum level of warnings available with your development tools.

- Use error-checking tools to find memory leaks, common coding errors and other potential bugs.

- Get in the habit of testing code immediately after writing it. This includes checking that the code fails gracefully in error conditions. This testing saves time by ensuring you have reliable code before you build on top of it. Do some testing after you've written a handful of lines of code, no more.

- Write code that checks for errors and reports them. If a piece of code expects to be passed some data, then check that it is. If it is passed nothing sensible, then have it return a failure, which should get logged or reported to the user. If you are expecting a variable to have one of a fixed set of values, then test that it does, and report an error if it doesn't. Don't write the code to simply do nothing if one of its basic assumptions is broken; this is almost as bad as crashing.

  Error-checking code needs to be tested just as code to handle normal execution does. The user will not thank you for software that crashes when the unexpected occurs, reports meaningless messages, or gets trapped in a state that cannot be escaped from. This is another reason to use unit test benches and special test data, which allow error and boundary cases to be explored easily.

- Use architectures and algorithms that will work reliably, not ones that 'seem to work'. For instance, if some function is not safe until the system has been initialized, then prevent it happening until the system is initialized; don't do something dirty like setting a timer that 'should give it time' to initialize.

This is not a book about coding, but solid coding can dramatically reduce the frustration and risk of development. For more on solid coding, see the references cited in the bibliography (SECTION 42).

▶ **Reduce the length of the design–code–test cycle.** It is essential that developers can write code, compile and test it, as quickly as possible. Not only does this lead to more efficiency, it also leads to higher quality, as people will be more willing to test after every small code change. In order to reduce the cycle:

■ Make sure that your developers get the fastest machines and use the best tools that your organization can provide. Make sure people know how to use the tools that they have.

■ Reduce dependencies:

– *In code:*

… Modularize and encapsulate so that changes to one module do not affect another.

… Write the code in a way that reduces the amount of rebuilding that happens when something is changed. This usually involves reducing the length of 'chains' of files included in other files. When a file is changed, the only files that should get recompiled are those that are really affected by the change.

In particular, never use a 'mother of all include files' that includes all your other files. Such a file is a useful thing to give to the customer of a component, but don't use it inside the component itself.

– *Between people:*

… Allocate different areas of responsibility to people so that people don't get in each other's way trying to work on the same files.

… If there are common bottlenecks with shared files then try to split those files up so that people don't have to wait for them to become free.

… Have unit test benches so that people can test their own work independently of the rest of the project.

– If testing is made slow by the need to connect to some slow source of data (such as a remote database) or some scarce resource (such as a test room), then make a dummy data source so that most testing can happen in simulation at each developer's desk, using the real data source for more formal testing at regular intervals.

▶ **Don't skimp on testing.** Informal testing should be an everyday part of developing software, and nothing should go back into version control unless it has had some basic testing. More formal testing should happen before every release and it should be documented and thorough. Automated test tools can save a lot of time and improve quality – see SECTION 39: UNIT TESTING OR FINAL TESTING?.

▶ Make regular releases of your product. If possible, make sure these releases get seen and used by your customer and by real end-users, and that you get feedback. The more feedback you get, the less likely you are to have a problem with the customer rejecting what you deliver. Even if nobody outside your organization wants to receive an interim release, it is still worth the time of making an internal release. Get everything tidied up, make sure there are test specs, user documentation and so on, and release the product, perhaps to your marketing department or QA department for evaluation. Although it may seem like a huge delay to stop the project and start writing test documents and performing formal testing, it can be very useful in providing a firm baseline for future work, based on a well-tested and documented product.

Too many interim releases would certainly cost an unacceptable amount of time, but if your project has undergone major changes then try to get a release of some sort out before embarking on yet more major changes.

▶ To stop your project coming in late, you must play your part as leader, and lead.

  ▪ Take responsibility, don't blame others, don't make excuses. If you realize you made a mistake then own up to it and put it right.

  ▪ Don't let others get away with spreading blame or making lame excuses.

  ▪ Do those things that the leader must do, even if they are unpleasant or dull, in order to allow the rest of the team to progress.

  ▪ If you know of problems then make something happen about them; don't ignore them or wait for someone to tell you to do something about them.

  ▪ Be the person on the team who can see the bigger picture of the whole project in its context. Details matter but you need to make sure that you can see the wood for the trees.

  ▪ Don't assume that managers 'must know' about problems you are having, make sure they *do* know. Don't go to managers with problems, go with solution options for them to choose between. Go to the management when you need resources or you need the support that they can provide.

- ■ If there's a decision that you can make, make it, without asking for management permission. If someone else on your team is best placed to make the decision, delegate it to them.

▶ If you start to fall behind, do something appropriate about it. Don't ignore it, but don't panic either. See the   infobar //   IF YOU DO START TO FALL BEHIND.

▶ Always be willing to spend time to save time. For example, suppose that to test your work you need to be connected to a slow database, perhaps over a slow network link. Developers sit and stare at their programs for minutes on end waiting for data to arrive, wasting perhaps an hour a day. Now you could solve this problem – you could set up mirroring of the database, or simulate it completely with a test bed. But you don't want to spend the time – let's say it would take someone two weeks to do this 'and we haven't got two weeks to spare!'. But think of the time it would save – an hour per person per day. For a team of five developers, those two weeks of effort would actually be paid back in only *three weeks*! If there are months left to run on your project, then speeding up the database connection would be an excellent way of saving time, and also improving morale. Yet many team leaders would be unwilling to spend the two weeks of time because they are in a panic about getting behind the schedule. Similarly, people cut corners to save time, skipping out thorough requirements capture for example in a rush to 'get started'. This nearly always ends up wasting significant time, by the end of the project. If you have an option to save time over the life of the project then take it, even if it means getting behind the scheduled plan in the short term.

Think about projects you've worked on. Why they were late, or how did they manage to be on time? What could have been done differently, to save time? It's vital to learn from previous projects, especially those in your own organization. It's important to have conviction in your own experience and apply what you learn to your own projects, even if the rest of the organization does not follow. For example, if you believe from your experience that one reason projects are late in your organization is that you are using the tools in the wrong way, then on your next project try to use them in what you consider to be the right way – even if the rest of the organization does not agree.

Even when competently led, staffed with excellent people and given adequate support from management, many projects are still late. That is

infobar // **IF YOU DO START TO FALL BEHIND**

If you find that you are getting behind schedule, then *do something about it*. Projects slip one day at a time. Don't let the slip build up in the hope that it will all turn out all right – usually it won't. If the project does start to fall behind, your options are:

■ Throw another person at it. Negotiate with your management to get another good person (permanent or contractor) onto your team. If your project is under-staffed, then this will have a significant impact on your speed of progress. However, if your project is already adequately staffed, then having more people on it will not have as much effect as you might like, and if your project already has as many people on it as it can really take, adding more people may actually slow it down. If you try to rearrange your project plan to accommodate another person, it will soon become apparent which situation you fall into. See SECTION 9: HOW DO I DRAW UP A PROJECT PLAN?.

If you bring in someone new you need to be certain that the person will be productive and will fit into the team. If you are recruiting someone for the job, whether permanent or on contract, do not panic into taking someone unsuitable. Getting the wrong person into your team is usually worse than leaving the vacancy empty.

New people take time to become productive, and they cause a disturbance to the team. So this option is only appropriate as a fairly long-term solution, if you realize that your project will need more people. Putting more people on a project is not a sensible solution to a short-term problem, such as meeting an imminent release deadline.

■ Drop features. In negotiation with your customer and your management you may be able to drop some non-essential features or move them into a future release, or to swap some hard features for some easier ones.

■ Get more time. Again, through negotiation you may be able to delay the delivery dates.

■ Work overtime. This can have quite an impact in the short term, but is only appropriate when there is a deadline approaching. It would be hard to persuade people to work overtime if there's months to go before delivery. Even if people were so persuaded they would soon become stale and tired, and would do little extra work but would make more mistakes and be miserable. See SECTION 20: HOW MANY HOURS SHOULD I AND MY TEAM BE WORKING?.

Those really are the only major options. In many cases, none of them are very appealing. You need to choose one option, or a combination of them, and

cont >>

>>

pursue it, even if it will make you unpopular. The sooner you do this and achieve a project that is running to its schedule, the better.

One reason that software projects are often late is that there are so few easy remedies when things do start to go wrong. Prevention is much better than cure.

certainly not an excuse for complacency. If your project is late despite your best efforts you can expect your management and your customers to have some understanding and to retain confidence in your abilities, but if it is late because of a lack of control on your part then you can expect that confidence to be lost, probably for ever. In the future, as more and more of the economy comes to rest on software, we can expect customers to become much less forgiving and to expect projects to be delivered strictly according to the timetables that we predict. The time when your actions have the most impact on the delivery date is when delivery is furthest away, at the start of the project.

12

MY TEAM IS WORKING CLOSELY WITH ANOTHER TEAM, BUT THE QUALITY OF THEIR OUTPUT IS POOR // WHAT CAN I DO?

Many computer systems interact with other systems created by other organizations or by other teams in the same organization. In addition, most development teams take their input from other people such as marketing teams or customer representatives. And there is always a customer of some sort, either an internal or an external customer, who will take our output but from whom we also need to obtain input and feedback. The problem is, the input or feedback we need is sometimes poor, late, or totally absent.

In a formal, procedural way this problem is approached by imposing tightly controlled specifications, defined responsibilities, formal testing and written acceptance. We'll get to all that in a moment, but really those 'mechanical' procedures are not the best way to approach the problem at all. Actually this whole issue is about people, and it's best tackled from that point of view.

People work best together when they have met face to face and got to understand each other a little in an informal context. So the first thing to do is to make sure that people who will communicate or work together meet up and speak together. If people can experience a little of each other's working lives and environments by some sort of exchange trip, that's even better. If relations are already bad, and that thought repels you, then it is even more urgent that you overcome that feeling and organize such a get-together.

The first thing on the agenda when you meet up is to make sure that everyone has the same understanding of what is to be delivered, and when, and of the priorities involved. Often people are so eager to agree that they gloss over issues and don't want to 'go looking' for problems, but to some extent you need to do this. For instance, **there is often a problem with words**, even if everyone speaks the same language. You might, for instance, agree that the other team will produce a specification for you to work from, but when it arrives you find it is useless junk. Could it be that there was not a common understanding of what a 'specification' was supposed to contain? For instance, the 'specification' for my car is something that was written after the design was complete, and gives the car's length to the millimetre. Is that the sort of thing you wanted? Or did you want something more like a marketing input, such as 'this vehicle should appeal to the younger and more affluent owner'? Or did you mean that you wanted an interface description of some sort? If such things are not stated then there will almost certainly be misunderstandings.

Whether it's software you're discussing or a document, the best way is to **agree an outline of what is to be done**. For a document this is a list of headings, for software it's an interface specification, preferably all the way down to detailed code. It doesn't have to be set in stone, but it gives you a starting point and gives everyone something they can take away and start working with. As well as specifying what is to be delivered, you need to agree *when* it is to be delivered.

Try to **keep deliverables clean and one-directional**. In other words, partition the problem so that, as far as possible, there are things to be delivered by the other team to your team, and other things to be delivered by your team to the other team, but avoid deliverables that sit on the fence and belong to nobody in particular. For those issues that must be worked on together, if at all practicable arrange it so that people are co-opted from one site to another and can work on the problem closely together, rather than having the work bounced backwards and forwards, or worked on remotely by two separate teams.

Sometimes you can find yourself receiving software from another team that is very poor and doesn't seem to have been tested to any degree at all. If you're lucky you will be able to persuade the other team to start testing more thoroughly, but usually this doesn't seem to happen. I think it's because quality problems often stem from the culture of the development team. If that team never tests anything (they're hackers), you'll be hard pressed to get them to stop developing and start testing. After an hour they'll be fed up and find some excuse to start coding again. **It is**

vital to avoid the situation where your team become the test team for somebody else's work. If you keep testing and re-testing other people's work, your team will look unproductive, the other team will look like they are churning out work, and you will be the one that suffers. One way to avoid this is to build a test bench for the other team's work. *They* should have done this, but be pragmatic and spend your time doing it for them. Make it simple to use, preferably just a single pass/fail test. The sort of test bench that lets you manually exercise the software is not what you want, because you'll never get the hackers to use it. Give the other team your test bench, source code and all. Make it clear that before you receive any more code from them, it must pass the test bench. This won't catch all possible errors, and you could still receive horrible code that manages to pass the test bench and little more, but it's still much better than letting them ship everything without even a cursory test.

If tension is mounting between your team and another then you need to involve your management. It's easy to think that managers must be aware of the tensions, but often they are not. Managers constantly hear whinging and complaining, and they learn to filter most of it out. So if the relationship with the other team really has become a problem, you need to raise it quite formally to your management, not as a minor moan, but as a *critical problem* that requires management authority to sort out. Before doing this you had better have facts available to back up your position – you can be sure that it won't be taken lying down.

Sometimes you make an agreement with another team that they will do something, and they just seem to ignore the agreement, or forget about it. They might deliver something that doesn't meet the agreement, or doesn't use the agreed interface. To prevent disaster, you need to catch this early, by having early deliveries of output. These early deliverables may not do much, but they give you confidence that both sides are still aiming in the same direction. It's good to agree a timetable for these deliveries at the beginning.

Similarly, so that you don't make the same mistake of delivering something inappropriate, it's important to get early feedback from your customers. Some customers approve early documents without really reading them, and the first really useful feedback you get is when you deliver a prototype. So make sure that you deliver something concrete, as early as possible in the project.

Of course the formal, procedural, quality control methods have their place. Formally agreed documents, meetings with recorded minutes, defined responsibilities, written acceptance criteria and so on all help to put a relationship between two organizations, or even two internal teams, onto a solid 'legal' footing. But these agreements are just as often breached as informal agreements, and are mostly useful for pointing the finger after the event, to avoid paying, or to apportion blame. Although you may have these agreements, it's best not to appeal to higher managerial authority or to lawyers, better to refer to the agreements in negotiations but keep the legal option in reserve for the case of a complete failure of the relationship. If you still need to work together and are still trying to do so, don't try to use the formal procedural approach, but concentrate on the informal, personal approach to the problem.

It's very easy to be critical of others, hard to appreciate their problems. Before you get too critical, *think about your own output*. Is it perfect? You know the reasons why you have taken some short-cuts, such as the urgent interruptions that came up, the person who left to get another job, and the honest mistakes that you made. You probably don't want to tell outsiders about all of these things. Think how things look to people outside, who can't see everything that's happened. Is your team's behaviour as seen from the outside actually that different from that of the team you're having problems with? Isn't it possible that *they're also trying to do their best*, but are having problems that you're not aware of?

It's all too easy for things to get nasty between people who hardly meet and who have different priorities and perspectives. Apart from giving the benefit of the doubt, try to avoid spreading discontent in your own team. It's frightening how a few caustic words can get a whole team into a self-righteous attitude of 'hatred of the enemy'. This sort of negativity and blame culture is always a hindrance to a positive outcome for the project, and it can make for a very unpleasant working atmosphere. Avoid attacking the people on the other team, but stick to tackling the issues, and learn to dampen down any mutterings and resentments.

From a purely selfish point of view, you probably need the other team and they need you, so it's in your interest to be a little flexible, as long as you're not taken to breaking point.

It's a bit like a marriage. There is a formal agreement in a marriage, but that's not what makes a marriage work. Referring to that formal agreement and getting the lawyers involved is something that you do only when the relationship has completely failed. It is not the way to make a rocky marriage work!

13

MY LAST PROJECT NEVER SEEMS TO GO AWAY, I'M CONSTANTLY DOING FIXES AND CHANGES TO IT // WHAT CAN I DO?

It has been said that a software project is never finished, it is merely abandoned. Usually, if you're working under tight commercial pressures, the project will be 'finished', with some unresolved minor bugs and some things that you wanted to improve but never had time to. This is normal, and from a commercial point of view it makes sense, because if any remaining issues are very minor, they are probably not worth the cost of putting right.

This section is about projects that reach a stage of 'almost good enough to stop working on', but get stuck in that stage for a long time, or which are declared to be finished, and then get reopened, over and over again.

Sometimes a project doesn't end, but keeps spluttering on. I'm not talking about a project that is simply late. I'm referring to a project that spends long periods of time in a state of 'very nearly finished', where people are working very hard but progress, especially as seen from outside the project team, seems to be slow, or where the project has been released but then costs as much effort in maintenance as it did in development.

Almost always, problems like this can be traced back to fundamental failings and mistakes made at the beginning of the project.

Of course, prevention is much better than cure. For advice on how to avoid getting in this mess in the first place, please refer to SECTION 11: KEEPING PROJECTS ON SCHEDULE. The rest of this section is concerned with rescuing a project that has got stuck in the 'almost finished' trap, whether because of mistakes made by the project team, mismanagement and misdirection from above, or circumstances beyond the team's control.

If a project has got into this mess then it is very hard, though not impossible, to rescue it. If the problem doesn't become apparent until the project is very obviously in trouble, then the best that can be done is to adopt the following approach:

▶ If you personally have been coding and not paying attention to project management issues, stop coding immediately.

▶ Postpone any short-term deliveries that are not essential. Try to get the team a breathing space of a few weeks when they can think about the issues without having to constantly deliver updates or give demos.

▶ Renegotiate the requirements and the delivery schedule with customers and management. Don't assume that there is no flexibility – if the customer is given the choice between a very late delivery and an interim delivery they may well prefer at least to receive something. Be willing to throw out requirements that are unnecessary or excessive.

▶ Make sure there is a plan in place that captures all the work that needs doing, including time for restructuring work. It may be best to throw away existing plans, starting again from the current position. Include some contingency for problems that have not yet been discovered – in a project that is in trouble, 30% might be a reasonable amount of contingency to add on top of realistic estimates of remaining work.

▶ Prioritize and order tasks so that things get done in a sensible sequence and people don't 'thrash' from one thing to another.

▶ If people are constantly stopping development, for instance to work on other projects, to do demos or to release interim fixes, try to get agreements with customers and managers that reduce these diversions.

▶ Make the time to ensure the development environment is efficient, by ensuring that decent tools are in use and people know how to use them, and that the design–code–build–test cycle is as fast as possible. Make sure there is a test environment that can be used without stopping development.

▶ Be willing to spend time to save time. If it is obvious that the architecture is weak, for example, but the team has been under such stress that it could not contemplate changing it, consider whether a redesign or partial redesign would actually save time over the life of the project. If people are constantly being held up by needing access to shared files or shared test facilities, try to reorganize things to allow more independence. If a redesign or reorganization makes sense, then incorporate it into the plan. Similarly, be willing to spend effort speeding up compilation by reducing interdependencies in code, or to speed up testing by building test benches or test environments.

The aim is to transform the project from one that is thrashing to one that is merely late. Once that happens, there may be some hope of gaining some time back by using more resources, doing overtime and prioritizing. Until that stage – while the project is still being transformed – avoid disruptive moves. For instance, it's probably *not* a good idea to bring in extra developers, or to get rid of someone who appears to be lazy, or to adopt

If management offer you extra resources, one place they might well be used without causing disruption is in strengthening the test team.

totally new tools, or to try to use a new technology that is supposed to speed things up. Do these things only if they are necessary to allow the turn-around to happen. For instance, get rid of a problem person if he or she is causing such friction that the team cannot work together.

The aim is to help the team to *get itself* out of the mess, not to foster a feeling that the team has failed. You want the team to feel it now has a chance to put things right for itself, and to avoid an air of gloom, failure and especially blame.

With personal tensions running high, customers and management getting upset, and good people likely to be demotivated or leaving, turning round a project that made fundamental mistakes early in its life is a tough job. It is likely that you will have to adopt quite an autocratic style of leadership to direct the project out of the mess. This is not going to be popular, especially if it was you who made the mistakes and got the project into the mess in the first place. It is absolutely essential that your leadership is backed up by support from your management. If your management do not accept that fundamental changes are needed, or do not support you in your efforts to make those changes, then it is likely that you will not be able to make them.

On the other hand, if you realize fairly early in the project that you rushed the early stages or that the project is becoming hacked, then there is every hope of turning things around before the problems become too serious, *provided* you can admit to yourself that things are wrong and get yourself the time to do something about it. Even if six months have passed on a one-year project it should not be too late to put things straight, if you realize that you made some serious mistakes.

In this case the best approach is for you to start back at the beginning, reviewing what was done and changing it where necessary. Don't try to stop the project! It may not even be a good idea to tell people that you are consciously questioning the things that were done. Start again from the beginning. Check that the requirements still make sense and are adequately detailed, checking with customers if necessary. Review the architecture of the project – is there one? Does it still seem appropriate? You and your team probably had to make some decisions at the start of the project that were based on best guesses and scant information – have you learnt enough to revisit those decisions and confidently change your minds?

As you consider an issue, think what needs to be changed. You can't change everything just because it 'would have been better' to have done it

See also SECTION 38: THE DESIGN OF MY PROJECT IS IN A MESS.

differently, you can only change things that are definitely wrong and will cause problems. Even if you limit yourself to things that definitely need doing, you are likely to meet heavy resistance from other team members, and from managers if you consult them. 'We can't change the architecture now, it's too late!' 'We have a demo to do next month and this feature needs to be finished' and so on. Obviously you will need to plan the work carefully, make time for it to happen, and limit it to the essentials.

You may also realize, as part of reconsidering the project, that the original plan was very optimistic. This is not the same sort of issue as those I've addressed in this section. The plan may be unrealistic in a way that will make the project late, but that's not the same as ending up stuck in the '80% complete' trap as described above. If you're constantly slipping because the plan is too optimistic then make sure that the plan is sufficiently detailed and the estimates are realistic, using the experience of what has happened thus far on the project to make a better prediction of what will happen in the future (see also SECTION 9: HOW DO I DRAW UP A PROJECT PLAN? for some tips on estimation). You may have to inform your customer that you will be late, and tell your management that you will need more time or more people. The sooner the issue is raised the better. You won't be popular, but you'll be even less popular if you ignore the warning signs and carry on regardless.

Prevention definitely is better than cure, and it's best not to get into this 'nearly completed' trap in the first place. If you do find yourself on a project that is thrashing because of fundamental problems, try not to get sucked completely into the everyday disaster recovery operations, but reserve some of your energy for looking at the bigger picture and for being the person on the project who gets the necessary fundamental improvements made.

The ability to understand details and make one's own analysis of them, but also to be able to step back from them and see the bigger picture, has been called the 'helicopter trait', which successful people often seem to possess. Don't ignore the details, but don't get bogged down in them and fail to see the wider picture either.

14 HOW CAN I GET A GOOD JOB DONE WHEN OUR PROCEDURES ARE SO BAD?

Software development does not lend itself to control by rigid procedures. The processes that contribute most to the success of the outcome – such as analysis, design and coding – cannot be standardized and proceduralized (thank goodness). In addition, software development is changing all the time, so procedures that are specific tend to get out of date very quickly, and if they are not specific then they are often so woolly as to be worthless.

It is important to understand the difference between *procedures* and *processes*. Procedures provide constraints within which everyone must operate, but processes are what individual people actually do. Procedures are poor at controlling creative activities, whereas appropriate processes can help creative activities to succeed. Procedures are usually organization-wide or department-wide and change quite slowly, but processes vary from project to project and can change quite quickly. Crucially, your boss is probably in charge of the procedures your team must work to, whereas you have much more control over the processes adopted on your team. Good procedures guide your processes and help the organization function, but should not dictate in detail how your team operates – you must do that.

Many engineers can't see the benefit of procedures at all. 'We know how to do our jobs, who needs the paperwork?' Good procedures are those that help you to get your job done, even if they do it by restricting you somewhat. For example, in the release process, good procedures will contain useful check-lists to remind you to do things that need doing (for example incrementing version numbers), will record things that need recording (so that a build is reproducible in the future), and will help to protect the organization's intellectual property. They won't make you do things that are stupid or have no benefit. If your procedures are getting in the way of you making a good job then your procedures need changing, but that does not mean that the whole concept of working to procedures is wrong.

Some engineers immediately blame the QA (Quality Assurance) department for all procedural problems. 'QA are useless! I read this document today, it's all signed off and everything, and it tells you to do things that any idiot can see are impossible!' This shows a misunderstanding of what Quality departments are for. They are NOT there to police the quality of everything that is done. That is for people to do themselves: quality is everyone's responsibility (and on your team, it is especially *your* responsibility). Quality departments are there to manage the quality procedures and make sure they are followed, and also modified and improved constantly so that they remain useful. Quality assurance managers manage the quality department, they don't (and can't) directly manage the quality of the work done in an organization. For instance, procedures can mandate that designs are documented and must be approved by someone with design authority. They cannot mandate that what is in the text of the document is actually correct or useful; that is the job of the author of the document and of the design authority. All the quality department can do is to mandate that the document exists, to make sure it is approved, and ensure that the date and issue number and so on are correct, before it is formally referenced elsewhere or sent outside the company.

If your procedures are too woolly, then it's up to you to create your own processes and impose some discipline on yourself and your team. If you decide that, beyond what it says in the coding procedure, every function definition should have a comment in the code, then impose that rule on the team and police it yourself. If you think it's important and worth the effort then go for it. The fact that your procedures don't mandate it is not an issue; you're the team leader and you control the processes adopted by your team. Of course, the processes you impose must fit within the constraints of your formal procedures.

If your procedures are difficult to follow because they are out of date or too restrictive, try to get them changed. You can't ignore rules just because you don't like them, but quite often procedures get so out of date that everyone knows they're wrong. If this is the consensus in your organization (not just your own opinion), then try to get them changed, and in the meantime go ahead and *bend the rules*! Don't be ashamed to bend rules that are actually getting in the way of doing a good job! Don't bend

Never write a document that is useless, just to 'keep QA quiet'. If the document is not needed or there genuinely is not time to write it, then explain this to QA, and you should be given permission to skip it or postpone it. If you are forced to write something anyway, then write something very short, maybe a few bullet-points, that sets out some main points but explains that this is an interim document. Never write some rubbish that looks good to QA but is actually unusable; it's an insult to everyone who comes along later and tries to follow what you did, and it's a waste of your time.

the rules because of laziness, or to cut corners, or to avoid scrutiny by others, but only to avoid rules that are stupid. For example, the change-control procedures I saw in one company insisted that nobody could take a file out of the version control system without written, signed permission, and they couldn't put it back without another signature. While this sort of control might make sense on a vital, legacy product where small changes are being made and need to be made carefully, it is a totally unworkable and stupid procedure during development of new products. Naturally, the engineers bent the system. They got permission at the start of the project to work on every file, and at the end they got permission to put them all back in again. Useful version control was still achieved because an electronic system was in place, so the procedures, which were written before that system was introduced and had not been updated, deserved to be ignored.

Of course, what should happen if procedures are inappropriate is that they should be changed. As team leader you shouldn't just moan about the situation, you should try to do something about it. When trying to change procedures, aim low. Suggest small changes. Get the ball rolling, however slowly, as the inertia is usually enormous. If you try to propose wholesale changes then almost certainly they will never get agreed and you will get bogged down in arguments and bureaucracy. It usually takes a very strong and powerful manager, with unwavering support from the top, to make large changes to procedures. If there isn't such a person around with a strong inclination to make large changes to the procedures, I strongly advise against trying to do it yourself. Instead, propose small but frequent incremental changes that don't cause too much aggravation.

At the end of the day, engineers are paid to develop software, not to create beautiful project folders. Follow the procedures in a way that is most appropriate to getting the job done adequately. Use your knowledge of your project to decide which procedures to impose rigidly (or to exceed in your own processes) in order to keep the quality high, and which to comply with using minimum effort. That doesn't mean you have a licence to miss out things because you're in a hurry, it just means that sometimes you can follow a procedure by doing very little work because not much work *needs* to be done. And sometimes you need to do much more than the procedure dictates because it is necessary. The procedures are a guide and a final constraint on your actions; you must not let them unthinkingly dictate your actions.

If you ever have to write or modify procedures, you'll soon find out that it is a difficult and thankless task. It's very hard to get right, and whatever

infobar // **STUPID PROCEDURES**

- First symptom of stupid procedures: **They make you produce write-only documents.** A typical example of a stupid procedure is a release process that makes you list all the files in a directory, when anyone who wants to know what files are in the release could just look in the directory, or coding standards that insist you fill in the file name, author, creation date, full change history etc. etc., every time you change anything in a file, most of which is never used by anybody. What little these procedures add to quality is more than lost in terms of wasted time and the disincentive they place on people making small but useful changes.

  Another way that a procedure can produce a write-only document is by dictating a huge list of subjects that it must cover, whether relevant or not, so producing a huge document where the useful content is lost in rubbish.

- Second symptom of stupid procedures: **They impose rules that try to replace trust.** An organization must trust its own people, otherwise it should not employ them. If an organization trusts its engineers to develop its products, then it must trust them to do their jobs without constant policing. Of course people occasionally do something silly or even deliberately damaging, but procedures should not be written from the assumption that people are typically stupid or malicious. They should act as a reminder to competent people of what needs doing, and allow someone to check that it was done. They should not enforce rigid control. (Procedures are a little like the rules of the road. Normally, the rules are there to prevent accidents, and people are expected to obey them. We have lights that tell us when we must stop, and we trust people to obey them. Only in severe situations is tight control used, such as having barriers to prevent cars crossing train lines when a train is coming. In software, we may have a rule that when code is put back under source control after a change, a comment must be written to explain what was done. We should trust people to comply with this rule, and remind them occasionally when necessary. Only in the most stringent situation, such as for safety-critical code, should someone need to check and authorize that this rule is being obeyed.)

  Similarly, poor procedures often try to replace trust in the leader, by replacing it with bureaucratic processes and committee meetings. See the   >skills box **HINTS ON PROCEDURE WRITING** below, and the Diagram 'Why the Neanderthals became extinct' below.

- Third symptom of stupid procedures: **They are hopelessly out of date.** The trouble with all bureaucratic systems is that after a while the people who enforce them start to believe that the rules must be correct because 'rules is rules'. If

cont >>

>>

you suggest that something different should be done, you get told that you have to follow the rules because they are the rules. Of course it's true that you can't break the rules just because you feel like it, but one of the major differences between a useful QA department and a useless one is that useful departments encourage other departments to constantly revise and change the procedures, albeit slowly and carefully. Useless QA departments block changes and insist on enforcing rules even when they are inappropriate or out of date.

■ Fourth symptom of stupid procedures: **They are designed to get accreditation first and foremost.** Good procedures are written by capturing the best practice from inside the organization, and from other organizations, and ensuring that everyone follows it. Usually, people adopt the practices first and then formalize them into procedures later.

A classic way to make really stupid procedures is to take a quality standard and translate it into procedures that are designed purely to gain accreditation to the standard, with any idea of helping people to do a good job being an afterthought. If you really want to make some procedures that are stinkingly awful, write them and enforce them without first giving them a trial run on a real project. Amazingly, that's how many managers try to go about it, and the result is procedures that impress an auditor but actually get in the way of getting the job done properly. **Good procedures are mostly about self-regulation, not about pleasing auditors.**

■ Fifth symptom of stupid procedures: **They are written by somebody who doesn't know how to do the job that the procedures regulate.** Engineering procedures should be written by engineers. Even the most well-meaning general manager, administrative assistant or QA person cannot write engineering procedures, there are just too many subtleties. Whoever writes the procedures, they should always be reviewed by the people who will have to follow them, and the review feedback should be taken very seriously.

> skills box

HINTS ON PROCEDURE WRITING

If you find yourself having to make major changes to procedures, it's worth doing your homework first. This is a huge area that is mostly outside of the scope of this book, so I'm only going to give a few hints:

■ Obviously you need to comply with any specific regulations that apply to the industry you are in, such as medical standards or standards for agricultural products. Get a copy of them, and get as much help as possible in understanding how to apply them – usually there are guidance notes to go with the documents, but also the regulators are usually quite willing to talk about the regulations they produce, and may also be able to recommend independent consultants to advise you.

■ If your procedures are intended to comply with some standard such as ISO9001-3, get a copy of the standard and the guidance notes that go with them. They are surprisingly readable. Also, contact the people who will audit you – they are often quite willing to help you through the process of writing your procedures, and they can often put you in touch with other organizations that have already got procedures in place that you might be able to use as a starting point.

It isn't possible to download a copy of ISO9001-3; it has to be purchased from your national standards authority (e.g. ANSI or BSI), or it can be purchased from organizations such as IHS (http://global.ihs.com).

If you are writing procedures from scratch, the organization of 'chapters' from ISO9001 is the ideal way to begin.

Procedures such as ISO9001 tend to specify the *quality of the quality system*, whereas process methodologies tend to help with the process and therefore with the quality of the software produced.

There are many different processes already fully documented that can be adopted. Browse the book shops or a good library and you may find a process already written that is almost what you want. The advantage of following a published process such as these is that it will come with pages of explanation and examples, and will have already been tried and tested elsewhere. Here are some process methodologies that you might be able to adapt:

– The 'Rational Unified Process'. Heavily based on UML (see APPENDIX 2: BRIEF INTRODUCTION TO UML) through all stages of analysis, design, coding and testing, this methodology is well documented in several books, is supported to some extent by the Rational tools, and can also be purchased as online help on CD. See www.rational.com/products/rup/index.jtmpl.

– The Software Engineering Institute's (SEI) 'Capability Maturity Model, Version 1.1'. Not an easy model to apply, it is mostly relevant if you have some commercial necessity to demonstrate achievement of a given level of maturity. See www.sei.cmu.edu/.

The quality standard ISO9001 is often misunderstood. It does not of itself increase the quality of what you do. It is a standard for the *quality system* of an organization, not a standard for the quality of what an organization does. ISO9001 got a bad press in the software industry a while ago, but with recent changes it has become much more useful.

cont >>

>>

- NASA's Software Engineering Lab's (SEL) 'Recommended Approach to Software Development, Revision 3'. Very formalized and full of critical reviews and so forth, but appropriate in a large project with only one chance at success. See fdd.gsfc.nasa.gov/seltext.html.

- The US Food and Drug Administration's 'Medical Device Code Of Good Manufacturing Practice'. This is a huge document, but well written. Although written for medical products, with a heavy emphasis on avoiding hazards, this code can be adapted (probably greatly cut down) to any other area of work. See www.fda.gov/cdrh/ode/software.pdf and www.fda.gov/cdrh/fr1007ap.pdf.

- The Dynamic System Development Method. This is appropriate if you have a very good and close working relationship with your customer, especially if your customer is better placed to test your work than you are. Only apply it if all the prerequisites for its use, which the method itself defines, are fully met. See www.dsdm.org.

- The 'Team Software Process', created by Watts Humphrey. A pragmatic process with plenty of well-defined activites, especially appropriate if you have a quite inexperienced team. See the 'process and procedures' section in the bibliography (SECTION 42) for a reference.

▪ Read up on project management concepts, such as the 'V-Model' (see the bibliography [SECTION 42] for books that will explain this concept). Incorporate ideas from these books into your procedures. But always be totally practical; don't try to push the frontiers of software development – remember that your organization exists for its own reasons (such as to make money), not to prove anything to anybody.

▪ Do not try to proceduralize every action that is taken on a project. There is no need to draw a diagram that shows 'Have I made a mistake in the design? – yes, go back and rework it, no...'. Nobody is going to use such a diagram, it is just useless paperwork. For an example of the sort of thing to be avoided, see the diagram, 'Why the Neanderthals became extinct' below. Your procedures should help people do a good job, not make them sit in endless meetings to discuss whether they did a good job.

▪ Coding standards often produce the most arguments. These arguments may be reduced by adopting some sort of standard that everyone is familiar with, or by adopting the same style of code as that produced by any automated tools you have. See the bibliography for some books on coding that give useful guidelines which can be incorporated into procedures. Failing that, it needs one strong and influential person to impose a coding standard.

▪ Reviews are also a source of friction, and here it is best to define different types of reviews, and leave it up to team leaders to decide what sort of reviews they hold and when. Mandate formal reviews only where they are always necessary to ensure quality or to maintain control. For instance, you might mandate that requirements must be reviewed and approved before design starts.

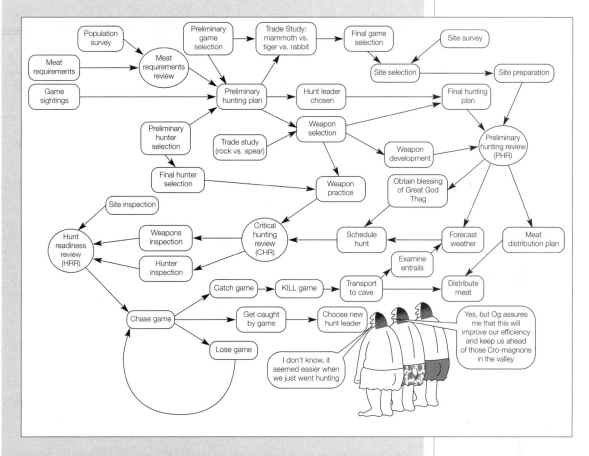

Don't go overboard on check-lists. Check-lists are useful for reminding people to do things that they otherwise might forget to do, such as to upgrade a version number when making a release. They are *not* good for structuring reviews. For example, don't have a check-list for code reviews that asks 'is commenting adequate?', 'is the code clearly laid out?' and so on – when you review code you work through it, in a way that is not compatible with going through such a check-list point by point. For code reviews, check-lists are useful for reminding you to check for compliance with coding standards, but you need to be careful they don't distract you from looking at the more subtle but important aspects of code quality.

In the worst cases, if presented with a long mandatory check-list, people will consider each point on the list, after which they will be too fed up to do the actual useful review work of trying to understand what has been done and considering whether it is appropriate to the task.

Template documents work very well. Create some sample documents and make these available as a starting point. Ideally, there should be a whole sample *project*, ready to be used as the outline for new projects.

Why the Neanderthals became extinct

I have tried to trace the originator of this drawing but have failed. If anyone knows who they are please let me know and I will happily recognize their genius on my website.

cont >>

>>

- Write out the new procedures, get them reviewed by several people, and then try them out in your own project first. Change them when you see improvements that you could make. Only try to get them formally adopted once they are stable and working on that project. Remember, though, that what works for your project may not be appropriate for all other projects now or in the future. Try to build in some flexibility so that your new procedures are not immediately out of date.

- Err on the side of less control and formality when writing procedures. If it turns out that some control needs tightening up then that can be done instantly by issuing instructions to people, with changes to the procedures coming later. But if you make the procedures too tight then either they will get in the way, or they will get ignored, or someone will have to keep writing waivers.

- Remember that the auditor is the least important person in the process. Your customer is the most important, followed by people in your organization, followed by other organizations you deal with – the auditor has a last veto on the process. If you get audited against your new procedures and you get through with flying colours, not even a minor problem, then there's probably something wrong!!! Usually, there's a compromise to be made between what you want to do and what the auditors want – it is right and healthy to balance that compromise as far as possible towards your customer's needs, just barely satisfying the auditor – and getting one or two minor audit discrepancies is not the end of the world, in fact it may be an indication that you got the balance about right!

you do, somebody seems to take extreme exception to it. It's not surprising then that procedures often get out of date as nobody wants to touch them, even the managers who are supposed to be enforcing them. But, as team leader, making difficult things happen that need to happen is part of your job, and unfortunately that means you may have to take a lead in getting procedures updated. See the >skills box HINTS ON PROCEDURE WRITING, above. Updating procedures is likely to be a thankless task, but one that will eventually contribute to the smooth running of your department.

Once new procedures have been put in place, people need to be made to follow them. They need to know that the new procedure exists, be made to read it, and be persuaded to change their behaviour to comply with it. Sending round an e-mail instructing people to go and find a copy and read it is not likely to work very well; people are much more likely to read a document if you send them a copy of the document than if they have to go and find it. Having read it, people still need to be persuaded to change their ways, and as team leader it comes down to you to monitor this during reviews and in day-to-day work. Most people will not change their ways unless given a little push in the right direction.

Poor procedures can slow you down, they can be frustrating, and they can fail to help you do a good job. But they cannot force you to do a bad job. Poor procedures can never be used as an excuse for poor quality work. It is your job as leader to make sure that the quality of work done on your team is up to scratch, even if you get scant help from your procedures.

>> **LEADING PEOPLE**

15

WHAT IS MEANT BY 'TEAMBUILDING'?
IS THERE SOMETHING I'M SUPPOSED TO BE DOING **TO BUILD A BETTER TEAM?**

Working in a team that has a good team spirit can be a great motivator. When people feel part of a team, they want to give it their best and to pull their weight. Team spirit is the one motivating factor that *you* have the most control over and are most responsible for. If working on your team is a miserable experience then people won't do their best. If people are glad they're on your team then the results can be dramatic.

'Teambuilding' was a bit of a management buzz-word a few years ago, and hundreds of books were (and still are) written about it. But it's not a separate activity that you do – if you ask someone what they're doing right now, they're unlikely to reply 'right now, I'm teambuilding'! Teambuilding is a set of skills, habits and attitudes, which is why it's hard to pin down (and therefore, a lucrative subject for authors of management books).

Firstly, it helps if you have a clear definition of what a 'team' is. We all know when we're in a team, but getting a good definition of a team gives some insight into the things that need to be concentrated upon in order to build up a team that works well. My own favourite definition of a team is '*a group of people working closely together to achieve a common purpose*'. This definition leads on to the following things you can do to build up a team:

▶ Teambuilding starts by getting a group of people together. It must be clear who is on the team, and people must be committed to being on it. People may be on the team full-time or just occasionally, but in either case they must be prepared to commit time and energy to the team.

It should be clear what each person's role is within the team. When a decision is to be made, it should be obvious who should make it. Everyone should know who they are working for and who works for them.

There are often problems for people whose main job is based in a departmental function rather than in project work. For instance, a purchasing manager may be assigned to the team, but may well feel more commitment to the purchasing department than to the project team. In cases like this, it's important that the team leader makes it clear to the individual's departmental boss that the person is needed on the team, and that this will take time, which other people in that department may need to make up. You need to do what you can to make sure that everyone on the team can give commitment to the team, without neglecting other commitments they have.

Teams only work for groups of people of a certain size – and it's quite a narrow range of sizes. It's hard to call a group of people a 'team' if there are only two of them. At the other extreme, it's very unlikely that 15 people will work together as one cohesive team – it would just be too complicated, and people will naturally bunch into sub-teams. This applies mostly to full-time team members – it's the size of the 'core' of the team that matters. Part-time team members could take the number of people involved in a team much higher than this without too many problems.

▶ **The people have to be able to get on together.** This doesn't mean they have to be similar in any way, or that they want to be close friends, but it is important that they can respect one another and *trust each other to do their jobs*. Friction and arguments are not uncommon when a team forms, but shouldn't go on too long. Back-stabbing and point-scoring have no place in a team, and if you see them happening then you need to put a stop to them quickly – try to find out why someone feels it necessary to put someone else down, and be prepared to come down hard on the offender if it amounts to nothing but personal politicking.

Sometimes there is someone on a team that nobody can stand, even though they are technically quite competent. My advice is to get rid of such a person as soon as possible as the whole team will suffer (and people will do whatever they can to leave it) if such a person is left in place.

Some organizations believe strongly in 'teambuilding exercises', such as out-of-bounds or wilderness experiences. I would not recommend that you try to organize such an activity as a way of trying to bring together your team, as most people would not accept this as an appropriate part of your job. Instead, if such a thing is organized by your management, try to split up your team and spread people out, so that your team forms bonds and contacts with other people in the organization.

Sporting activities, free lunches, or just bringing some doughnuts to a boring meeting *do* work, especially if they are fairly spontaneous things. Any organized 'teambuilding' event will fail if people feel pressurized to attend it.

▶ **The team needs a purpose, right from the outset. The purpose must be clear, it must be seen to be achievable, and it must be perceived as worthy of achievement.** Never play down your team's purpose, always stress the value of what it is doing. That's not to say you should pretend there aren't problems, but you should always stress the importance of trying to reach the goal.

This is why teams of developers often work best if they form once the project requirements have been clarified, rather than *while* they are being clarified. It is also important that the team's purpose is constant – see the infobar // CHANGES OF DIRECTION.

When someone joins your team, spend plenty of time with them, explaining what the project is about. Don't give a narrow focus on the technology or on the specific work that the person will be doing, until you have explained the bigger picture of why the project is needed, why it is happening now, and where it fits in to the plans of the organization or its customers.

People need to understand both the long-term goals of the project and also the short-term priorities. They need to know where they are going and how they are going to get there, and what they should be doing 'right now'.

▶ The team members need good communications in order to work closely together. Preferably, they should be located very closely together. A few metres makes a big difference to communication. A wall presents a large barrier to communication. And if people are in different buildings, they might as well be in different cities for all the close communication that is likely to happen.

Try to assemble your team physically close together. If this is not possible and people are dispersed, then maintaining good communications and a sense of working as a single team will be one of your primary responsibilities and something you will have to put significant effort into.

The team needs a common language, both a common tongue and a common understanding of technical terms and jargon. Barriers of language and culture can be real problems that are difficult to tackle, but it can help if you can agree a common set of terms.

infobar // **CHANGES OF DIRECTION**

The team's purpose is so central to its existence that if it is changed at all, people are likely to feel stressed by the change, and to try to resist it. Even if people can understand the change, they still react against it emotionally. This is one reason why 'moving goalposts' are so disruptive, and why requirements changes need to be very carefully handled (see SECTION 26: CHANGE REQUESTS).

When the requirements do change, it is useful for the leader to identify those things that have remained common and remain central to the team's purpose so that people continue to feel bound to the team. For example, if you have put a lot of effort into demonstrating that you can use a new operating system but management order you to use an old one anyway, it is worth encouraging people to recognize that the purpose of the team has not changed, its primary goal is the same, it will simply be achieving it through different technology.

Even changing the *name* of the project or product can cause significant loss of morale – people identify with the project name, in the same way that soldiers identify with their battalion name, and changing it can make people upset (which is something that marketing departments rarely appreciate).

Good communication is usually informal and frequent. A certain amount of chatting is necessary and desirable, because people work best together if they get to know each other as human beings. If you are working with other people mostly by e-mail, try to arrange to meet them at the start of the project if possible, and speak to them on the phone (or even better, use videoconferencing) at regular intervals. This greatly reduces the chance of conflicts occurring.

Never try to control or centralize communication, either within the team or between your team and other people. Encourage people to talk to people they need to talk to, even if they are quite senior or located at some distance. If someone needs to call a meeting then encourage them to arrange it themselves. As far as possible, let people organize themselves as they see fit, moving desks, swapping computers, whatever it takes to organize working together more closely. **Give higher priority to people working together as an effective unit than to them working efficiently as individuals.** A team that spends time chatting over technical issues is far more likely to succeed than one that constantly works in silence.

On multinational projects the physical separation, plus differences in culture, language and working practices, make misunderstandings and disagreements very likely. Meeting up, and using videoconferencing, is especially important on multinational projects.

Discourage habits that damage communication. Working from home, working offset hours, and hiding away in a closed office all have their place when they are needed, but they do a great deal of harm to communications and shouldn't be encouraged.

▶ The team **needs to feel that it is progressing** towards its objectives. When your team has achieved something significant, then celebrate a little. Take time to enjoy the experience. Go to the pub. Reward yourselves for your achievements. So often in software development, the time pressures are such that when we finish something the main feeling is one of relief, and of wanting to get home at last, rather than pride and pleasure. This takes all the sense of achievement out of the work – so give yourself a little break when you've done well.

When the team's achieved some milestone, no matter how small, tell management about it. It only takes an e-mail. Why not give them some good news for a change? It might help you, when things don't go so well, if they've heard something other than bad news from your team.

You need to be taken seriously, so don't keep spouting on about how well things are going if they're not. But it's worth occasionally reminding people of the good points of the team and its work – people notice the bad things all the time, but the good things get taken for granted and undervalued. It's worth talking them up, just occasionally.

▶ People must be willing to **sacrifice their own objectives** to those of the team. Joining a team means working to a common objective, and that means that you're not working to your own personal objectives and hidden agendas. People will only do this if they can see that it will not last long, or if they can see that the team's objectives actually aid their own and deliver some reward.

A key personal objective for many engineers is to keep their skills up to date, or to put it more crudely, to get some interesting stuff on to their CV. This is one of the objectives that may have to be sacrificed to the team's objectives, and people can find it hard to accept, for example, sometimes using an older technology on a project.

People are far more willing to subjugate their own wishes to those of the team if they feel that they 'own' the problem. For example, people will be more willing to use an older technology if they themselves were part of the decision to adopt that technology, rather than having the decision forced upon them.

Early in a team's life, before the team members have committed themselves to the team and the way it will work, decisions are far more likely to be influenced by personal objectives than they are later. So when important decisions, such as a choice of technology, are being made early in the project's life, it is appropriate for the leader to be quite firm and strong, otherwise vital decisions may be made for all the wrong reasons. Involve and consult people, to aid in them feeling ownership, but be firm in ensuring that decisions are made for the right reasons.

If it's obvious that people are not getting much out of working on the project, then you need to provide additional rewards from the project work. This might simply be in the form of a better social atmosphere, or being more flexible over the work, or of making sure that people get recognized by management as making a contribution, which might help them progress within the organization.

Usually, you can accommodate people's interests and aspirations to some extent by letting people work on aspects of the project that they find interesting, and by allowing flexibility in how they tackle the work. But sometimes that isn't enough and people try to pull the project onto a direction that suits them, even if it damages the project – see the infobar // THE DARK SIDE, below.

▶ The team must be able to achieve its purpose. This means it must have sufficient people, the time and resources necessary, and be seen to have commitment from management. The people must between them have the necessary skills to achieve the purpose, or else (much less ideally) these skills must somehow be available to the team from some outside source.

These issues are covered in more detail in other sections, such as those concerned with planning and requirements capture.

If your team is struggling without the resources or the commitment it needs, you should approach management to try to get the priorities sorted out.

▶ A team needs a mix of personality types. Some people are better at having insightful ideas, but not at implementing them. Some people are good at design concepts, while others are better at implementation. Some people enjoy finishing off and 'polishing' the product, while others hate it. You need a mix of people so that for every task you can find someone who is at least willing to do it, even if it's not their idea of heaven.

If the team is very lacking in one type of behaviour – say for instance that nobody seems to quite finish things off properly – then you can and should try to get people to do those aspects of the work that they dislike, if it makes up part of the whole job – but you also have to accept that you as leader will end up having to do some of the jobs that nobody else is doing. For example, if you have a team where nobody is very 'organized', then it will be down to you to maintain folders of documents, tidy up the structure of the project and clear out junk, make sure that a safe copy is taken of work before it gets radically changed, and so on. If you have a team where everybody wants to do things just the same old way, and you need them to adopt new methods, then you will have to be the one who reads the books, makes prototypes to test out new ideas, and so on.

If your team is made up of people who all have a similar outlook and skills, it will probably feel very cosy, but *look out*, because it isn't likely to come up with the best solutions.

▶ **Teams are held together by a social bond.** You cannot have a team if no time is allowed for chatting and idle banter. It only takes a few 'unproductive' minutes out of each day to make a huge difference to the quality of working life. In any case, social chatter often has a work aspect, and there are many times I've learnt more in the coffee break in the middle of a meeting than I have in the meeting itself.

▶ **The team leader must adopt the appropriate leadership style.** See SECTION 16: LEADERSHIP STYLE.

Teambuilding is a subtle process, and most of it just happens by doing your job and working with the other people on the team. Every decision that is made on your project affects not only the quality of the products, the time-scales and budget, but also the people, individually and as a team. The effect on the team members needs to be balanced with the other factors when you are making a decision.

A team doesn't have to meet all of the above factors completely in order to work well, but the better it fits them, the more enjoyable the teamwork is likely to be, and the better the output produced. If you can see deficiencies in your team, see if you can do something about them. If you can see strengths, try to build on them.

I have been told that that some Japanese companies build in dissonance, just enough conflict to make things interesting without being disruptive.

infobar // **THE DARK SIDE**

Even a strong team can have its problems.

■ Weak or quiet people can get ignored, and can be oppressed or bullied into doing things they don't want to do. This is especially true if there is a range of seniority in the team – junior people will tend to shut up in front of people who are very senior.

Sometimes, decisions get made on the basis of who shouts the loudest.

If someone doesn't want to speak in a meeting then don't bring attention to them or force them to speak up, but have a quiet chat with them afterwards to hear what they have to say.

■ Teams can become very inward looking, existing for their own sakes and ignoring the rest of the world. They can continue to strive towards an objective that is no longer relevant, because they choose not to change direction. They can convince themselves that they know more about the issues than their customer does and so will ignore the customer and do what they think right.

As leader, you must keep the team focused on the needs of its customers, and maintain an outward-looking perspective.

■ Teams usually make more risky decisions than individuals. Taken to the extreme, 'group-think' can set in. This is where a team of people make decisions that are stupid, but they convince themselves that they will work. The team members constantly support and encourage each other, and look inwards for their feed-back, ignoring or rejecting anything that they don't want to hear from outside the team. They become convinced that they, the team, are in the right and the rest of the world is wrong.

Usually this happens when a strong leader is surrounded by weak acolytes, and gets constantly encouraged no matter how stupid the decisions become. It can also happen if people desperately want to get into, and stay in, the group, and will accept any decisions made by the rest of the group in order to be accepted by it. It is much more likely to happen if the team is made up of people who all have quite similar backgrounds and attitudes, than if there is a mix of people with different abilities and opinions.

When group-think starts up, any team members who are sceptical and don't join in the process are likely to get ostracized. These are of course just the people who are needed to retain stability, but they are likely to get pushed out.

cont >>

>>

If everyone on your team seems to be agreeing with one another and telling themselves how brilliant they are and how dumb everyone else is, *look out*. Seek out the dissenters that are being given a hard time, and listen attentively to what they say.

■ In order to get on, people avoid subjects that they know are contentious, rather than raise them. In this way, important issues can be left unresolved until far too late. If you know of problem issues, try to get them sorted out; don't let them get papered over.

■ The team can be used as a vehicle by people to achieve their own ambitions, enhance their CVs, or to avoid work. If everyone has the same personal agendas then these are likely to dominate over the official objectives of the team. As leader you are the final safeguard against the team going out of control, and you must operate that safeguard, even if it makes you unpopular for a while.

16

SOMETIMES I THINK I'M BEING A SOFT TOUCH AND LETTING PEOPLE WALK ALL OVER ME // OTHER TIMES I THINK PEOPLE RESENT ME FOR INTERFERING // HOW DO I KNOW WHEN I'M GETTING THE STYLE RIGHT?

see the infobar //
**COPING WITH
DISCOMFORT**.

The more feedback you can get, both from the team and from the product, the better you will be able to respond to it. If you don't interact with your team very often or take notice of how they are behaving, or if you don't independently check out the product, you may not realize that something is wrong until it has gone quite far. If something has already gone quite wrong by the time you notice it, it's easy to over-react, and this starts the oscillation effect going. Subtle and frequent feedback both from people and from the product is the key to avoid the oscillation.

When you first start leading other people, it's very hard not to bounce between being too laid-back and being too autocratic. The first time I led a project, I tried letting people get on with things their own way, and everyone seemed happy, but later I found that some people had wasted their time on unimportant tasks, and had produced something that didn't impress me. So then I gave out smaller tasks, and went around checking up on people more often, but I got some unpleasant feelings from people who felt they were being 'controlled', in an autocratic way.

It's hard to know when you're getting it right, and it is *not* a matter of finding the style that seems most comfortable, either for you or for anybody else. The most comfortable style is not necessarily the most productive, and as team leader you may have to accept being a little uncomfortable at times to get the work done.

Remember that you are trying to balance the needs of the people on the team with the needs of the project. So as well as listening to the people on the team, 'listen to the product' by frequently playing with the software that is being produced, pretending to be an end-user trying to use the product, to get a feel for the software in use. Knowing the product very well (and comparing what it does to what the customer wants it to do) gives you a very solid foundation for knowing what you really want to change and what you can live with, and this gives you more confidence and credibility when dealing with the other people on the team.

The right leadership style depends on the following things:

▶ **The person.** Each person will work best if treated in a way that is appropriate to their seniority, their temperament and their abilities. A dedicated, capable, senior team member will probably rightly expect to be able to get on with large chunks of work without any need for approval by you. All you need to do is to be aware of what they are doing and to steer them in the right direction occasionally, by making sure they are aware of the project priorities and time-scales. A more junior engineer on the other hand may well need to be given small tasks, precisely described, may need to be mentored in how to tackle them, and their output may need to be reviewed in detail to keep the quality up and to help them learn.

Of course everyone has some things they are good at and others where they need more help, and so people need to be given freedom in some areas and need walking through others. It's a mistake to think that a senior person is necessarily best left alone to analyse, design and implement a large chunk of work unsupervised, just because they are senior. Some people need help with the early stages, while others are good architects and designers but lousy coders. You need to look at their output to find out what they are good at and what not. Don't be embarrassed about looking over someone's work, as everyone should expect to have their work reviewed, it's not a personal insult (see also SECTION 4: WHEN SHOULD I REVIEW OTHER PEOPLE'S WORK AND HOW?).

There are a few people who like to be spoon-fed, even on issues they are competent at, either because of lack of confidence or because of wanting to avoid responsibility. All you can do is to give out as much responsibility as the person will take, and also try to build it up to higher levels by making sure that the experience of responsibility comes out as a positive one. You need to do this because you shouldn't have to spend your time spoon-feeding work to people, but build up the confidence and responsibility slowly, otherwise confidence could be damaged even more.

A more common problem is the person who has an inflated opinion of their own abilities, and believes they have a right to do whatever they like without supervision or review. Whilst you can be a little flexible and adapt to the person, you cannot allow shoddy work to happen just because someone is awkward. Everyone else on the project would suffer if you allowed this. Even if the person is competent, you need to understand what is happening on the project and what progress is being made. So there really is no choice: find out what each person is good at

You also have things you are good at and some things you are not good at. Be honest with yourself about what you are good at and what not. When you have to do something you're not good at, get help (from someone on your team, if possible) so that you do it better. **Admitting your weaknesses does not make you a weak leader, it demonstrates good judgement.** Equally, on the issues that you know yourself to be good at, be confident in reviewing other people's work and strong in pursuing your objectives.

> skills box

LEADING JUNIORS

It's great to get young, recently trained people into an organization. They breathe new life into it, bring in energy and enthusiasm, and (let's face it) are often very good value for money. However, it is absolutely vital to be very selective in the recruitment process. Lots of people go into engineering because they like playing with computers, and they think the money will be good – many simply don't have an engineering attitude and cannot design at all.

If someone has not got enough experience to be left to get on with a reasonable size job (say, a week's work) alone, then they count as a junior engineer. It's not a matter of age, and there isn't a direct relationship with experience – some people cease to be 'junior', according to this definition, within a few months of starting work, while some people barely manage it at all. It's not just about skills either. You might get someone straight from college who is a brilliant programmer, and even (less commonly) a great designer. But they may still be junior because they haven't learnt some of the basic lessons that we all learn the hard way when we start working. Things like, 'test what you do before you've done too much' or 'start simply and work up to the complex stuff'. Even the best recently-trained engineers can take time to adapt to working in a team and working in industry. Until they have learnt how to cope, you can't let them entirely off the reins.

The less experienced and able a team member is, the more of your time you will have to devote to them. That's only fair and natural. As well as more help and guidance, they need to be closely supervised, and controlled – that's a harsh word but it fits in this context. The trick is to achieve the necessary control without getting up the person's nose.

■ Never treat juniors as cheap slave labour to fix other people's dirty work. People should fix their own bugs, not expect others to do it. Don't expect juniors to complete half-finished work either; this is very hard for anyone to do as it is hard to get into somebody else's code, and it can be especially hard for a junior to get to grips with terse code written by an expert. Be prepared to give out important and interesting work to junior team members, and accept that they will need more help and more time to complete it.

■ People straight out of college don't just need to gain technical experience, they also need to learn how to behave in an environment that may be new to them. Make sure that they are familiar with the way things work before expecting them to conform; for instance, let them sit through other people's design reviews so they know what to expect, before their work is reviewed.

■ Respond to the problems, not the person. If someone messes up because they didn't know how to do something then it's not their fault, you can't blame someone for not knowing something that they have never been told. Make sure they will know it next time, and make sure you are accessible if advice is needed. If some work is poor quality, don't just criticize it, suggest improvements and explain why they matter. Never criticize the person, only the work.

■ This is going to sound very touchy-feely, but it's true: you can tell a lot about how most people are progressing just by looking at how they are sitting at their computer. Most people, if they are stuck or in a mess, will be sitting all tensed up, looking frustrated. They may be taking an awful lot of breaks, or alternatively they may be taking no breaks at all and working into the night. If you notice that someone seems tense, don't leap up at the first sign of trouble, but give them a couple of hours to try to figure things out for themselves, then wander over to check if you can help.

■ Act as a coach and mentor, or make sure somebody does; don't leave people floundering for days on end. This is especially important when a junior person must do creative, unstructured or open-ended work, like analysis, design, user-interface layout, or writing proposal documents – junior people often find it hard to know where to start if faced with a blank sheet of paper or a multitude of options. This is where someone with more experience can get them started, and this is best done by doing the work *with* them to help them understand how to go about it.

■ Give out tasks that are as large as the person can confidently cope with. For a fresh graduate, these might be very small! Make it clear what you want done, how you want it done, how long it should take, and at what stages the person should come to you so you can check what they have done. Make the targets difficult (for them) but realistically achievable. Make sure the person knows that they can ask for help whenever they need it.

■ Review the work. You *have* to do this for junior engineers. It might just be a glance over the engineer's shoulder – you can't completely avoid looking over people's shoulders! Avoid picking on small points, in fact don't mention them at all. Just pick up on things that you really cannot live with, and help the person to feel that they are learning, rather than that they are out of their depth. If someone has tried hard, even if the result was not very good, give warm and positive feedback – even if the best you can say is 'well done for trying so hard, but I can see you need a bit of help'. If you give negative feedback then next time the person may just say to themselves 'there's no point busting a gut, whatever I do he'll just tell me to change it'. See also SECTION 4: WHEN SHOULD I REVIEW OTHER PEOPLE'S WORK, AND HOW?

Most juniors learn very fast, and quite soon you will be treating them pretty much like their more senior colleagues, but maybe just giving them rather smaller, more tightly contained tasks.

Although most people who take up software development are pretty bright, avoid 'dropping them in at the deep end'. Some people will flounder and lose confidence if you give them tasks that are too hard. Others will rapidly find a pragmatic way to solve the problems they come across – but in the process, most likely they will take short-cuts, learning just the snippets of information they need to get the job done, rather than learning the subject thoroughly. Try to encourage junior people to take things slowly enough to really understand what they are doing, so that they get proper training out of the work they are doing.

cont >>

>>

There are a few engineers who come out of college with egos the size of Jupiter. They know more than anyone, will be told nothing, and want to change everything. Stick to the rules of giving out tasks that are no larger than you want to give them, and review the results, commenting on the work, not the personality. Keep control of the work even if you can't control the person. Most graduates will soon work out that they need to prove what they can do before they will be allowed more freedom, and most will go on and prove it pretty quickly and get the freedom they crave. Many of us were like this once – and we ended up being OK – so give them a chance to get it out of their system. A few juniors with huge egos really can't stand being treated as juniors even though they quite obviously are junior, will get very upset, and usually will leave quite quickly (saving you the trouble of getting rid of them).

Leading people who are more junior than yourself takes up time, but it's a good use of your time, transferring some of the experience and 'software wisdom' you've gained to someone else, who will start to use it on your project. It can be a very rewarding experience.

and not so good at, and if people are not good at a particular task then take more control over how they do it and spend more time reviewing the results. You have to work with *your* opinion of how brilliant a person is, not the person's own opinion.

See also the >skills box LEADING JUNIORS above.

▶ **The urgency of the job.** When deadlines are tight but people are arguing about issues without a consensus emerging, and there just isn't time for any more argument, then you can and should direct people to do things your way, in quite an autocratic manner.

Most people will accept this for a short time if it gets the job done.

See also SECTION 19: WHEN SHOULD I LET SOMEONE DO A THING THEIR OWN WAY? and SECTION 3: I AM THE MOST EXPERIENCED ENGINEER ON THE TEAM.

When an issue is not so urgent, *even if it is important*, you should be more willing to let people make their own mistakes and learn from them. If the issue is important then give the work to someone who you think is capable of doing it well, and make sure that any mistakes are found later by testing and reviews. Providing that you give people work that is within their capabilities, the fact that an issue is important is not a good enough reason to take tight control of it.

▶ **The phase in the project's life.** It makes sense to take more control at the start of a project when the requirements capture, architecture and outline design are being settled, the first framework code is being written and so on. These things have a critical impact on the success of the project and they benefit from being done in a single, consistent manner. You may want to do most of this work yourself or delegate it to other people whilst keeping tight control by reviews and approval. This is quite autocratic but it is appropriate.

Also it is much easier to implement unpopular policies, such as 'we will have regular code reviews', early on in the project. If someone joins a project team and they are told 'we have code reviews on this project', they will accept it much more readily than if such a policy is imposed later on.

In the middle part of the project, during the 'design–code–test' increments, you can be more relaxed about things and just steer them. You need to keep enough control, but not too much.

Later on, as you near a major release of the project, you will again have to take tighter control, to ensure that bugs get fixed, documentation gets done and testing is thorough. Most people will accept that somebody has got to take tight control like this to achieve a successful release.

▶ **You.** Everyone has their own preferred style. Most engineers will tell you how much they believe in delegation, but when they become leaders their style is actually quite autocratic, as they like to be in control. Be honest with yourself and accept the way you are. If you try to adopt a style that doesn't come naturally, it will make you miserable and it simply won't work. The right style is not necessarily the one you find most comfortable (see the infobar // COPING WITH DISCOMFORT), but it should be a style that you believe in.

If you have been lucky enough to work for a competent team leader, then use them as a role model, and try to make things that worked for them work for you too. Beware, however, that what works for one leader with one lot of people on one project may not be appropriate for another leader or another lot of people or another project.

These four factors have to be balanced together to find a style that is appropriate for a given situation at a given time. Note that your leadership style should NOT be influenced by the degree of formality on the project. Even on very closely controlled projects, such as military projects, where approval in writing is needed for every change, you can still adopt a personal style that is trusting and relaxed. The formal procedures are

infobar // **COPING WITH DISCOMFORT**

The people on your team will be wanting and expecting you to take on the leadership role you have been given. They will be hoping that you will be a strong leader who will get things done and make things happen. Of course, they may also believe that they personally don't need much leading and should be left to get on with their job without your interference, and may be hoping that all the unpleasant tasks go to somebody else.

Getting people to do things that they really would rather not do, like having their work reviewed, is one of the sad facts of life for a team leader. You can't afford to be a soft touch. If a document wants writing or someone's design needs changing, then you are going to have to get it done, and this may feel uncomfortable.

But there is no need to get heavy or to get formal. Reviews should not be formal affairs, and neither should the task of allocating tasks to people. Just tell people what you want them to do and why. Be honest – if you don't like what's been done then say so. Concentrate on the work, but don't appear to be apologetic if you don't really feel it, and don't blame managers or procedures or make other excuses – if the work is to be done because *you want* it done then say so. It *is* possible to make it clear what you want, to be polite, and to be firm, all at the same time!

New leaders often feel bad about interrupting people or pressurizing them. At the first sign of someone looking uncomfortable they volunteer 'Don't worry, we can talk later' or 'if you haven't finished it today, that's OK, I'll come back on Monday'. This is usually a bad habit to get into. If you know someone is really busy then don't interrupt them unless you have to, but if you need to, then just do it and don't make any fuss about it. If someone seems to be taking a long time to finish something, then make sure you find out exactly where they are at present. Give them half an hour to get something ready to show you if necessary, but don't pretend that you're quite happy for days to go by before you find out what's going on.

It's not always comfortable being the leader, but it's your job. You may feel like a lonely, sad tyrant at times, although this reduces as you get practice. You must either do the job, or step down and let somebody else do it. A leader who can't stand being uncomfortable and making themselves unpopular on occasion is a liability to the team and an irritation to the people on it, not a help.

infobar // **A BIT OF THEORY**

This infobar describes, *very* briefly, a particular theory. It's more of a theory of psychology than of management, you may be glad to hear, and is concerned with the way people feel about their work and about how this motivates them.

This theory is called 'Hackman and Oldham's theory of job satisfaction'. It is based on a study of the behaviour of, and interviews with, several hundred people, mostly professional office workers.

The diagram shows that the fundamental attributes of someone's work ('core job characteristics') affect the way they think and feel about it ('critical psychological state') and this in turn affects how well they do the job and how much they enjoy it ('personal and work outcomes'). It also shows that the degree to which a person can achieve a satisfying job and experience pleasure from their work is governed by several 'moderators', such as their technical abilities ('knowledge and skill'), how much that person strives to improve themselves ('growth need strength'), and how much job satisfaction they get from peripheral aspects of being at work ('context satisfactions').

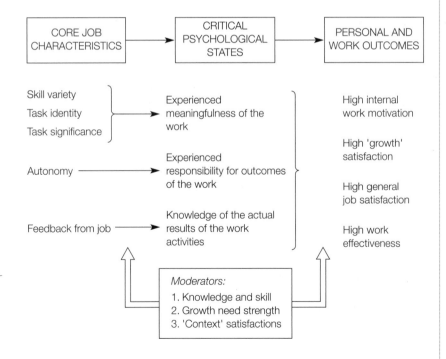

Source: 'The complete job characteristics model' from *Work Redesign* by Hackman/Oldman.

cont >>

>>

The meaning of the other phrases on the diagram is as follows:

Skill variety – the variety of activities and number of skills used in the job. Too little variety leads to monotony. Too much variety leads to fragmentation of effort and frustration.

Task identity – the extent to which the person completes whole tasks that they can identify as belonging to them, rather than contributing effort to a pooled result. People like to feel that the result of their work will be something that they can identify as their own.

Task significance – the extent to which the tasks contribute to the overall outcome of the project or success of the organization. The degree to which the tasks are worth doing.

The above three factors add up to 'intrinsic motivation' (motivation originating from inside the person, not imposed by other people). Generally, all three factors are needed in order for intrinsic motivation to happen.

Autonomy – the amount of freedom and discretion that a person has. The extent to which they 'own' the task, and the *extent to which a person can set their own objectives*. The optimum level of autonomy depends on the person and how well they are prepared.

Feedback from job – knowledge of how well the job was performed, and how much it was appreciated. Feedback can come from other people, from automated systems, or from self-regulation and checking. If someone sets themselves high standards, then testing their own work against that standard provides highly effective feedback. Timeliness of feedback matters greatly – feedback long after the event is of little value.

Experienced meaningfulness of the work – to what extent the person perceives the whole job as worth doing, either for themselves, for the organization, or for society at large. The degree to which time at work is perceived as time well spent.

Experienced responsibility for outcomes of the work – to what extent the person believes that their own actions have an impact on the finished product.

Knowledge of the actual results of the work activities – how much the person is aware of the effects of their actions. Also, how quickly they find out about the results of their efforts.

High internal work motivation – describes the way in which people can become highly motivated to perform well at work, due to their own psychological state rather than due to pressures or promises made by other people.

High 'growth' satisfaction – feeling good about developing and learning as a person.

High general job satisfaction – enjoying the job.

Hackman and Oldham state that the need for personal growth is the reason that many people are not satisfied by a job that they can do easily, but are motivated to do something more difficult and to learn. By harnessing this motivation to develop, a leader can direct a person's energy towards the objectives of the organization.

This theory rejects any contradiction between job satisfaction and motivation, whereas some other theories claim that people are motivated to do better largely because they are *not* satisfied with what they have got. According to the results of Hackman and Oldham's study, the people who were highly satisfied by their jobs were usually also the ones who were highly motivated to try hard. Hackman and Oldham's study proposes that people's need for development and growth is what links satisfaction with motivation.

You might like to try to analyse the situation of the people on your own team, according to this model. How much skill variety, task identity and task significance is there in the tasks that they are doing in your team? How much autonomy do they have over their work – to what extent can people set their own objectives? What sort of feedback about their performance are they receiving? How strong are their growth needs? The whole point of a theory like this is that you can apply it to your own situation and use it to identify things that ought to be done differently. What factors in your own team's practices are reducing people's job satisfaction and work quality?

there to prevent mistakes, they are not there to replace trust, to enforce a strict hierarchy or to prevent people taking on responsibility.

The aim of adopting the appropriate style for each situation is to achieve a team that is *relaxed but productive*. People should be doing the right things and be under enough pressure to be working suitably hard, but should not be demotivated or stressed by your actions. You need to keep some pressure on people, otherwise tasks tend to take a very long time, but too much pressure is counter-productive. Try to keep the level of pressure fairly constant, increasing only as urgent deadlines approach.

17

ONE OF MY TEAM MEMBERS IS AN EXPERT IN AN IMPORTANT ASPECT OF THE PROJECT THAT I KNOW LITTLE ABOUT // I FEEL LIKE A FOOL TRYING TO LEAD ON THIS ISSUE // WHAT CAN I DO?

In any leadership position, it's common to have people working for you who know more about some things than you do, or who are simply better at some things than you are. This is normal and healthy. If it's new to you, it's a sign that your career has just taken its first step onto the leadership ladder. The higher you go on that ladder, the more you will have to get used to leading people whose jobs you don't fully understand. Think about the most senior person in your organization, who probably has experts in finance, marketing, engineering and so on reporting to them – can they really be an expert in all these fields themselves?

It is also very healthy to delegate areas of responsibility for aspects of the project to other team members, and if you have a ready-made expert then they naturally would expect to make the decisions in the area that they know most about.

But delegation doesn't mean abdicating control and letting people do whatever they like without question. This issue of leading an expert usually only becomes a problem if you have someone on the team with whom you're having trouble. Some people think that being an expert excuses them from scrutiny by others who are less 'qualified'. This is simply not an acceptable attitude. Organizations are hierarchies, and everyone is responsible to someone else, so you shouldn't feel uncomfortable about making sure that, in broad terms, you understand and approve of what your 'expert' is doing, how they are doing it, and what progress they are making. As leader, you will be held responsible for everything that happens on the project.

Let's do this by way of an example. My fictional example project includes some image processing work which (let's say) I know little about. A new team member, John, is about to join my team, as an image processing expert.

The first thing I do is to make sure that John understands what the project is about. Not just the image processing but the bigger picture of the project as a whole. I also explain the architecture of the software that we've designed and where his work will fit into it. The image processing is an important part of the project and I especially want John to get a feel for who the customer is and what they need, so I ask him to arrange to visit the customer in person.

When John returns from that meeting, I talk to him about his discussions with the customer. John has informally agreed to add certain new features to the product. We discuss what these involve and I have to decide that although we want to do a good job, we can't actually do some of the work that John has agreed to, because we don't have time and nobody is paying for it. So I have to phone the customer and explain that they won't be getting some of the features after all ('in this release') – it's better to do this as soon as possible and be honest about it rather than leave them with unrealistic expectations. Meanwhile, I ask John to put together a document describing the features he is going to implement, especially from a user-interface point of view.

After a couple of days, John has not got back to me and I'm getting an uncomfortable feeling. Should I leave well alone, or start hassling him? The image processing is important, and John is new to the team, so I want to be sure that important decisions are not being made now without any review, as they might not be appropriate for the project. I ask John to tell me what he's up to, and he shows me a prototype he's knocked together to test out some ideas. I don't understand the details of the algorithms he's talking about, but by questioning him I can work out that John thought of two basic approaches that would work, and has chosen one of them. I want to understand what the options are about, but John is rather evasive and keeps playing with his software rather than talking to me, so I walk away.

But I don't let it drop. I know this is important and I want to feel that it is under control. I book a meeting room and after allowing a few hours for things to cool down, I ask John to go with me to talk about it. There's only John and me present, but getting him away from his computer and into a meeting about the image processing options means that he can't evade the issue.

John tells me that there are two options he considered, and he starts telling me the sequence of operations in each. Here's a snippet: '… then with this binary image I could do a generalized Hough transform to detect the parallel segments, following which…' – which is too detailed for me to see what the options are basically about. It's tempting to disguise my ignorance and just let him do his own thing, but I know that I would never have any control ever again if I did that.

I let him finish but then I still want to get to the bottom of what the options really are. I draw a table on the whiteboard with the names of the options on the top and 'pros and cons' down the side. This is what I really want to get at. After a few false starts and with John getting pretty fed up with me, I've understood that option 1 is quite a clever, fancy self-adjusting algorithm that will be more robust once it's working, but will take longer to finish and will be harder to get working at all. Option 2 is cruder and based on some approximate rules-of-thumb that happen to apply in most cases of interest. It will be quicker to develop but not 100% reliable, and will need tweaking if the user changes the environment of use, such as the lighting conditions under which the images being processed were taken.

This is a general principle to apply in almost all decisions: there is no 'good' and 'bad', there is only 'appropriate' and 'inappropriate' for your project.

Now I must resist my own preconceptions about what is a 'good' and a 'bad' approach, and instead consider what is appropriate. What matters is the consequences for the customer.

In this case, the customer is not expecting 100% reliable results, whereas they are very concerned about getting something as quickly as possible, and will be willing to pay for any tweaking. It seems to me that approach number 2 is the more appropriate in this case, and I'm relieved because that is the one John has chosen (although, in talking to me, he has learnt some things about the application that I had forgotten to tell him before, and changed his mind on some technical points).

Just to be sure, I phone the customer and discuss the options. They agree with our approach and now I'm much happier about it.

Now that I understand more of what John is doing, I understand more of what I was looking at when I saw John's prototype, and I'm worried about his approach. I think it will be very hard later to separate the algorithms from the user interface. Working together, John and I work out an outline design for the image processing system and its API interface to the rest of the project. By making some changes elsewhere, I can make the image processing API cleaner and so make John's work more self-contained. John isn't very interested in this stuff, he doesn't really see the problem and his head is full of much more interesting image processing algorithms right now. So I go away and code up the framework code myself, and add on a dummy user interface to call the image processing module through its API. By the time I hand this over to John, he's already coded some impressive image processing stuff.

But when I next check in on John, I only have to look at what he's done to the user interface to realize that he just hasn't understood about the idea of an API interface to his code, and sure enough when I look at his code with him, I can see the user interface calling straight into the guts of the image processing module, bypassing the API. It's a mess.

So now I've learnt some things about leading John. I can delegate important algorithmic decisions to him, although I will have to make it clear that I still want to understand what he's doing. But clean design is not his strong point, he's not a natural at encapsulating and organizing. On the implementation side he needs both helping and watching.

I sit down with John and we spend an hour moving code around until it fits in with the module design and is reasonably well structured internally. I also tell John that I want regular code reviews, to look at the details of each algorithm once he's finished it. He is not pleased (nobody likes code reviews), but code reviews already happen on this project and he can't really find an argument to get out of them.

As it happens, when we have the first review about a week later, although the detail of John's code is a bit scruffy, it is readable and reasonably well commented, it has lots of error checking, and it fits in with the architecture. I'm pleased, and I decide not to write down any of my minor niggles, but to simply sign off the review with no changes required. I am tempted not to ask for any more reviews since this one was so good but experience tells me that this is not a good idea. We do have reviews after that but usually they are very brief and I only write down one or two things that I'd like to be changed, so they're not too painful (code reviews are never pleasant).

I hope you have taken something useful from this tale. I have tried to make this a tale of success (with a few tense moments), in the hope that you can use it as a model for success in your own case. Of course, you may be able to find ways that work better for you, or that are more appropriate to the environment you work in and the people you work with.

One thing that often worries people about managing experts on their team is the worry that they are being bullshitted – that the expert is using their expertise as a barrier to communication, is doing things their own way for their own reasons and is out of control. Normally, this is actually not a problem in itself, but a symptom of a more fundamental problem of trust. People who are good at something are usually very happy to talk about it and try to explain it in simple terms that allow you to understand what is happening. They may need guiding sometimes, to avoid wandering off into interesting but inappropriate work, but they will often come to you *asking* for a 'sanity check' when they have made an important decision.

It's actually those that are *not* very good – those that are *pretending* to be experts – that are the problem. They may try to disguise the shallowness of their knowledge by refusing to talk in simple terms that you can understand, or by refusing to communicate at all (and of course doing everything they can to make you feel uncomfortable and guilty about questioning them). So don't worry about controlling the technical expertise at all. As a technical person yourself, you will be able to detect bullshit when you hear it, and that is why the pretend-experts try to make sure you hear nothing comprehensible at all. If someone cannot or will not explain things in simple terms you can understand, it is not because you are stupid (as they might try to imply), but because there is something really wrong with their skills or their attitude, or they are trying to use the project as a vehicle to do work that they want to do even though it is not appropriate for the project.

Think about the quality of interaction you're having with someone to determine whether the situation is healthy, don't worry about the detailed area of expertise. With experts, as with everyone else, you should aim to trust people and to respect their judgement – and if you find you cannot trust them, then take tight control, or preferably get them off your team altogether.

18

I CAN'T GET MY TEAM TO DO ANY DESIGN OR DOCUMENTATION, THEY JUST WANT TO CODE // WHAT CAN I DO?

For a summary of why design and documentation are worth spending time on at all, see the infobar // WHY NOT JUST CODE? below.

Whilst you do occasionally come across a team of people who are very strong on theory and don't know when to stop analysing and designing and to start coding, it is far, far more common to find teams that are best at coding, or at least keenest on coding, and start it far too early before they know exactly what the design will look like.

There are plenty of software engineers around who think that software is unlike other engineering disciplines, in that you can implement it without designing it. These people usually seem to believe that software code is self-documenting, as if source comments are sufficient to describe how a system fits together. This is of course just hacking. Good engineering practice applies as much in software as in other disciplines, and that includes the importance of careful design in a structured way, and the need to document the design so that others can understand it. Hacking wastes an enormous amount of time in later rework, and as team leader you cannot tolerate it. Unfortunately, hacking has its own rewards. **Hacking is addictive, and a difficult habit to break.**

Of course, the amount of design and documentation you do is up to you (within any limits set down by your procedures or by the contract with your customer). For instance, regarding design, there is a scale from the basic minimum design to the maximum sensible amount:

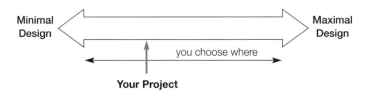

I would define the minimum design as consisting of:

▶ A block-diagram-level structure, broken into smaller component units, down to the module or class level, where each component is identified with a name, and has defined responsibilities.

▶ The architecture of processes and threads and the outline of interfaces between these.

▶ The relationships between the units (for instance, which units use or own which other units).

▶ Some analysis of the dynamics of the system in use (message, data-flow or sequence diagrams).

▶ Basic design policies such as naming conventions and error handling strategies.

You can always do this much, and so this is the minimum. Not to do even this much would always be asking for a large amount of time to be wasted later in rework. See the infobar // WHY NOT JUST CODE?.

The maximum sensible amount of design is:

▶ A design carried to a level of detail where you are totally confident that it can be implemented and will work as designed, but you can go no further without implementation.

In most situations this is considerably more detail than the minimum design, and would include detailed definition of individual operations (including inputs and outputs, error reporting, preconditions and postconditions), dry-runs of typical operations, and possibly detailed user interface layout.

I am **not** talking here about the amount of design done before *any* code is written. I'm talking about the amount of design that gets done *before each iteration* of designing and coding. Even if you aim for a heavy-design route, you might still want to take an iterative, prototype-driven approach, if that makes most sense for your project with the people that you have.

With a minimal-design route, the team focuses on coding, with design providing little more than an outline structure to work within. Future iterations will fill in the design some more, but at each iteration the focus is on doing enough design to get the structure sorted out before continuing to code. The maximal design approach on the other hand stresses the importance of design over code. The idea is to get the design complete before the coding starts, in each iteration. The mental effort, the fun, is in the design, and the coding becomes a routine matter that should proceed smoothly and quickly.

infobar // WHY NOT JUST CODE?

Here are the reasons why you need to design before you code. The design that you do should satisfy all of these requirements, to the extent that is appropriate on your project.

- To ensure that all the issues have been addressed and the best solutions chosen.

- To avoid wasteful rework caused by having an initial arrangement of code that is not suitable for all the functionality required.

- To be able to estimate and plan the coding, testing and documentation, by working out what tasks are involved. This in turn will allow progress to be more accurately tracked.

- To identify areas of high risk so that these can be mitigated as much as possible, for instance by starting work on prototypes to investigate technology that is not well understood.

- To provide confidence to the team, and to its managers and customers, that the software will provide the features that are specified, without stumbling over some unforeseen problem later on.

- To enable coding work to be allocated and delegated in a clean way, so that each person can work independently on a separate unit of code, and yet the units will all fit together without problem.

- To evaluate the eventual software against important goals such as maintainability, robustness, reusability or consistency with company strategy, before coding starts.

- To have a master plan for the code which fulfils all requirements, so that code is fitted into place rather than being constantly chopped around as new requirements are implemented.

- To provide the opportunity for interested parties to review the direction of the project, at an early stage. Such reviews add to quality and to confidence.

- To enable others to do their jobs, for example so that test-writers can define unit tests for components.

- To enable the project to be modified or built upon in future with minimum effort and greatest confidence.

Here are the reasons why you may need to write a technical document. A document should satisfy all of the reasons that are appropriate in the given case. If none of these reasons apply to a given document, then it probably doesn't need writing at all.

- To communicate knowledge about the software to those that may need it, such as other developers, testers, reviewers, managers, customers or maintainers, in a form that is accessible and useful to those people.

- To avoid interruptions to team members by providing a source of information for other people to reference.

- To record important facts that should be available after the original team has dispersed.

- To allow a given situation, problem or action to be repeated or replicated in future if necessary.

- To provide a 'friendly' explanation for those people that can't or don't want to read code, for example explaining how to use some interface or operate some function.

- To capture knowledge that was gained, for instance to prevent mistakes being repeated.

It's for you to decide what point on this continuum from minimal to maximal design is appropriate for your project, and this will depend on the nature of the project, how well specified it is, how well you understand the technologies involved, and on the people who will do the design and the coding. Do not aim for the minimal end of the continuum, even on the first iteration of your design–code–test loop, just so that you can 'get on with it'.

Many books will tell you to keep designing until you can go no further – in other words, *always* to aim for a maximal design as I've defined it. This makes sense *if* the project is appropriate and the people have the necessary skills, because then the heavy-design route will get the project finished sooner, although it will seem to get off to a slower start. But to me, the advice always to aim for a heavy-design approach is too simplistic. If your project is not very well defined and needs lots of prototyping, and many of the people on your team are not strong on design, then trying to take a maximal design route will probably be a mistake. It makes sense to do less than the maximum possible, *less even than the team is able* to do, because the project and the team would gain more from implementation and iteration, and coming back to the design later, than it would from trying to do more design in each iteration.

Some engineers claim that they 'do the design in code', in other words they have a mental image of the design, which they implement without drawing. The problem with this approach is that nobody can review the design, and no documentation will be created. Worse still, the mental design tends to change and mutate over time in a way that doesn't happen to a drawing. If someone tells you that they have a mental image to work from, ask them to draw it for you and to keep the drawing up to date.

When I first heard this concept expressed, it sounded to me, as someone who believes strongly in designing before coding, like an appalling set of excuses and cop-outs, but having experienced several teams where a strong design approach simply would not work, I've come to accept it as the reality of leading projects. You have to do the best with what you've got.

The following diagram is intended to sum up the advice I'm giving regarding design. There are four criteria on which your project can be rated, and you need to judge where your project sits on each of the scales. This has been filled in by hatching the scales for a hypothetical project, as shown below:

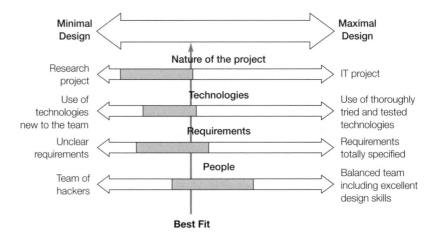

This example shows a project that is quite researchy and will use technologies that are new to the team; the requirements are not brilliantly clear, and the team is not a bunch of hackers but neither is it a perfectly balanced team with excellent design skills. The best fit has been drawn with the solid arrow. While the team members may want to do more design up front, the use of new technologies and the researchy nature of the work means that it will not be sensible to proceed along a strong-design route. The best-fit is somewhere down the middle, and means that a serious amount of design should be done in each iteration around the design–code–test loop, but there will be no point in going as far as could possibly be done, filling in every single detail. The team will probably learn more about the technologies and about the project in the next iteration, which would make some of the detail obsolete before it was even implemented.

Note that I have drawn the arrow almost as far right as it can be drawn. If there is a range of 'best fit', then my instinct is to do as much design as makes sense, not as little. Another way to use the diagram above is to try to analyse what factor is preventing you from doing more design than you would otherwise be able to do. If you can tackle that factor and do more design, your project is more likely to progress quickly and smoothly.

Whilst I think that as team leader you should take quite strong control over the overall architecture of the project and the defining documentation such as the requirements, it's a different matter for detailed design and documentation – detailed design should be done by individual engineers or by small groups of people, and everyone should document their own work. You can't and shouldn't do everybody's designs for them, and even if you tried you'd probably find that the designs were either ignored or were misunderstood to the point of being useless. People would get bored and demotivated. They need to participate in the design and have some ownership of it in order to understand it and value it. Similar logic applies to design documentation, which should capture in detail how the system works, and test documents, which should explain how to probe the details of operation, and these are best written by the person who made the detailed design decisions.

So what *can* you do if your project lends itself to strong design, but you can't take a strong-design route because the people can't be made to do the design or prove incapable of it when they do try? Or if the team isn't even up to achieving the minimal level of design?

Whilst it may not be achievable, it's worth discussing with your management whether you could change one or two people on your team. If you are literally the only person on the team who wants to design before coding, you're in for a tough time. See if you can obtain the services of at least one more person who's not going to hack.

This is especially important near the start of a project, when the most important design decisions are made and the first code gets laid down.

Many people are keen on designing in principle, but just don't know how to go about it, especially if faced with a blank sheet of paper. You can help such a person by sitting with them and doing their detailed design *together* with them. Try to fill in the details of how the design will work in action, not just the static structure of the thing. People who are not used to designing often have an attitude that 'it doesn't matter what we do at this stage, it'll all change when we code'. You need to shock them out of this attitude! The best way to do this is to work closely with the person, designing the system – both static names and interactions, and dynamic

This section is concerned with fundamental problems in a project team. Hacking also happens when deadlines approach and quick fixes are needed, even in a capable and well-balanced team. That is another issue, quite distinct from those raised in this section.

Some people hack because they have no design skills, but some hack simply because that is what they have been used to doing. Often, if someone is immersed in a team that is busy designing, they will get into the habit. A possible way to give a boost to your efforts to increase the amount of design your team does is to get one of your team members seconded to another team, one that is taking a design-lead approach, and then brought back.

To my mind someone should not be treated as 'senior' if they cannot design.

operation – and then implementing it. Initially this would be a fairly minimal design route, you would design the outline architecture, no more, and then code the empty shell. Maybe you can start the process off, and then hand it over to the person to complete. It's vital to get the message over that the design and the code must be consistent, and that if you find problems with the design, you make design changes and loop round to the code only when the design is fixed, you don't abandon the design as obsolete and start hacking!

You have the power to make design and documentation happen. If it's not happening on your team, then it's your responsibility to do something about it. You have the authority to allocate tasks to people – or not to allocate them until the previous task has been documented! You are the gatekeeper of new tasks. You can deny someone the relief of leaving behind the mess they've just created, until you're happy that it's tidied up. You can, if you choose, insist on reviewing the design before the coding starts.

Of course, some people may be better just left to code. If you have someone on your team who can't be made to design or who is simply useless at it, then make sure someone else does the design. Use this non-designer as a coder, whose job is to fill in the implementation details of a design done by someone else. This rule has to be applied even to a senior person.

Don't let people design if they can't do it, and don't let them code anything that hasn't been designed.

There are a few people who are so clueless about design that even if you give them a design and a framework implementation, when you come back to their work later you find that the code bears no resemblance to what you designed. Some people just can't be made to see the design as anything other than worthless paperwork. Ideally, you need to work quite hard on these people, sitting together with them, mentoring them, showing them how an object in the design gets turned into an object with the same name and the same behaviour in the code. This may not be possible – you may not have time, or the person may be quite senior and not someone you can teach like this. **Such people must not be allowed to work on production code.** If you've got some new technologies to investigate, user interfaces to prototype, or research to be done, give it to them (but don't use any of the code later without a thorough review!). If you haven't got any such work to do, and you have someone who can't follow a design, let alone create one, then you should try to get them off your team. **The days when software could be done by people who don't have a basic engineering aptitude are over.**

There are some engineers around who think they have some right to write code, and then let other people test it and debug it. This is simply unacceptable. Everyone must test their work before putting it under version control. Everyone must fix bugs in their own code. Getting people to *test* their work – to do the informal, day-to-day sort of testing – is actually easier then getting them to design or to document. If you make sure that there are usable test benches available for people to test their code, and you make sure that people fix any bugs that they introduce, then most engineers will soon learn to test their code before letting others see it. Having test tools such as runtime checkers and syntax analysers can also help.

Documentation has some properties in common with design, except that it's less rewarding. You still need to decide how much is appropriate – who will use the documentation, and what for? It's very tempting to say 'there isn't time' and put it off till later, but then of course by the end of the project there's a huge pile to be done, no time allocated to it, other projects with higher priorities, and nobody can remember why they did certain things any more. The best way to get round this is to create all the documents you need at the start of the project – even those that are only really useful towards the end, such as installation notes – and keep adding to them, keeping them live, as you go through the project. Even if you only keep notes rather than finished documents, it helps to have somewhere ready to jot down important points. See the `infobar //` **HOW MUCH DOCUMENTATION DO I NEED TO DO?**

One way to make sure documents are usable is to try to use them occasionally! For instance, try to install the software using the installation notes, or better still, get someone else to do it who hasn't tried before. This is a far better check of a document than just reading through it. Try to build the software using the build manual. Try to test it using the test notes. If they're not up to scratch, get the person responsible to update them. Documentation bugs are bugs just like code bugs, and the person responsible for a bug should fix it. Don't do it yourself even if it's quite easy to do.

If a heavy-design route is taken, documentation tends to be produced as a by-product of the design process, with little detail needing to be added later.

Don't succumb to the 'husband's gambit'. A well-known and effective technique for getting out of work you don't like is to mess it up well and good the first time, like the newly married man who drops all the crockery on the floor the first time he has to wash up – from then on, he doesn't even need to avoid being asked, he can even offer to help, in the certain knowledge that his offer will be refused. If someone does a really bad job of writing documentation the first time, don't just give up and get someone else to do it for them next time – keep reviewing it and getting them to improve it until it's good enough.

infobar // **HOW MUCH DOCUMENTATION DO I REALLY NEED TO DO?**

Most developers are not great fans of documentation. While they might concede that it should be done, they can also usually find something 'better' to do with their time.

When it comes down to it, many managers are not great fans of documentation either, since they would rather have people being 'productive'. Although they will often pay lip service to the necessity for thorough documentation, they are often happy if it is quietly forgotten. Although they understand that documentation will be needed to maintain a system, they can usually find something 'better' for their subordinates to do with their time, and documentation is never seen as urgent.

Of course, there are times when documentation must be done, maybe to fulfil a contract, or in a highly regulated industry such as medicine, to satisfy an auditor. But even then it is all too easy to write something that apparently satisfies the need, but in fact is useless and is done just to keep people off your back. For instance, I once needed to rebuild quite a complex bit of software, and I found that there was a 'build manual'. When I opened it, I found that it was just a list of all the files in the build (which I didn't need to know), but didn't give any instructions at all. When I asked the author of this document, he told me that the document was written 'to keep QA off his back' – the real build instructions were actually written as notes on a piece of paper on his desk. What a total waste of his time, and of mine. Never write (or let someone else write) a document that is not needed, just to keep the procedures happy. If a document is not needed, then argue the case and don't do it. (If you're not sure whether a document is needed or not, check with the list of points in the infobar // WHY NOT JUST CODE?) Sometimes you have to write something, to 'fill the hole in the system', in which case you should write a document that is very tiny and just explains why there is nothing to say.

The rule with all documentation is do enough, and no more than enough, for those who will need to use it. It seems obvious that you should write a document for the person who needs it, but it is easy to forget who that is. Quite often I've found myself describing a design, telling the reader, who I imagine to be another designer, about bits that I'm proud of, and justifying the decisions I made. But then later I've realized that nobody wants to read that! If anyone does anything on the project in the future, they will be trying to fix bugs, or to add new features. They don't want to read about how clever I think I was or why the design is the way it is, they just want to understand how it works so they can get in and change it quickly without messing it up.

Even if you're using a design tool that almost writes the code for you, the content of the design is not enough. The tool shows people what is there now, it doesn't usually explain how it all fits together or highlight important things that are 'easy to break'. Equally, a team often starts off with an intent to make the system work in a given way, but that intent is thwarted by some issue and cannot be realized. It is a good idea to record the original intention as well as what was actually done, as an opportunity may arise to implement the original intention.

For these reasons, I don't like to make a 'Design Description' document. I would prefer to make two documents:

- A 'Design Proposal', which is written at the start of the project, for people who will review the design. It may be a document or a design made using a design tool. Once the design is decided upon, this proposal is no longer of any use and should be archived. No effort is put into keeping it up to date as design changes occur. The design itself is of course worked on but the justification of it in words is not maintained. Of course if nobody is going to use such a document to review the design then don't write this document at all.

- 'Maintenance Notes' for engineers who will look after the project after it is released. During the project development this is a living document, and probably quite scruffy, full of outline information and things to remember. After the project is released this is tidied up, fattened out and brought up to date. The final document should include an outline description of the design that was finally arrived at, complementing any detail in a design tool, so that maintainers can find their way around the design and understand the intention in the mind of the designers. If your maintenance team is used to looking at the design then these notes may be incorporated as text notes or as an explicit maintenance section in the design itself.

Note that neither of these is a design description that is supposed to be correct at all times as the project develops. I have never found the need for such a document as such knowledge exists in the team members, more accessibly and in much more detail than any document would contain. If I have to make a document called Design Description, I fill it with Maintenance Notes.

Quite often, people justify the fact that they have not written a document by saying that it would be very short and so not worth the bother. It's very tempting to skip something if you feel there's not much to say, especially if you have to work under heavy procedures and you know that you will have to spend ages getting the document officially registered, approved and so on. But actually the short documents don't take long to write, and they can be very useful. I once wrote a build manual that was about three lines long – it just told you to get a

cont >>

>>

certain project out of source control, double-click on the appropriate file and do 'rebuild all' – and some months later I was thanked by another developer for having written it. 'You were out and I needed to rebuild the project,' he said. 'I found the notes and it gave me confidence that I was doing the right thing.' The fact that the document took me only two minutes to write would not have been a good reason to avoid writing it!

Issues always seem more obvious to you when you're in the thick of a project than they really are. To keep on the example of build manuals, there's usually something to remember, some file that needs copying or some version number to remember to change when you do a release. When you're involved in the project, these things seem obvious, but if you don't write notes, when you come back to it in a year's time, you won't have a clue. The best way with this kind of 'living document' is to write something at the very beginning of the project, and keep using it yourself and improving it slightly as you go, keeping it up to date. Don't put such documents under formal control too soon if that causes problems updating them, as you need to be able to change such things very easily. Have them handy, and get them formally controlled only when the project is about to release.

If you've bothered to write a document, make sure it can be found in future, not just by someone going to look specifically for it, but also by someone browsing through the project who may not know to go looking for it. Make some hyperlink or shortcut to the document, or make a document listing all the other documents on the project, or put a little text file in with the source code, listing what documents there are to find. There's nothing more annoying than wasting days trying to work something out for yourself, only to find that you could have just read about it, only nobody bothered to tell you where.

At the end of the day, you're paid to develop good software, not to make beautiful support documents (user documents are a different matter). You're also paid to make sure that you leave a project that can be maintained in future. Remember the poor maintainer to come – it might be you.

Some organizations like everyone to keep things written up in log books. Whilst these are good for jotting down ideas and lists of things for one person to remember, they are almost always totally unusable by anyone but the author. Therefore, important information should always be written up, and never just left in a log book.

19

WHEN SHOULD I LET SOMEONE DO A THING THEIR OWN WAY, AND WHEN SHOULD I MAKE THEM DO IT MY WAY?

You may feel that being a team leader puts you in a very difficult position. You are responsible for the outcome of the project, but you don't have the degree of control you would really like to get things done properly. You have to rely on persuasion, cajoling and appealing, because you have little power.

Actually, most positions of leadership are like this, even senior ones. Good leaders rarely give orders, even if they have the power to do so. It just doesn't lead to a pleasant or effective working relationship. This is one of the great dilemmas of leadership: there are times when you should insist on things being done your way, and there are times when you should let someone do it their own way – how do you tell which applies in any given situation?

If you want a job doing your way, then you have to say so when you allocate the task. It is no good letting someone do a thing their own way, and then later reviewing their work and complaining that it was not done how you wanted it done – if you want it done your way, you have to say so up front. The hard part is knowing when to give strict guidance, and when to leave it up to the person to make up their own mind.

Even when you have a very competent person working for you, they may have different ideas about how a problem should be tackled. Often they are no more right or wrong than you are, and it is important to recognize this; they just have a different opinion.

▶ If the issue is not very important, then let the person do it their own way. If they make mistakes and learn from them, then that is a positive outcome. By doing this you demonstrate trust for the individual and you create a relaxed atmosphere. Even if the task is 'your job' and you have delegated it to someone else, you should give other team members the freedom to make their own decisions.

▶ **If the task is urgent, *and* you know how to do it much better than they do, then have it done your way.** Note that I said 'urgent', not 'important'. The reason for getting things done your way is that there is not time for the explanations, mistakes, reviews and so on that would occur if you let someone else do the job.

If you constantly take control then people will not learn to do the work for themselves, and you will be constantly interrupted by urgent work. When a job is not urgent, even if it is important, let people have some freedom, and then review their work, so that they learn and develop.

Unless something is urgent, it's even worth letting people 'reinvent the wheel'. If you try to tell someone why their way won't work but they can't see it, or you try to show them a better way but they can't understand the problem, then let them go a little way with their own solution. They will get to understand the issue the hard way, and be much more willing to listen to what you have to say.

▶ **Don't accept arguments that have nothing to do with the project's priorities.** Never give in to someone wanting to do something a given way, if the reasons they give are of the following kinds:

- ▪ 'It's more efficient.' Unless you are dealing with the inner loop of a time-critical process, code that is robust and supportable is far preferable to code that is merely fast. Many appeals to efficiency are completely spurious. For example, developers sometimes complain that it's not efficient to call a routine indirectly, instead they must call it directly to save the time taken by the indirection. Typically this time actually amounts to a few nanoseconds and is absolutely irrelevant.

- ▪ 'It will be faster/easier to code.' Unless you are very close to a delivery deadline and some bug must be fixed urgently, it is sheer laziness to do something 'the easy way'. Do it the right way.

- ▪ 'It's more OO/it's more cool/it's the latest way.' So what? Is it a project priority to make code that is more object-oriented, or is most in fashion? Being more object-oriented may be a good thing – it may be more appropriate – but it is not a reason in itself.

■ 'It allows future-proofing flexibility'. Some future-proofing and flexibility is a good thing, but beware advocates of radical structures and approaches that promise 'enormous flexibility – you could do anything with this method!!'. Usually, there will be an awful lot of effort involved in achieving this flexibility, far more than these advocates will have you believe, and unless this level of flexibility is required for your project, this effort will be unjustifiable. Remember that if you provide such flexibility, you will have to test that it works, because someone will go and use it.

■ 'It will create a library module that other projects will be able to use.' If it is well structured, parts of most software projects are fairly general purpose and potentially reusable. However, turning those sections into code that is *actually* reused involves a huge amount of extra effort in expanding the interfaces to be full enough for every likely use, in documentation, and in thorough and independent testing. If part of your code can be made independent of the rest then that is a good idea, but don't be driven by a desire to create libraries just because you are able to do so. Creating a reusable library will be a huge burden for your project; don't weigh your project down with that burden unless it has been agreed with management and you have been given the resources necessary to cover the extra effort involved.

■ 'You must do it my way because I'm the expert.' Sometimes, a team member will propose a solution that you simply do not understand. It may be based on unfamiliar technology, or they may be using words whose meaning you are unsure of. No decision should be made without understanding the options; you need to understand what the other person is saying before you can either accept or reject the idea. If you don't understand what someone is proposing, then say so and get them to explain it to you. Keep asking for clarification until you do understand. Summarize what you understand back to the individual, to make sure you have really got it. If in the end you cannot understand the option being presented, that is good enough reason to reject it. If you don't understand it you will not be able to lead it, and that is sufficient reason for rejection. (See also SECTION 17: LEADING AN EXPERT.) Never go with an option you don't understand, as you will not be able to control it.

■ 'I'll shout and scream if you don't do it my way'. Never give in to placate awkward people – this just builds up an expectancy that petulance will win, and rewards behaviour that is not acceptable in a team.

What matters is: 'which way is more appropriate to achieving the project's objectives and priorities, and which is more in keeping with the project's principles?'

Most situations are not perfectly clear-cut and will not fall neatly into one of the above categories. Being an effective team leader requires you to balance various factors. In this case, the issues at stake are the needs of the team members (who will benefit in higher morale and in learning if you let them do things their own way), and the needs of the project (which will benefit if things are tightly controlled and done in a single consistent way, provided that you are good at your job and that you are constantly available). This does not have to be a win–lose struggle. Quite often, by thinking around the issue and *using some creativity*, a solution can be found that satisfies the project's needs and also provides a challenge that enables the individual engineers to maintain their self-esteem.

Often, the reasons that someone gives you don't seem very solid, and yet they are adamant that they must do it their way. This is a sign of a hidden agenda at work – there is some reason why the person wants to do something their way, and it's not all about the project. It is important to try to understand what the hidden agenda is. It may have to do with a desire to get a particular technology on their CV, or it may be because they have done things a certain way in the past and are unwilling to change.

Understanding the motivation behind a person's attitudes is a vital part in making a decision as to whether to allow someone to do something their own way or to insist on them doing it yours. Do not make the decision purely on technical grounds. That you believe your solution to be superior is not sufficient reason to make an autocratic decision. The damage to the individual's motivation, and the lost opportunity to develop the person, must be weighed into the decision, and the technical superiority of your approach must be large and certain before you override these things.

Of course, you are the team leader and it is for you to make these decisions. It is for you to decide whether your solution is superior and if it is sufficiently so to override your team member's wishes. The team member may not agree with you, *nobody* may agree with you, but it is still your prerogative to make the decision whichever way you feel fit, even if you are in a minority of one.

Before deciding that you know best, you might like to ask yourself why *you* want to do it your way. Do you have some hidden agenda yourself? Are you just wanting to do things the same old way, when in fact your

Sometimes, you may have someone on your team who is actually more senior than you are, or who has 'friends in high places' and could overrule your decision or get it overruled. My advice in this situation is to ignore this dimension and make the best decision that you can. If you are overruled then you will have to live with it, but it's better to hold out for what you believe to be correct than to give in because of a mere threat that your decision will be reversed. If you are constantly overruled, there is something severely wrong with the structure of your team and this would need addressing.

team member may have seen a better way? Do not underestimate your own resistance to change! There is no excuse for making decisions on the grounds of your own feelings of personal comfort, and certainly not for the benefit of your own CV. Your personal needs do not outweigh those of the other people on the team. The only factors to be balanced are the well-being of the individual and the well-being of the project. Your own feelings don't come into it.

Never let anyone railroad you into doing things their way. This might take the form of 'I've already nearly finished doing it my way', 'there isn't time to decide now', 'I talked to the expert/the boss/my priest and he told me this way was best'. None of these statements should be taken at face value, as they almost always represent some hidden agenda at work. You are the team leader and you must be allowed to perform your unique role within the team, which includes making decisions. If someone has done something you don't like and presented it as a *fait accompli*, then review what they have done and if you don't like it, get it changed.

Having more power and authority would not actually make any of these issues easier, nor improve your relationship with the rest of your team. In fact, having more authority might throw up a barrier between you and your team members. Informal control is what leadership is all about, at any level of seniority. You have a position of leadership within the team, and that includes a role of decision maker. But the other team members are not your underlings to be directed at your whim, they are your fellow team members. You need to exercise your roles of decision maker and of leader, whilst giving people the freedom to make their own decisions whenever possible. You must allow people to make, and learn from, their own mistakes.

20

HOW MANY HOURS SHOULD I AND MY TEAM BE WORKING?

In most software development environments, pressure comes in waves, although there is *always* more work that could be done, more features you could pack in if you had time. As leader you will be acutely aware of the pressures to get the work done, but you may also feel uncomfortable with the idea of asking people to do overtime.

In the normal course of events, if your project is going well then you should allow people to work any hours they choose as long as they meet the contracted times. Some people will work exactly the minimum contracted hours (especially contractors) – this is fine as long as they are spending those hours productively. Most people tend to work just a little over the minimum required. A few will work much longer.

If you find that your team is routinely under such pressure that people are working very long hours – say two hours a day extra or more – then there is something seriously wrong, and it is unlikely that overtime is the right solution to the problem. Perhaps there are simply not enough people on the job, but usually that's a symptom, not the real problem. Perhaps unrealistic plans are in place. Maybe people are trying to do work that doesn't actually need to be done – it's amazing how often people think that the customer 'must need' something, without checking. Perhaps some risk materialized. Maybe circumstances have changed, like someone has left the team, or large feature changes have come in, but nobody has re-planned and changed the expectations of delivery. Working very long hours for weeks at a time is not acceptable under most circumstances. People get tired, they get stressed, the quality of work suffers, they fall out with one another. Illness and even divorce are not unknown consequences. Quitting is quite a common response.

In these circumstances you need to step back from the immediate crises and look at the bigger picture. What has fundamentally gone wrong? What can be done about it? Something has got to give. Extra effort can be used to solve short-term problems and crises, but it is not a solution to a longer-term problem. Long-term problems often manifest themselves as a sequence of short-term crises, hence the need to step back and see the bigger picture. Even if the problem originated with one of your own decisions – perhaps one of your mistakes – you have to admit that there is something seriously wrong and look for ways to sort it out. Can it be solved with more people (perhaps contractors)? Can requirements be renegotiated or pushed into a later delivery? If nothing else, has a longer time-scale got to be acknowledged? You need to sort out some radical and realistic proposals, and implement them. This may require agreement from your management and from the customer. It is important that you obtain this agreement, even if it is a painful thing to go through. You are the leader and it is your job to face up to the situation you find yourself in, and you owe it to the rest of the team to negotiate a workload that is reasonable, as soon as possible.

In some organizations it becomes normal for people to work long hours, and you can feel guilty about leaving before others in the evening. My advice is to leave on time anyway if there is no immediate crisis to keep you there. Set an example as someone who works well, gets the job done, and also manages to have a life. Most frequently, people work these extra hours because everyone else is doing it, and if you break the pattern you can find others following suit.

There are some organizations that have a 'macho' culture, where colleagues (or managers) actively pressurize people to do one or two hours a day, or more, extra. This is called a 'sweatshop attitude'. If you knew things would be that way when you took the job then fair enough, you can't complain about it now. Otherwise it is unfair and you should fight it. A worse menace is the manager who works long hours and believes that all team leaders should work them too ('to show commitment'), as if you can't lead a team without being in a constant flap. This again is rubbish and should be resisted.

It's not unusual to find that the team leader ends up working slightly longer hours than other people on the team. This is normal. But you should not need to routinely work excessively long hours, otherwise there is a problem with the way you are delegating or allocating work. If you

I heard about one manager who always complained that he was the only one working at weekends. It turned out that he only came in at weekends because his marriage was in a mess and he wanted to get away from his wife. He didn't need to be at work. But that didn't stop him from pressurizing everyone else to come in!

enjoy your work and want to work longer hours then that's fine, but make allowance for the fact that other people may not want to. This does not demonstrate a lack of commitment on their part, it simply shows that they have other calls upon their time, outside of work.

Of course there are times when extra hours are needed to get the job done, like when a release is promised, when a show or demo is coming up, or when a disaster needs to be averted (or recovered from). Under these circumstances it is reasonable to expect people to do longer hours for a few days. Even if the problem is not of the team's making, it is still normal for a professional person to work longer hours, often without pay, in order to meet the organization's commitments. For most people, this is accepted as part of the unwritten rules of working as a professional engineer.

When overtime is needed, you need to ask people to do it. **Overtime is too much to expect, but it's not too much to ask.** In other words, you can and should ask people if they will do overtime, you should not shirk from trying quite hard to persuade them to do it, but you should be willing to accept their decision if they say no.

By far the easiest way to ask people is to tell people how much extra time you will be putting in, and then ask them what they can manage. **If you expect others to work overtime then you should do it too.** Even if you can't contribute much, if you expect others on your team to work extra hours then you should be there with them. If nothing else, you can fetch the drinks and order the pizzas.

Some people simply will not do overtime. This may just seem like awkwardness but often there are good reasons outside work for it. People with young families, those who care for elderly or disabled relatives, or who have personal or marital problems, often won't. Some people feel that they have been taken for a ride in the past, having done lots of extra hours without any recognition of the sacrifice, and so have vowed not to do it again. Whatever the reason, they may not want to share it with you, and may just appear stubborn. Voluntary overtime is just that, voluntary, and although you can ask people quite directly to please do overtime, you should not penalize them if they choose not to. If you trust people enough to work on your team, then you should trust them enough to decide for themselves whether they can put in extra hours.

Some organizations have reward schemes where people can nominate colleagues for bonuses for working 'beyond expectations'. If yours has one, consider nominating your team for it, if they do long hours at your request.

21

I WANT TO PRAISE PEOPLE WHEN THEY DO WELL, BUT IT SOUNDS SO CONDESCENDING // HOW SHOULD I REWARD GOOD WORK?

People need feedback from their work, in order to feel that people care about what they do and how well they do it. Feedback is also essential in allowing people to learn and to improve what they do.

People may receive feedback (in the form of praise, or of dissatisfaction) directly from customers, and they may also be subject to annual reviews by managers. Neither of these sources of praise directly relates to an engineer's everyday work. Customers see only one aspect of the work, and often have little understanding of the problems faced in software development. Managers are not directly involved in day-to-day development and often get their opinions second-hand. In any case, feedback in an annual review is usually so long after the event that it has little value.

It is therefore essential that everyone receives feedback *from the rest of the team* as to how well they are doing their jobs. Most importantly, if someone is weak at one aspect of development, for example they don't test their work enough, clear but polite feedback will help that person to focus on improving that aspect of their work in future.

Positive feedback is also very valuable in encouraging people to continue to do good work. If you try really hard to do something well, and nobody seems to care, you are likely not to try quite so hard next time. The team leader ought to be somebody who does care, and who makes this clear.

Praise, just like criticism, should be directed at the work, not the personality. Just as criticizing work is likely to be taken personally, so is praising it – so you can use this to your advantage. It is necessary to give praise indirectly, because direct praise would often sound condescending. For instance, suppose someone has just reorganized the code to make it simpler. If you praise the person, for instance by saying 'well done, you've done a great job, that will make everybody's life easier', it's like patting someone on the head – and likely to be equally badly received by anyone except the most submissive individual. But you can get away with praising the work rather than the person, for instance 'Isn't it amazing how much junk we had? It will make life much easier now it's gone'. There is not much praise there, and what little there is is directed more at the new organization than at the organizer, but there is enough praise and the message is positive enough to be correctly interpreted.

The truly condescending remark is the sort that says or implies 'you did that almost as well as I could have done', or 'you did well considering how little experience you've got'. It's all too easy to fall into this mode of talking with very junior engineers, and the mode of talking is a reflection of a mode of thinking. It's this mode of thinking that you need to stop yourself using. The condescending way of thinking leads you to be amazed that someone managed to do something well, and that's how the resulting praise comes out. If you start out having high expectations of people, then when these are achieved praise is hardly necessary. It is adequate to acknowledge that the task was hard and was important and has been completed well.

Another form of indirect praise is to ask for advice. This implicitly states 'I value your judgement'. Asking someone for advice on an issue implies that you recognize that they know as much, or more, about it than you do, or that they have equal intellectual ability to bring to bear. The best sort of praise is the sort that comes from one's peers, not from people who think that they are your superiors. Asking someone's advice, as one engineer to another, demonstrates trust and respect.

The natural time for praise to be given is in reviews. If you've looked at someone else's work, and picked holes in it, it is also good practice to comment on the things that were good about it. It's all too easy in a review to concentrate on things that need improving. It is worth spending a moment commenting on the things that are good and don't need to be changed. If you encourage people to review each other's work, encourage them to identify the positive aspects of the work they review, as well as the problems.

Be sure to take the opportunity of praising your team members to your managers, especially if the person in question is listening. It doesn't do much for anybody's motivation to overhear their team leader say 'I've got three juniors on my team, can't you find me some more resource?'. Why not say, 'I've got three really good engineers on my team, but even so, we still need some more help', or better 'Can you find me someone else who's as good as Jim?'. You can get away with more overt praise of someone when they are in the third-person than you can when you speak to them directly. Strange but true.

Giving praise can be just as uncomfortable and unrewarding as giving criticism, although you do get used to it. Just as with criticism, while you need to tread lightly, you shouldn't avoid the act altogether. Some sort of acknowledgement is all that most people need in order to feel that their hard work did not go completely unnoticed.

22

I'VE GOT SOMEONE ON MY TEAM WHO'S A REAL PROBLEM // WHAT SHOULD I DO?

Having someone on your team who drives you nuts is one of the real nightmares of team leadership. Once you get into this situation it can be very difficult to get out of it, and if you are new to it, it can keep you awake at nights.

It's very easy to decide that someone is simply 'no good' and should be got rid of. Whilst this might turn out to be true sometimes, often this would be a big mistake and a huge overreaction.

It's especially important not to act too soon. Whilst you can't let personnel problems drag on for months, it's a mistake to think that you should try to sort them out in a matter of a day or two. You can't judge someone's behaviour that quickly, and you can't expect people to modify their behaviour that fast. Everyone has bad days, and bad weeks. Especially at the start of a project, people get into arguments, sometimes quite vicious arguments. Usually, these heal over and people will work together afterwards. It's also worth bearing in mind that there are times when you should keep someone who is a pain – see the infobar // 'THE DEVIL'S ADVOCATE'.

It's very important with personnel issues to try to get to the root cause of the problem. Often, what appears to be a personnel problem with one difficult person can in fact be a symptom of problems in the team as a whole, or with the way work is structured in your organization, or that you are putting a person into a situation they can't cope with.

For example, you may have a team of senior developers. Someone has got to do the donkey work of repeated testing and verification on the project,

infobar // **THE DEVIL'S ADVOCATE**

It can be annoying to work with someone who seems to challenge everything you say. It can also be very helpful. It depends whether the challenge comes from someone who is trying to help get a better job done, or someone who would disagree with you whatever you said.

In a famous psychological experiment, several groups of people were given a problem to solve. In half the teams, one person had been told (unbeknown to the other team members) to challenge the rest of the team as much as possible, pointing out problems with the way they were tackling the problem, and proposing alternatives.

The teams that had a 'devil's advocate' solved the problem significantly better than the teams where nobody was told to act this way.

In a second stage of the experiment, each team was told to choose one member whom they would remove from the team. In every case, the 'devil's advocate' was removed. In every case, the teams performed worse without this person than they had with them.

Having someone on your team who challenges everything may not be pleasant, but it can be very useful. If you remove that person, your team may not do its job so well. If you have such a person on your team, rather than getting rid of them, you should find some positive way for them to channel their opinions and energies, without disturbing the rest of the team.

and once one person has started, they are likely to end up stuck with that role for the rest of the project. They may at first have welcomed the job, and felt that they were doing the rest of the team a favour, but may become very disenchanted with the work after some time. You might expect that someone in this position would simply talk to the leader about their dissatisfaction, but often people feel unable to do this, or they have simply not analysed the situation objectively enough to see what the issue is that is making them unhappy. The result can be a person that is constantly negative, point-scoring and sarcastic. But it is not a problem with the person's character. It is a problem caused by them being given too much work to which they are not suited.

The fundamental problem in this example goes further than job allocation. The root cause is that the team is unbalanced. It has too many people of one type; everyone wants and expects to do the interesting work. In this situation, the boring, unglamorous (and still highly essential) work will get done by someone unsuitable, or (if the leader is not strong) it will not get done at all.

As with many personnel problems, working out the root cause of the issue is the major part of the solution. You may be able to reallocate the work, take on some of it yourself, automate some of it, draft in another person to do it, or at the very least, talk to the person and demonstrate some support.

Similarly, structural problems with the way a company is organized can often be manifested in individual stress and negativity. For instance, in large organizations it is not uncommon to find that the design engineers and the support engineers report into totally separate branches of the organizational hierarchy. People on the ground, trying to work together, may be working to totally contrary priorities and perspectives. Usually, the individuals involved do not see it that way, they just get stressed by the individual issues, the apparent unhelpfulness and inflexibility of the 'other lot'. If you can see past the tension to the underlying issues, even if you are unable to broker some sort of compromise between the camps, at least you will be able to understand an individual who appears to be negative, but is in fact constantly facing a stressful situation.

Having looked at the wider picture, you might still conclude that there are no excuses, you just have an individual who is not working properly. They may be producing poor quality work, or spending far too much time chatting and browsing the internet, or be difficult to work with. You have still got to see if you can find the root cause of the problem. For example, if someone is dragging out work, they may be doing so because they are not looking forward to the task that is coming next, or they may even believe that there is no more work waiting for them to do and they might fear losing their job. If someone is always chatting, they may be bored with work that is too easy for them. Someone may have very poor time-keeping because of marital problems which mean they have to take their children to school sometimes. People become difficult and uncommunicative if they are under too much stress.

You need to *talk to the person* to find out what is going on. This is a very difficult thing to do. It has to be done informally and sensitively. If the person thinks you are attacking them, they will get defensive. You need to keep the focus on the problem, not the personality. Talk about what is happening, and ask why it is happening. Explain why it is causing a

See also SECTION 24: ONE OF MY PEOPLE IS SPENDING TOO MUCH TIME CHATTING AND WEB BROWSING, and SECTION 27: I'M VERY STRESSED AT THE MOMENT, AND SO ARE SOME OF MY TEAM.

problem to you. This sort of discussion can rapidly degenerate into a shouting match despite your best efforts, and if this happens, you will probably not get a second chance. In this case you will either have to tolerate the issue, or escalate it to higher management.

Poor performance, of course, may be due to poor training or poor coaching. No one can do a job well if they are not confident of the skills required. Frequently, bosses 'drop people in at the deep end', not realizing that this suits some people but not others. For many people, trying to do a job without prior training saps the confidence and reduces morale. Once a person has started doing the job, they will find it hard to justify any training for skills that they are apparently already using, and so they may go on for years, getting by on a reduced set of skills, with greatly reduced effectiveness. If someone is sinking rather than swimming, they may need moving to the shallow end of the pool. You should give them work that is easier and which helps their learning. Build up their confidence and give time and training to bring them up to speed.

Poor performance can also be caused by poor leadership. You need to be sure that you are not actually the cause of the problem. The person might well turn round and say it's all your fault. This can lead to self-doubt, which is one of the agonies of leadership. Whilst you need to listen to what they say, and be humble enough to consider if you are to blame, you also need to keep your confidence. If you know your job then be confident of it and don't accept blame where it is not due.

For example, people who want an easy life sometimes fob off the leader and avoid reviews and discussions by using delaying tactics, such as 'just give me a day to tidy it up'. Next day it's still in a mess and not the right time for a review, and so it goes on. You might feel bad about constantly chasing someone up for a review. They might make it clear that they consider you to be oppressive. But be honest, is this your fault? No – it's the person's delaying tactics that are at fault. Continue to demand that review, in fact why not demand to have it right now, 'warts and all'?

If someone is not doing the work you require, you need to get *more rigorous, and a little more formal*, about the way you allocate work to them. Make extra sure that the person knows what you expect them to deliver, and when. Make any constraints or preferences clear. You want to avoid the situation where a person does not try because they think you have it in for them, so 'whatever I do he won't like it' – if you don't spell out what you want, you cannot complain if you don't get it. You also need to

If you know that a review is going to be painful, it's tempting to involve someone else as well, so that it's not just 'you versus him'. I find that this usually doesn't work, because other people are not likely to help fight your battles for you. If you're really worried that the relationship between you is too bad to cope with a review, consider arranging for someone else to do the review – but make sure that it happens and is done properly.

If you have two people on the team who cannot stand each other, it's probably advisable to tackle both of them equally, and if necessary get rid of both of them, rather than 'picking a winner'.

allocate smaller tasks, and to review the work more often, to give a chance for the person to learn what is required without having to do huge amounts of rework.

In this situation it can be very hard to decide what is acceptable and what not. The only fair way is to **insist only on those points that you specified when you allocated the work,** and no more. For instance, if you review some code and find it has no error checking, then explain the value of error checking, and be clear that you expect it to be done, and *next time* you can expect it to be there. This way, you can avoid getting into arguments about style, or about different approaches; if the work fits the requirements you spelled out when you allocated the task then it is good and you cannot complain.

Most people under these circumstances will be far from happy, and it is a very stressful and uncomfortable time for the leader as well. This situation is unstable and can only go two ways. The person will either realize what is expected of them and start to perform, or things will deteriorate completely. For this reason, you must **start off gently**, giving a *little* more guidance and being a *little* more formal. It should be hardly perceptible at first. Escalate it slowly if necessary. If you go in too hard, you will be open to the accusation of victimization.

Keep your bosses informed at all times. If you don't put your side of the situation as it unfolds, you may find yourself in hot water if things go wrong.

When all is said and done, there are still some people who are simply in the wrong job. Note that I did not say 'there are some people who are useless' – nobody is useless, but some people are pretty useless at the work they are currently being asked to perform. Some people are simply incompetent and don't have what it takes. Others have attitudes that are not compatible with working in a team.

Whilst you want to be fair to the individual concerned, you also have an obligation to others. If someone is not pulling their weight, it is not fair on the rest of the team, nor to your customers or the rest of the organization, to allow it to continue. In these rare circumstances, you may have to get the person thrown off your team. This might even result in the person being sacked. If you cannot get someone's behaviour or performance to improve, despite your genuine efforts, *even if the person is apparently trying their best,* you really have no option but to get rid of them.

To me, the defining question is '*do I trust this person to be on my team?*'. Trust is vital. You should always start off with the assumption that people are trustworthy and can be allowed to get on with things in their own way. But if you find that you really cannot trust somebody on your team, then you should get rid of them.

If you come to this decision then it is time to talk to the individual's boss. Make it clear that you have come to a decision after careful thought and after trying to find other solutions. But make it clear that this is a decision that you want to make; you are not just coming to voice concerns, you want action. You will probably have to justify this decision very robustly, especially if the outcome will be that someone loses their job. If you are convinced that you are doing the right thing then you should be able to do this, and most bosses will respect your wishes and take the person off your team. You should feel proud, not guilty, about doing this, if you are acting in the best interests of your team, your customers and your organization.

Most personnel issues are not black and white; people are not either 'good' or 'bad', 'brilliant' or 'incompetent'. Often, able people are given the wrong jobs, get poor training, or are put under intolerable pressure, and many respond by becoming negative, unproductive or disruptive. With careful thought and sensitive consideration, many such problems can be resolved. But there are people who are in the wrong team or the wrong job and cannot be trusted to continue, and these people should be removed.

23

I THINK ONE OF MY PEOPLE IS GOING TO LEAVE // HOW CAN I PREVENT THEM FROM GOING?

Software is a very dynamic business to be in, and people don't tend to stay in one job all that long, especially at the start of their careers. Within reason this is a good thing, as people build up a rounded experience and a full set of skills by moving from one environment to another. But it's in any organization's interest to hold on to good people, and losing a key person in the middle of a project can be a real headache, as it will often be impossible to replace them for some time and the project will suffer badly.

For contractors, pay may be the only issue in deciding whether to stay at the end of a contract.

Let's get the issue of remuneration out of the way. Some people do leave because of pay, although other things usually have to be quite bad as well for this to happen, at least for permanent staff. For most people, high pay does not motivate particularly well, although it can help to retain people. If you pay people very well, above the market rate, this does not tend to make them work any harder or be more committed, but it can make it more difficult for them to leave. Paying very well therefore makes sense for the people you cannot afford to lose.

If you pay peanuts, you get monkeys. If you pay through the nose, you may just get taken for a ride.

On the other hand, poor pay does demotivate and reduces commitment to the organization. Poor pay makes people resentful and unwilling to give more than the minimum effort, and is likely to make the better people leave.

Since the whole job of creating software depends upon the commitment of the people on your team, you want to have people who are being paid a rate that is commensurate with the skills, knowledge, experience and professionalism that they are bringing to the project and to the organization as a whole.

So if someone on your team is seriously upset by their pay, you should bring this to the attention of management. Replacing someone is a costly and time-consuming business, and you can never replace the experience that a person builds up doing their job. So it makes sound financial sense to pay a person what they are worth.

Beware, however, that there are a few people who are quite skilled at pumping up their pay by letting it be known that they might leave (they usually let it be known at a time when you can least afford to lose them). Before you rush off to management, think carefully about how much that person is really worth in the job market – can they actually better their pay? Also, consider the feelings of other people on the team – is it the right thing to be seen to be pushed around by someone who is making a big fuss? What will this do for the motivation of the other team members? If the whole team feels underpaid, they might appreciate your involvement in an important issue. But beware defending someone who is just a mercenary playing for more cash.

When it comes to staying in a job, for most people there are more important things than cash. **Trust, and respect from others, as well as self-respect that comes from personal development,** are the key factors. Showing a team member respect at work is not just a matter of personal interaction. It's about giving someone as much responsibility as they can comfortably handle, and trusting them to use it. People need to stretch out into new areas of skill and knowledge, and they need to feel that their experience is respected (see also SECTION 19: WHEN TO LET PEOPLE DO THINGS THEIR OWN WAY?). Delegation is a key way to extend people, and by doing so make them feel more valued and more likely to stay. **Give each person an area of responsibility, as big as they can cope with, and allow them to progress it their own way.** Most people far prefer this to being spoon-fed with small tasks.

There are a few people, and it is only a few, who like to avoid responsibility and prefer being told what to do. If you want to develop this sort of person in order to keep them from being bored and wanting to leave, then you need to do it very carefully, little by little. Keep the incremental increases in responsibility very small, and give lots of honest and fair feedback about the results. Make sure there's lots of positive feedback, but give a little criticism where it is needed.

One of the most common reasons given by technical people for leaving a job is that it didn't live up to the expectations they were led to believe when they were recruited. In other words, the job was over-sold. If some-one seems to be thinking of leaving, it's always worth talking to them about why they came to the job and what they expected of it. It may be there is some work you can give that goes some way to meeting their aspi-rations, or perhaps this is possible in another team. Even letting someone leave your team to go somewhere else in the organization is better than having them leave altogether.

When someone accepts a job as a software developer, there are some assumptions they usually make about the physical environment they will work in. These include assumptions that:

▶ They will be treated like a professional person – given sufficient desk room, a telephone, reasonable quality furniture and so forth.

▶ They will have a fairly fast computer, probably no more than two years old, with plenty of disk space and memory, and a decent-sized monitor.

▶ They will have free and instant access to e-mail and the web.

▶ They will have control over their computer (administrator rights and so forth), and be trusted to use the IT network, floppy drives, CD-ROM drives and CD copiers without scrutiny.

Complying with these assumptions is essential if you want to show an engineer respect and trust. An organization that employs a software engi-neer and gives them a four-year-old computer is saying to that person 'we don't care what you do with your time, spend it getting frustrated waiting for things to compile, it doesn't matter to us'. An organization that restricts access to e-mail or the internet is saying 'we don't expect you to be committed enough to work hard during the day (and we don't trust ourselves to be able to notice if you don't)'. An organization that restricts an engineer's access to their computer's operating system or its drives is saying to that person 'we don't trust you to use the tools of your job'. There are many organizations that don't accept these assumptions. Often these organizations have a large number of semi-skilled users who don't understand computers very well, but that is no justification for treating software engineers like idiots. If someone is going to leave because of frus-tration with organizational policies, there will be little that you can do in the short term. In the longer term, you may be able to persuade your management that software engineers are a special class of user, and maybe get the restrictions lifted.

17 inch is the minimum size for a developer's monitor. Trying to do software development on a 15 inch monitor is stressful and inefficient.

Social isolation is a common reason for people, especially young people without partners, to leave jobs quite quickly after they start them. For example, a new graduate may move across the country to take the best job they can find, but then find they have no friends and nothing to do outside work. Some people in this situation make friends easily, while others don't care, but for many, moving back to where their friends are is the easiest way to 'get a life'. If someone seems to be wanting to leave because of isolation outside work, you could try arranging some social occasions for your team. Work can satisfy at least some of a person's social needs.

Engineers need and expect to continue to be trained. In this business, you need to keep up with new technologies if you don't want your career to nose-dive. If someone is dissatisfied because of lack of training, then find some new work for them to do for which they will need training, and get them properly trained. Training doesn't necessarily mean going on a course, it could involve reading or self-paced training or just learning on the job, as long as new skills (not just knowledge) are gained. Make sure they use the skills that they receive – giving someone new skills and then not giving them opportunities to use them will make the person more frustrated, and actually make it easier for them to leave.

I was told the following way to remember the difference between education and training. If your daughter comes home from school and says she's had sex education, that's OK. If she comes home and says she's had sex training, that's something different. Knowledge is one thing, experience is quite another.

Having said all of the above, many team leaders worry too much about people leaving. If you worry instead about your team members' skills, their development as individuals, the variety of work they are getting, the level of responsibility they are being given, the cohesion of the team as a whole – in other words, **if you think about the people on your team as much as you think about the technical aspects of your work** – then job satisfaction and retention of people will happen automatically.

24

ONE OF MY TEAM IS SPENDING TOO MUCH TIME CHATTING AND WEB BROWSING //
WHAT SHOULD I DO?

Some amount of social chatter is normal and healthy among colleagues. This is the social 'glue' that keeps a team together and gives a sense of belonging and comradeship. But chatting causes interruptions and distraction, and it shouldn't go on long enough to impede progress significantly.

The most important indicator that somebody's not really trying very hard is that the work doesn't get done. You need to consider this over a period of several days, because some people go through periods of intense effort, followed by periods of relaxation and recovery. If the work is getting done, and if these 'recovery' periods are not interfering with other people, then leave well alone and accept that the person has this pattern.

But there are some people who get into the habit of loafing and don't get out of it. Not only are there the traditional ways of relaxing at work – chatting, phoning friends, reading magazines, taking long breaks, going for a cigarette – but new technology has provided wonderful new ways of looking busy whilst achieving absolutely diddly-squat. If someone is not pulling their weight on the team then you need to do something about it. Even if the person has valuable knowledge or skills, you can't allow them to be lazy while others work; it is an insult to the rest of the team.

It's best to avoid the 'subtle but pointed remark', such as 'taking a break again so soon?'. This rarely works, and it makes a poor impression on others who overhear it. Instead, you must get the person in private and point out your concerns. It is not an easy thing to do, it isn't comfortable, but you can't ignore the problem and hope it will go away. Don't try to get someone else to do something about it for you either, it is your

infobar // **TAKE EXTRA CARE IF...**

If any of the following apply, take extra care – involve management or Human Resources, or a trained counsellor, from the outset, or you could find yourself in difficulties:

- The person has 'friends in high places' or other political power within the organization, that could be used against you.

- Timekeeping is involved, e.g. arriving later for work. This is a different matter from laziness at work, because there are valid personal reasons why people sometimes have timekeeping problems, such as problems with childcare or illness, which they may not want to discuss with you.

- Suspicion of serious personal problems such as alcoholism or drug abuse.

- Other disciplinary problems are involved, e.g. violence, bullying, discrimination or harassment.

concern and you should take the first action (but see the infobar // TAKE EXTRA CARE IF... above). This doesn't need to take more than a few minutes, just explain that you think that the person is spending too much time chatting or whatever, explain that there's work to be done, and leave it at that.

If the person reacts angrily, or if after a few days nothing has changed, then it's time to get some backup. Involve your management or the Human Resources department. Even if things improve somewhat, but not enough, don't go for a second meeting with the person until you've involved your management. If things don't get better then this will become a disciplinary matter, and this is a private thing between a person and their boss – your involvement will be to keep management informed.

Most people, once given a kick like this, will change their ways. Wasting time becomes a habit more than anything, and once it is broken a new habit, involving more work, can be formed quite easily. Of course, there are some people who won't change their ways, or who change for a few days and then go back to how they were. These people must be removed from the team.

See SECTION 22: SOMEONE WHO'S A PROBLEM for more advice. Remember, though, that someone who is doing a little too much chatting or web browsing is not a problem person, they just need a bit of a prod. You should not treat such a person as a 'problem', just have a quiet word with them. Only if things don't improve or if the atmosphere becomes poisoned should you start treating such a person as 'a problem'.

>> REQUIREMENTS CAPTURE

25

WHAT IS MEANT BY 'REQUIREMENTS CAPTURE'? HOW DO I GO ABOUT IT?

Requirements capture is the process of finding out what your team has got to produce.

A very common reason that software projects fail is that they don't make a good job of requirements capture, but instead rush through it as quickly as possible in order to start on the 'real work'. If you don't do a good job of capturing the requirements, the requirements are still there – you just don't know about them. So you are likely to produce a product that the customer doesn't want, and then have to do more (unplanned) work to put things right when the customer complains. This is not a sensible way to go about developing a product.

This section is a brief introduction to the process of requirements capture. Whole books have been written on this topic (indeed, a couple of good ones are included in the bibliography at the end of this book [SECTION 42]).

The process is always the same (as set out below), but depending on whether you are creating a product for the market, dealing with an internal customer, or dealing with an external customer, the *emphasis* will be different:

▶ When dealing with an external (paying) customer, you will usually have quite a well-defined brief. This comes from contracts, bids, marketing materials and from meetings with customers. Usually, the bidding process will have involved some discussion and revision by the customer to clarify issues to some extent. The requirements capture process is then one of filling in extra details, getting agreements on the technical approach to be taken, and quantifying issues that have been left quite open. Doing some analysis is a very good idea (see SECTION 34: ANALYSIS), but building up a good relationship with the customer and gaining their agreement is the most important part of the task.

▶ When working for an internal customer, it is usual that the requirements are not very clear when you start the project. For example, you may be given the brief of automating the company's purchasing system, without much guidance as to how far to go (are you just replacing paper forms with computer screens, or are you adding new functionality?). In this sort of situation it is wise to invest significant time in an analysis phase, to determine what people really need and expect, and to avoid upsetting people who will be affected by the change.

▶ When creating a product for the market, you may have been given some input from your marketing department or elsewhere, but you may need to clarify this a great deal and make it more technically strict. If you can get access to real users, rather than relying entirely on internal contacts, you may gain a better understanding of what users really want. Whilst you still need to pin down the technical specification of the product you are going to make, the priority is in finding out what users' priorities are and what will be important in selling the product. It would be a very good idea to do some analysis of how the users will actually use the product, and you may be able to involve real users in this process. In making products for the market, it is very important to get an understanding of the marketplace – do you need to get something to market quickly, or do you need to make a 'killer app'? Often, phased deliveries are important when releasing to the market, and an indication of these phases should be part of the requirements specification.

The steps to performing requirements capture are as follows:

1 **Create a repository to hold the results**. This might be a document, or it might be a database (see the infobar // REQUIREMENTS DOCUMENT OR REQUIREMENTS DATABASE?). In either case, *it needs to have some structure* so that as you discover requirements, they can be slotted into the repository.

If many of your requirements are coming from a document that is quite structured and formal, such as a bid document that contains numbered paragraphs, then it makes sense to adopt the same structure and the same numbering for your own document (this is not relevant in the case of a database because a database record would usually record this information anyway). This makes it easy for customers who are familiar with their own document to understand your document. If necessary, invent your own detailed numbering scheme – every requirement should be identifiable by its own number, such as 'section 3.1.2, point 3' or 'requirement 128'.

If you are inventing your own structure for your document, try to group the requirements into common areas that are related to the way the product will be used, not based on a guess of the software architecture. For instance, details of the user interface for driving a function are best collected with other details of that function, rather than having all the user interface details collected into one section.

I was taught that a requirements document ought to be divided into functional requirements (things that the system must do) and non-functional requirements (which typically cover such issues as the operating system platform, arrangements for backups of data, and speed of operation). Personally I have never found that this structure adds any clarity to a requirements document, it just adds a level of headings. I also think that the distinction can be misleading. For instance, if a function takes far too long to operate then that is a bug – the function does not work properly – so to me, speed of operation is a functional requirement. Use the functional/non-functional structure if you think it has some merit, or if your procedures require you to do so, but otherwise don't get too worried about the distinction between functional and non-functional requirements.

2 **Trawl for requirements**. Often, many requirements come from a primary source such as a marketing document or a bid. These can be copied into the requirements document (and clarified in the next step). But usually there are other sources of requirements – other documents, other people who should be involved.

Go out of your way to find requirements! Make sure that all the people who should have had a say have been able to contribute. Involve end-users if possible. In a manufacturing environment, make sure that people in departments such as production and support are consulted, as they may have ideas for making the product cheaper to manufacture, or for adding diagnostics to aid testing. Don't be afraid of capturing requirements such as these that are 'invented' in-house – you can always give them a low priority or push them into a later release, but they should be captured none the less.

It is usually worth spending extra effort clarifying user interface features, for instance by creating prototypes and getting them reviewed by end-users. This not only helps get the user interface right, but often clarifies other requirements, and may even reveal some requirements that had been implied or assumed by the customer but not understood by the developers.

Put all the requirements you discover into your requirements document or database.

Sometimes it is useful to be able to identify where every requirement came from. This could be done by having a 'traceability matrix' that maps from requirements to their sources, or it can be recorded with each requirement as part of the text or as a database field. If you want to have this traceability, then build it up as you create the repository, don't try to fill it in later. Generating this traceability takes quite a bit of effort, so you must decide right at the start whether it will be needed or not.

3 **Clarify the requirements**. This is the stage where the requirements get transformed into something that makes sense to an engineer. Vague marketing terms need to be translated into specific technical proposals. Assumptions need to be made explicit. You need to identify what you will do, and also explain a little about how you intend to do it.

People sometimes get upset over the difference between a requirement, a specification, and a design issue. Certainly you shouldn't go too far and start including design solutions, because the requirements document is about what you must do, not about how you must do it. But in reality, some solution-domain decisions must be included. My rule is: 'If it matters to the customer, it ought to be in the requirements document'. For instance, if you decide that you will use a certain database (which will be part of the solution and not accessed by the customer directly), then tell the customer in the requirements document, because they will have to pay for it. You don't have to say much about how it will be used, but it should be included (as an intention, if nothing more), even though it is a solution-domain issue.

Requirements fall into one of two categories:

▶ **Hard, specific requirements.** Where possible, requirements should be specific and they should be quantitative (in other words, using numbers). For example, a marketing requirement that 'it should be obvious that the system is busy' should be translated to something more specific – is an 'hourglass cursor' enough, or do you need a 'progress bar', or what? A requirement that 'an image should be produced quickly' might be translated to 'within 5 seconds'. The intention of such requirements is that they are sufficiently precisely defined that *they can be used in acceptance testing.* Even if your organization or your customer doesn't work that way, the best way to produce really useful requirements is to structure your specific requirements so that they are suitable for acceptance testing.

It is vital not to tie yourself to specific requirements that are unnecessarily stringent. Be specific, but be mediocre, in your requirements document. Suppose that the marketing requirement says that 'images must be produced quickly' – don't specify 5 seconds if 30 would probably do. Specify a product that is adequate, not brilliant. Hopefully you will be able to exceed the requirements in places and produce something that is really good. It's tempting to say to yourself 'I want to make a good job of this' and so specify something impressively good – this is usually a big mistake, as it limits your freedom and sets you up for a failure. Do you really want to have arguments with a customer who won't pay because the feature that takes 6 seconds should have taken 5, when it's not really that vital at all? Remember, write the requirements as if you will be held to them by an acceptance test. Is it sensible for the software to fail its acceptance because it took 6 seconds to do its job? If 30 seconds would be OK, then say 30 seconds. This is better than saying 'fast', and it's better than committing yourself to something unnecessarily difficult. Of course, if it has to happen in 5 seconds, then say 5 seconds, no longer – specify the mediocre, but not the unacceptably poor.

▶ **Intentions and priorities**. If something cannot *or should not* be made specific and quantitative, then make it clear that it is an intention, not something that you will be held to. It is useful to include in the document phrases such as 'we intend to use 128-bit encryption if the relevant legal issues can be resolved' or 'the image warping will be as fast as possible; however, compression ratio is more important than speed'. These things cannot be tested against, and must be phrased to ensure that they cannot be held against you, but are worth including to show that you have registered the existence of an issue that matters.

Requirements are clarified in the following ways:

▶ **By discussion**. Don't be afraid to telephone your customer and ask them for clarification, or even to explain that a requirement is hard to meet and ask them how important it is – usually, there is some

> skills box

PRIORITIZING REQUIREMENTS

Here are three different ways to prioritize a requirement, and they can be used or combined as required.

1 The obvious 1,2,3 approach. All priority-1 requirements are more important than all priority-2 requirements, and so on. Equally good is 'Major, Medium, Minor'. Simple and effective.

2 The MoSCoW approach. This rates each requirement as either:

Must do – an essential requirement

Should do – not essential but needed to make a good quality product

Could do – low priority but worth doing

Won't do – rejected as outside the scope of the requirements

In practice this usually has to be combined with the 1,2,3 approach, as you can have a requirement, for instance, that is Minor but Must be done (for example, a requirement to include copyright details in the Help About box).

A useful summary if used in combination with the 1,2,3 approach.

3 The want it/need it approach. Here you rate, or ask your customer to rate, each requirement on two scores:

a) How upset will you be if this requirement is not fulfilled?

b) How happy will you be if this requirement is fulfilled?

If somebody will be very happy if a requirement is fulfilled, but not very upset if it isn't, then it's a 'nice to have', whereas if they will be upset by it not being fulfilled then it's a 'must have'.

In practice I find that this approach takes a long time, and the rating of each requirement on two scales doesn't lead to a clear prioritization. Use this method in discussions if you want to understand what is really important to the customer, but make sure that a more basic prioritization, using one of the other approaches, is recorded as a summary.

flexibility available even when a very formal specification has been placed before you (if there are commercial sensitivities involved, then involve a senior manager first!).

▶ **By analysis.** Think through what the user wants to do with the system, and how they want to use it. For example, suppose that an operation will take a significant length of time to complete. Will the user need to cancel it before it is finished? If the requirements document doesn't say anything, then don't simply assume that the ability to cancel the operation is not needed – if it's going to be needed in order to make the system pleasant to use, then it's best to realize that now, because the customer will only demand it later in any case. Your document should explicitly state one way or the other, for instance 'there will be no functionality for the user to cancel this operation'. This makes the decision visible, where it can be explicitly accepted or rejected, not left undecided.

Analysis includes making prototypes, either for yourself or to show to users. See SECTION 34: IS 'ANALYSIS' REALLY NECESSARY, OR CAN I GO STRAIGHT INTO DESIGN?

▶ **By review.** Get your document reviewed both by people in your organization and by the customer. The requirements capture process is your opportunity to clarify issues, and get contentious items sorted out. Don't paper over the cracks and hide issues in order to get your document accepted, those problems will come back and bite you later. Get issues out into the open where they can be approached in a businesslike manner.

4 **Prioritize and phase the requirements**. Frequently, you will be required to deliver interim releases before the final shipment, either for review or to actually be put into use. Even if this is not specified in any source documents or meetings, you should still open the issue by stating something in the requirements. Interim deliveries can help to relieve time pressure, and they often make for a better customer relationship, but of course they also cost extra time and money.

Requirements should always be prioritized. Understanding the customer's priorities is part of learning about their needs in the wider sense. If you work on the highest priorities first, to the extent that this makes logical sense, then you will soon have something useful to show to the customer and to use for demos, and you will be able to make a useful interim delivery if necessary.

There are actually several different ways to prioritize requirements; see the >skills box PRIORITISING REQUIREMENTS above.

5 **Get your document formally accepted**. Whether you are working for a paying customer or for some internal customer such as a sales or marketing department, always make sure that the requirements are thoroughly reviewed and that they are accepted by the customer. In the case of an external customer this must mean that someone signs that they accept. For internal customers this may not be possible but it is worth trying to achieve.

Often, there are confusions about the relative importance of the various requirements sources (especially on larger projects), for instance whether the requirements document takes precedence over the bid document or not. If possible, get formal, written acceptance that *the requirements document you have written takes precedence over all other requirements documents*. Since your document incorporates and builds on those previous documents, this should not be impossible to achieve. It is essential to resolve this type of conflict. Quite often you see requirements documents that state something like 'where this document differs from the bid document, the bid will take precedence'. This is absolute nonsense and should not be done – if your document is written after the bid document, why would it say something different, unless a decision has been made to change something?

It's not uncommon for some commercial renegotiation to take place during the acceptance phase, in fact it's almost inevitable on a large project. By your analysis you may have discovered that there is more to do than was originally budgeted for, and in reviewing the requirements, the customer may have demanded new features. For this reason, during the review process, every time you send a copy of the requirements to the customer it should include a disclaimer, something like 'we do not warrant that the requirements contained herein will be produced to the currently agreed cost or timetable'. Then when the requirements are stable you can talk about money and time again.

Making sure that there is a good requirements document that summarizes what the project is about and formally records what you must do is a vital part of ensuring that a project runs smoothly. It is one of the tasks that is *uniquely under the control of the team leader* – making a good job of the requirements is entirely and directly under the software team leader's control. Make sure you spend the time that is necessary on this process, as that time will be repaid to you many times over as the project proceeds.

infobar // **REQUIREMENTS DOCUMENT OR REQUIREMENTS DATABASE?**

Requirements need to be recorded in a way that makes them accessible. There are basically two ways to do this:

1 In a document, which can be read 'cover to cover' and also used for reference.

2 In a database of individual requirements, each of which might include:

- An explanation and description

- The source of the requirement: what document or which person, and a reference

- Change history of this requirement: how it was modified, by whom, when and why

- Status of the requirement (e.g. 'implemented')

- Whether the requirement is to be 'visible' to the customer or is an internal issue (e.g. the need to reuse and improve certain in-house technology as part of the project would not be visible to the customer but is a requirement nonetheless)

- Other information concerning each item, such as cross-references to test specifications, risk or hazard analyses or bug reports.

A document is very useful for explaining to people such as new project members what the project is about. A document is also far better than a database for communication – most customers don't respond well if you send them a database file and ask them to review it! It is easy to circulate a document and have people mark changes on it for your consideration. Databases can of course produce reports but these are not normally as flexible as 'real' documents (for example, in the ability to include cross-references and hyperlinks, tables, diagrams and so on).

The database has the advantage of being easily searched, for instance to find all requirements created since a given date, or all those that came from a certain source. It also has the advantage of being able to produce views and reports that filter the information according to the need of the moment. There are commercially available packages that are designed for requirements capture, and these can usually integrate with testing, bug reporting and configuration management packages as well.

Personally I think that, even if a database is the primary requirements repository, there always needs to be a document, at least to introduce, explain and cross-reference the project. To my mind you always need a document as a top-level overview. For many projects, especially smaller projects, the database is more cumbersome than it is convenient. The database is especially useful for projects that are either

- Fairly large (say, a detailed requirements document would run to over 100 pages), or

- Commercially risky, political or contentious, where the database is useful to record exactly why and how a requirement was entered, while at the same time having the facility to hide information from reports that might be produced.

It doesn't really matter whether a project is very formal (e.g. military) or informal. A database can be useful on informal projects and a document can contain everything that is needed on a very formal project.

If your procedures don't dictate a detailed approach, it's usually acceptable to start off with a requirements document, keeping it updated and annotated as you require, and start a database if this becomes too cumbersome.

Some organizations have standard database templates and these can get quite large and cumbersome, with dozens of fields for each entry. Often they have fields for all sorts of data that is relevant on some projects but not others. In this situation, it is a very good idea to decide, early on, which fields are to be used on your project and which not. The database must be used consistently, otherwise people get lazy and forget to fill in some fields, damaging the usefulness of the database for searching and reporting.

26

THE CUSTOMER KEEPS ASKING FOR CHANGES AND IMPROVEMENTS // CAN I REALLY SAY 'NO'?

Feature-creep is not confined to software. For example:

■ In the military there is an effect called 'mission creep', which refers to the way in which an army can get increasingly pulled into a conflict. The same thing often happens in software projects. A project can get increasingly complex as the customer strives for more integration with its existing systems, and the new software is 'pulled in' to the client's organization.

■ In architecture, there is an effect called 'gold plating', which refers to the way that an architect will specify fancy superficial trimmings at high cost to try to impress the customer, while neglecting the more important but less glamorous features of a building, such as air-conditioning. Software engineers are frequently guilty of gold-plating.

Feature-creep is unavoidable. Markets move as competitors and customers change. Technology advances, making some things obsolete and providing new opportunities. Organizations change and reorganize. Ideas get clarified in the process of being worked on. People simply (and quite correctly) change their minds.

So there is no point trying to insist that no changes can happen. Your customers and your organization need some flexibility from you. What you can do is to keep the changes to a minimum, to organize the project so that changes can be accommodated, and to approach changes with a commercial attitude.

You should never say 'no' outright to a change request. Sometimes you may simply accept it, but more usually you should treat a request as the start of a negotiation for more time and money to allow you to make the change.

Keep changes to a minimum by:

▶ **Having clear requirements**. Perform analysis and requirements capture at the start of your project to make sure you understand what the customer wants and how the product will actually be used. Make sure the requirements are formally approved by your customer or by your marketing department as a definitive statement of what you will deliver. See SECTION 25: WHAT IS MEANT BY REQUIREMENTS CAPTURE?

▶ **Finding out how vital a requested change really is**. It is tempting to treat complaints from the customer as of high priority, especially if they come out of acceptance testing. But many requests are no more than passing comments or 'wish-lists', that can be noted and maybe pencilled in to be 'considered for the next release' (which means, 'we'll consider them in the next release if you pay for them'). Ask the customer to prioritize a new request against existing requirements by asking which features are more important and which they want to have first.

▶ **Always replying to a change request by giving an indication of the time, cost and quality implications**. It is not a case of being dogmatic or selfish, just tell them the truth of the matter and co-operate in finding the best way to use the available time and money. Remember also that a delay to your project may cause a knock-on delay to some other work that is expected to follow afterwards; you may need to make this clear as part of the discussion as this can greatly increase the actual cost of a delay.

Identifying delays is especially important if you are making a product to be sold on the market, rather than for a particular customer. Often, marketing departments put higher priority on time-to-market than on anything else and so, if you point out the resulting delay, may choose to wait and have the requested feature in a future release, or may agree to trade the feature for some other feature that they can live without.

Often, a customer will refuse to accept the cost implications of the changes they request. They will demand changes but quibble over the cost. If your relationship with your customer is covered by a fixed-price contract, you should refuse to do any extra work under these circumstances. This doesn't mean that you must stick rigidly to the original specification, making something that the customer no longer wants, but if the customer will not pay for the changes they are asking for, some other features will have to be dropped to compensate. You can put the options to the customer and ask them to choose, but all the options should make commercial sense. If necessary, involve someone from the commercial side of your organization, who is unlikely to be very generous in doing work for nothing.

On the other hand, if your customer is internal, or is paying by the day, they may try to insist that you 'do what they want' and insist that you make changes without introducing delays. If something cannot be done *to adequate quality* within the time allowed then don't agree to it and don't be told what you must do. If the customer cuts off the work they will get an unfinished product, and you can warn them of this in advance. Don't even think of giving them a 'finished' but poor quality product.

Some people moan about 'moving goalposts', as if the customer or the marketing people are unreasonable and stupid by making change requests. Sometimes they are unreasonable or stupid, but often a change is needed, or is at least desirable. Often the people who grumble about moving goalposts grumble to themselves, but do not reply to change requests with any specific cost or time implications. *The customer then learns that they can make change requests for free.* This encourages them to continue to make change requests. If you want to end this cycle, you have to consistently reply to requests with specific implications of the change and ask for approval to continue – if the time and money are not approved, don't do the work. The customer will then learn to think rather harder about change requests and to prioritize rather more.

Accommodate changes by:

▶ **Having contingency in your plan** (both in time and in money) to cope with unplanned tasks and problems. If the requirements cannot be pinned down or the customer seems prone to changing their mind then include a *large* contingency.

▶ **Making interim deliveries to your customer,** or delivering prototypes, to get feedback from the customer, and preferably end-users, as early as possible. The sooner you hear about changes, the better.

▶ **Keeping the architecture of the software clean**. Good encapsulation and structure allow changes to be made quickly and with minimum knock-on effect. If code blocks are self-contained, they can be moved around easily. If code is full of back-doors, side-effects, assumptions and spaghetti-like interconnections then implementing changes will take much longer and cause much more mess.

▶ **Having a mechanism for coping with change requests**. If you have a standard process for accepting or rejecting change requests, the customer may accept this as routine rather than as you being negative.

Take advantage of changes by:

▶ **Treating changes as commercial opportunities**. Don't simply accept change requests without question. Always work out how much time and money they will take to implement, and use this to start a negotiation with the customer. You can sometimes make a healthy profit from change-request work, especially if it's needed urgently. Of course, it is petty to do this with small requests.

The most infuriating sort of feedback is the 'I don't know what I want but this isn't it' type of comment. It's an absolute killer if you get to the end of a project and you find that the customer really doesn't like what you did but can't tell you what to do about it, they just want the whole thing to be redesigned. You need to prevent this happening by confirming that you're on the right track as early and as frequently as possible.

There is no doubt that feature-creep is a major reason for many software projects finishing late, or being perceived as finishing late. Frequently, engineers don't help themselves because they are too willing to accommodate changes without any negotiation or response. Your response to change requests should be positive, but not passive.

>> STRESS AND CONFLICT MANAGEMENT

27

I'M VERY STRESSED AT THE MOMENT, AND SO ARE SOME OF MY TEAM // WHAT CAN I DO ABOUT IT?

This is a book about software development, and it's not appropriate here to talk about diet, exercise, relaxation techniques and so on, although these are very relevant to reducing and handling personal stress. See the SECTION 42: BIBLIOGRAPHY for an excellent book concerning general stress management.

There are many reasons people get stressed at work, and software has its own special problems that can really wind you up. This is bad news, because stress is not only disagreeable and unhealthy, but also results in some pretty lousy work quality, and an unpleasant working environment. As leader, your aim should be to build a team that is highly productive and applying maximum effort, yet is not overly stressed.

Stress is not the same as pressure. As a leader it is often necessary to pressurize people to some extent, as some people will not work very hard unless the need to achieve a deadline or to please an important customer is impressed upon them. Most engineers enjoy a little pressure, and good engineers tend to put pressure on themselves to achieve what they set out to achieve, but when the pressure becomes too great, when it crosses a certain threshold, then it becomes stress.

The level at which this threshold is reached depends on the individual concerned. Some people hate to be rushed and respond very badly to pressure, other people don't seem to register the pressure until it becomes quite heavy. Unfortunately, this can mean that even if everyone in your team is under the same pressure, some people may take it well and others may be highly stressed.

Here are some things that **you as a leader can do** to reduce the stress in your team, including reducing your own stress:

1 **De-couple the work of people on the team**. The way to do this is to allocate areas of work to different people, so that each person is working in their own area as much as possible.

The key to achieving this de-coupling is to break your architecture down into clean blocks and to give these blocks clean, thoroughly designed interfaces.

The job for each person then becomes one of implementing a given block, or in other words of implementing the interfaces that the block has.

Breaking the work down in this way, and using test benches where possible to test each unit in isolation, not only reduces stress caused by people getting in each other's way, it also improves quality and saves time in the long run, both of which also reduce stress.

This approach also tends to allow more delegation, so that individual team members feel much more 'in control' of their own work. A feeling of lack of control is one of the major reasons for people to experience stress. By delegating, you allow more control and so reduce stress. You will also reduce your own stress, as you will have fewer interruptions.

2 **Set targets that are difficult but realistic**. It should be clear how much time is available for individual tasks, from the project plan. It should also be clear which tasks are critical and which are less critical. So there is no need to demand that everything be done in overtime.

If someone is working hard and working smart, but still missing the deadlines, then the time-scales in the plan are wrong and you need to revisit the project plan, not put the person under more pressure or demand longer hours.

3 **Don't be afraid to spend the time it takes to keep the quality up**. Find time for design reviews, code reviews, thorough testing and adequate documentation. The result will be that you don't get stuck with a pile of bugs and integration issues at the end of the project, because these will have been addressed as the project progressed, and you won't get lots of service calls interrupting you in the future when you're in the middle of another urgent project. All of this reduces stress considerably.

4 **Make sure that people understand what is expected of them**. People get stressed if they are unsure of what they are doing and worried that they might be messing things up. This is most relevant to junior engineers who may not know where to start on a task. When you allocate work, even if you do this very informally, make sure that the person understands what is required.

With junior staff it is often worth spelling out the steps involved in finishing the work, to give some guidance and also to give the person a sense of progress as they complete each step.

5   **Give feedback to people** so they know how they are progressing and don't get anxious that they are under-performing. Make it fair and helpful, never simply critical, and give praise where it is due, as long as it is sincere. See SECTION 21: GIVING PRAISE. Again this is most relevant with junior staff, or with someone who has had a bad experience recently and feels rejected at work.

6   **Make sure people are adequately trained**. While some people cope well with being 'dropped in at the deep end', most people actually don't cope too well and get overloaded and stressed. Trying to do something that you don't understand leads to a sense of inadequacy and loss of control, and an expectation of failure. Train people and give them time to learn the skills that they are expected to use.

7   **Manage your managers and your customers**. It is important to give regular feedback to your customers and managers, and to ensure that the feedback is honest. You can use this feedback to regulate the expectations that people have of your team. If you tell someone that a task will be finished 'tomorrow', then you cannot blame them for interrupting you tomorrow lunchtime to ask if the results are available. If the task is not finished then the person working on it will perceive that interruption as pressure and it will get them stressed. So, for example, if you think that a document you are working on is going to be finished by Monday evening, then tell the person who needs it that it will be ready on Tuesday morning. This will not delay the completion of the document, but it will avoid disappointment to your 'customer' and unnecessary pressure on your team.

8   **Shield people**. If someone is showing signs of being stressed, or has an especially heavy workload, it is not unreasonable to ask other team members, and also managers and customers, to give them some respite from interruptions. You could also allow someone to work in a different location or to work from home for a short time if they must get away from interruptions. If you do this, you will have to field the interruptions yourself, and you will have to live with the worsening of communications that will result.

9   **Act as mediator between different groups**. Sometimes, stress is caused by structural problems and different priorities and perspectives in an

organization. If another group that you depend on seems to be uncooperative and unhelpful, make an effort to understand the priorities that are driving that team and the stresses that they are under. Maybe you can compromise and give a little if it helps to get the job done and reduce tension. But make sure that your priorities get understood as well, don't get taken for a ride. See also SECTION 12: WORKING WITH A LESS ABLE TEAM.

10 **Be prepared to say no**. It's part of your job as leader to handle requests for extra features, for demo work and other unexpected tasks. If there are better things to be getting on with, be prepared to say so. Don't let other people relieve their own stress by pushing their priorities or their pressures onto you or your team.

Here are some things that **everyone can do** to reduce their own individual stress level:

1 **Prioritize**. Do the most *urgent* things first, and the most *important* things second (and the rest when you have time).

If you are constantly doing urgent things, and important things are left undone, that is a sure sign that you are overloaded. In this situation you need to step back and see if there are some fundamental things you can do about it, such as delegating some tasks, asking for work to be taken back off you, or re-estimating time-scales.

2 **Manage interruptions**. Turn off all indicators on your computer that show when new e-mail has arrived, and instead get into the habit of checking your mail at convenient times during the day.

If an issue needs discussing with several people, schedule a meeting so that everyone can talk about it. This causes fewer interruptions than having multiple conversations on the same subject with several people.

If you get constantly interrupted and you have something urgent to do, get away from your desk by hiding in a meeting room and working there, or working from home. This should be a rare occurrence – stress and interruptions go with the job, so you should only abandon your desk if there is something truly vital to be done that cannot wait.

3 **Keep your own private 'to-do lists'** of tasks that you personally have to do. Have separate to-do lists for each project or component that you are working on.

I use bits of paper, but no doubt electronic organization would also work well. On each to-do list, indicate for yourself the priority of the tasks to be done.

These prioritized task lists not only help organize your time, they also reduce stress because they reassure you that you are making the best use of your time.

If you find yourself with a whole pile of lists each with many tasks to be done then it is likely that you need to get rid of some tasks onto somebody else, otherwise they are not going to get done.

For more help on managing your time, see the excellent reference cited in the bibliography (SECTION 42).

4   **Don't thrash between tasks**, instead allocate your time. You might decide, for example, 'I'm going to work on project A today'. Then if interruptions come in for project B, handle them if they are urgent, and put everything else on project B's to-do list, to be handled when you get round to that project.

5   **Take a break**. A ten-minute tea break can provide an enormous stress relief. Getting out of the building is even better. If you're working so hard that you really think you can't stop, why not say to yourself, 'I'll have that ten-minute break, and I'll just have to stay ten minutes later tonight'. Very often I find that when I come back after a break in these circumstances I find I was about to do something really stupid because I was so stressed out, and so taking the break actually saved me time.

Always try to have a lunch break. Skipping the lunch break reduces your productivity and builds up tension. If you're under pressure then reduce the break but always take one.

6   **If something is stressing you out, try to put it in perspective**. A good technique is to ask yourself 'when I look back on this in a year's time, will it seem that important?' Sometimes the answer is yes, but often this technique helps you realize that you've just got yourself wound up over something that is really no big deal.

Often it's friction with other people that gets us in a rage, and this technique is good for putting that into perspective. If you get an e-mail from your boss saying that you should have tried harder to finish some work, when in fact the reason it wasn't done was that you were working very hard on something more important, it's very easy to fly off the handle and send a 'flame' reply, or to grind your teeth and think dark thoughts involving pins and voodoo dummies. But when you look back at this in a year's time, will that e-mail seem so terrible? Better to send a firm but polite reply to your boss, and it will probably turn out not to be a big issue. When you look back in a year's time it will all be a storm in a teacup.

7   **Be prepared to say no to meetings**. Obviously you can't say no to all meetings, as what may be low priority to you may be important to other attendees, so you can't be too selfish about it. But you should decline to attend a meeting if you are not really required, if you will not have time to prepare for it, or if you think the meeting is not going to be useful because the wrong people are attending or the agenda is inappropriate.

It is best to decline a meeting soon after you get the invitation rather than later, and it is rude to pull out of a meeting at the very last moment unless something terribly new and urgent has come up.

If you can't attend a meeting then don't send someone in your place unless they can contribute just as much as you could. It is pointless to send someone in your place who can't do the job, it wastes everyone's time and reflects badly on you.

8   **Recognize stress in others**. It's worth remembering that when people are being uncooperative or unreasonable, the reason may be that they themselves are under stress. If your boss is being a tyrant it may be because he is getting it in the neck from his boss. If one of your team members is being awkward it may be because they don't want to admit to themselves or to you that they've got a problem they can't solve.

If you can recognize the forces at work then it's likely that you can be more sympathetic and understanding, rather than being badly affected by somebody else's stress.

High stress levels can be tolerated, and even enjoyed as exciting, by most people for short periods, but should not be allowed to continue for weeks or months. Prolonged stress is highly damaging to individuals' health, to morale, to the quality of work, and to the chances of retaining good people.

A highly stressed developer usually develops poor software. A highly stressed team leader will usually lead the team badly. As team leader you have a responsibility to manage the stress levels of your team and of yourself.

28

MY TEAM SEEMS TO SPEND TOO MUCH TIME ARGUING // WHAT CAN I DO?

Some disagreement and even downright arguing is normal and healthy, particularly at certain times in the project's life.

When people first start to work together as a group, there is a certain amount of posturing and jostling for position. People come to the project with different preconceptions about how it should be tackled, and they bring different viewpoints to bear. They also have their own hidden agendas and their own personal priorities that they hope to pursue on the back of the project. These various differences come out fairly soon after the real work starts, and are manifested in arguments about work and in personal friction.

This is normal and natural behaviour for human beings. It does not mean that you have an unworkable or disruptive group of people. Quite the opposite, it shows that you have a group of people that is starting to gel into a team. Indeed, you should be far more worried if you find yourself in a group of people who sullenly avoid talking to each other, or who keep going off for furtive discussions in private cliques. A *lack* of open discussion and disagreement would indicate a serious problem.

I would go as far as to say that **a team cannot work effectively unless it has been through the arguing stage.** But that stage has to be handled properly by the team leader. The arguing stage should subside once the direction of the team is established and people have work that they can get on with, but it is necessary to go through that stage, to get issues out into the open and resolved. If you try to suppress arguments, they will rumble on for a long time, surfacing periodically to disrupt the project. Better to get them out in the open and settled at the beginning.

It is the leader's role to mediate in conflicts. You must be seen to be taking note of the opinions raised, and to be *listening* openly and fairly to them. You must balance the needs of the project (especially as seen from the customer's point of view), the needs and desires of the individuals making the argument, and the needs of the other people who have a stake in the outcome.

You must not give in to individuals who are jostling for more responsibility than they deserve. Nor must you allow the project to be pulled off course because of a desire by one (or even all) of the engineers to further their own priorities, such as building up their CVs.

It is during this early argumentative stage that *the guiding principles and priorities of the project should emerge*. Indeed, it is the emergence of a consensus about these principles and priorities that eventually causes the arguments to cease. So at the start of the project, you should be constantly ready to state, and sometimes to modify, the principles of the project. These principles may cover both technical and organizational issues.

It is for you as team leader to galvanize arguments into a decision, and more than that, it should be a decision about a clearly stated basic principle, not just about the specific issue. For instance, if some of the team are arguing that a new technology should be adopted for this project, while others are arguing for a more well-understood route to be taken, then you have the opportunity to state a principle, such as 'we will do it the old way because there are so many other new factors on this project to worry about that we shouldn't risk using that new technology as well' or alternately you might decide 'we should use the most productive tools available to us even if it takes time to learn them'. It is for you to reduce the specific arguments down to a choice of more general principles, and then use the project priorities to decide between the possible principles.

Far from suppressing arguments in the early stages of a project, it is your job to get them out in the open where they can be discussed maturely, and not to allow them to become personal or entrenched. Many people prefer to grumble, or to make snide remarks, rather than raise an issue directly. *You should act as a catalyst*, airing issues that you see to be contentious, listening to the opinions, and where necessary forcing a decision to be made that everyone on the team can live with.

It is worth remembering that the arguments may start all over again if a new person joins the team. After a little time you will notice friction building up between that person and the rest of the team. Whilst the team may be polite in the new person's presence, they may be scathing behind his or her back. Do not panic. The person is not being rejected, in fact they are starting the process of being accepted.

Another time when disagreement is to be allowed or to some extent encouraged is during reviews, especially design reviews. Engineers often have quite large egos concerning design issues and patterns and can find it hard to accept that other people may have a different approach that is as good as their own, or at least good enough. Very often a better design will emerge from a clash between opposing viewpoints, *if a little creativity and humour are also thrown in*. It's the team leader's job to mediate in these discussions, ensuring that everyone gets a fair hearing and that the discussion stays professional and doesn't become personal. Good design meetings are often full of banter and good-natured insults.

Beware, however, that shy people can be inhibited by a 'robust macho' atmosphere and may be alienated if it goes on too long.

Arguments may be healthy in some circumstances but they should not be allowed to go on too long or to happen at inappropriate times. If the same argument has been repeated three times, there is no point in having it a fourth time. In this situation you should quickly review the decision that has been made, and then make it clear that the decision is made and the team must move on. If decisions turn out to be wrong then they will have to be reversed, but they must stand for the time being. If someone on your team absolutely refuses to accept the consensus of the team and continues to be disruptive, you have got a personnel problem to deal with, either with that person or with the make-up of the team as a whole – see SECTION 22: SOMEONE WHO'S A REAL PROBLEM.

Sometimes there can be problems where a person *suppresses their disagreements*. This is quite common with contract staff, who often feel it inappropriate to disagree with the consensus of the team or with its leader. This is an unhealthy situation, as someone will not work effectively if they don't believe in what they are doing. However, it is very hard to remedy. Demanding to hear a person's opinions is likely to be very counter-productive. The only solution is to encourage a relaxed and supportive atmosphere in the team, where opinions can be voiced safely, without fear, by all members. Always act against any tendency for people to put others down, score points, or take an 'us and them' attitude, either across a split within the team, or with regard to other teams or organizations that you work with.

As the team matures, the number of arguments should reduce. In a healthy situation this is because the project's principles have been defined and accepted by the team and there is no need for further discussion on them.

When a team works well together, everyone gets a reward in the form of a more relaxed, productive and sociable working day. For most people, this reward is worth sacrificing some of their own personal agendas and preferences, and so most people will soon commit themselves to the team's common approach if they think that a real team atmosphere and a successful project are going to result.

>> RELATIONSHIP WITH MANAGEMENT

29

I WANT TO TACKLE THE PROJECT IN A PARTICULAR WAY // HOW CAN I MAKE SURE THAT MY MANAGEMENT WILL LET ME?

Sometimes, you may want to run your project in a different way to the rest of the organization. For instance, you might want to try a rapid-prototyping route that has not been used in your organization before, or you might want to apply a methodology you've read about. Or it may be that you want to give your software quite a radical architecture, or use a new language, and you don't think you should go ahead without first consulting your boss.

▶ The first question is, 'Is it really worth doing?'. Before doing anything else, consider the good and bad points of the options you're considering. There are always at least two options, since there is always the 'do nothing, carry on as before' option. Think the options through realistically, don't overemphasize the good points of your idea and play down the bad side, but *be objective*. Think what objections are likely to be raised and consider them carefully. If possible, be specific and quantitative – for instance, don't just guess that your approach will be faster, try to estimate *how much* faster. Very few choices are one-sided. A new approach that has benefits usually brings with it some problems; be honest about identifying these.

Ask yourself honestly, *why do you want to do this?* Are you trying to do something in a way that is definitely better, or simply in a way you feel more comfortable with, perhaps a way you did it before? If it's the latter, you need to be careful – why should the whole organization adapt to your wishes, why don't you adapt to it? If your way is just *a little* better, you shouldn't make too much fuss about getting other people to change; you should conform to the way things are normally done in your organization.

To force through a change you want that has little benefit is just egotistical and is not worth the disruption. Only forge ahead if there are definite, sizeable benefits. This may sound very conservative and complacent. What I'm saying is, be conservative or complacent about unimportant issues, save your energy for pushing through changes that actually matter.

▶ The next question to ask is 'Do I need management permission?'. Often, we put constraints on ourselves that are simply unnecessary. We don't try to overcome a barrier, because we think it too difficult or not worth the effort it will take, when in fact the barrier is not there in the first place. *It may be that you don't need anyone's permission, you can make the decision yourself.* If other people are affected, you may be able to negotiate directly with them, rather than involving your boss. For important decisions, you should at least keep your boss informed (this is sometimes known as the 'Jesuit approach' – do it first and ask forgiveness later).

But be careful. Even decisions that seem straightforward need to be considered carefully if they affect people outside of your team – whether other engineers, others in the organization, your customer, or whoever. *You can't just make a decision that is convenient for you, without considering the consequences for others.* For example, you may want to move to a different compiler. But if you do that, engineers who are using the old compiler may not be able to rebuild your code. They may not be willing to change compilers right now for good reasons of their own. In situations like this, you need to get an agreement from your manager or directly from the people affected by your decision, before you implement it. Normally, you shouldn't decide to adopt a new language, tool or technology without your manager's agreement, because it has an impact on people's training needs, the flexibility of moving people from one project to another, and the ethos and strategic direction of the department.

Of course, if money is involved then the question of whether you need permission may be even easier to answer: if the amount is above your own spending limit, you need permission.

▶ If you are still willing to go ahead, get someone else to review your proposal, as this almost always helps to clarify and improve your ideas. You should have a good idea of:

■ Exactly what it is that you are proposing

■ Why it's worth doing

If your idea is something that involves taking a risk – a risk that you consider to be worth taking – then use the 'expected benefit' approach, see SECTION 33: TAKING A RISK.

- What problems it will cause

- How it will affect other people

- What it will cost

- How to implement it – how to bring in the changes

- How other people will react to it

Let's suppose you've got past these hurdles – you want to do something that you feel is well worth doing, but for which you need permission, either because it affects other people or because you require approval to spend the money. So now you need to **persuade your management**, starting (and possibly ending) with your boss.

▶ The first step in persuading your boss is to **'sound out' your boss by raising the subject informally**. Find some excuse to raise the subject and to mention that you've been thinking about it, but don't be very intense, and avoid giving away your ideas at this stage. The aim is to find out if your boss has any strong feelings on the subject, which you'd have to take into account when presenting your ideas.

It may turn out that your boss is fundamentally opposed to what you have in mind. Even if this is the case, if you believe your idea is sound then you should pursue the matter and not be dissuaded without even presenting your ideas (unless your boss is the vicious sort that will act vindictively against anyone who disagrees with them). If your boss is a fairly reasonable person, it will do you no harm to present your views. If your arguments are reasonable and well presented then they may swing your boss's opinions, and even if you fail in this you will probably make a good impression just by the effort.

▶ Having sounded out your boss and thought what to say, it's time to **make your pitch**. You don't need to start off by doing any sort of formal presentation, but you do need to do more than just have a chat in passing. Managers get an awful lot of interruptions and they are forever being given suggestions of how they might do things better. Managers learn to ignore most of this otherwise they would never get anything done. You need to make sure that you get your boss's full attention for a little while, and make it clear you need a decision. Sending a few e-mails is not enough. Mentioning something in the corridor or putting your head round the manager's door is no good either. **The sad truth is that to get a manager's attention, you need to get them into a meeting.** It may

> skills box

THE THREE OUT OF FOUR TRICK

This is a trick for persuading a decision maker, such as your boss, to be 'sensible'. In other words, to make the choice that you want them to make.

Let's say that you have a module of legacy code that's in a real mess, and you want to rewrite it rather than keep trying to live with it. You have to involve your boss because it will require significant investment of resources.

You could present this choice to your boss:

1   Do nothing new, keep fixing bugs as they appear.

2   Total rewrite.

Your boss may choose option 1 outright. You are unlikely to get option 2 accepted unless the case is absolutely overwhelming – nobody wants to spend effort replacing existing work, and your boss may have seen attempted rewrites in the past that ended up producing something as bad as what they were trying to replace.

If your boss is in a positive mood and being creative, you may well be asked to consider a third choice: a partial rewrite. You may even be pressured to accept this as a decision, there and then in the meeting, without any real chance to think it through. Even if you are allowed to go away to think about this partial rewrite option, it is very likely to be the option chosen by your boss, no matter how much you dislike it – if you think the situation through then I'm sure you'll see why this is almost always the case.

A better way to go about things (in other words, one more likely to get the result you desire), is to **present four options, in ascending order of impact or risk, with your preferred option as third on the list**. After all, this is only fair – if you are going to include some options that don't go as far as you would like, it is only reasonable to include an option that goes further than you think is necessary.

So you might present the options as:

1   Do nothing new, keep fixing bugs as they appear

2   Partial rewrite of the worst internal parts of this module

3   Clean rewrite of the module's implementation, keeping the current interface

4   Redesign and clean up all the module's interfaces, then rewrite the module and make minor changes to the other modules affected

Presented in this way, your boss is far more likely to consider option 3 as a sensible and realistic option, indeed as being a compromise solution in itself.

Make sure your option 4 is realistic, indeed make it something you would really like and can honestly enthuse about.

cont >>

>>

And keep a straight face.

I learnt about this trick by having it done to me. I knew I'd been suckered when I saw everyone smiling as they were leaving a meeting where I'd just 'persuaded' them to take the option that apparently wasn't quite all they wanted. It worked! In fact this trick works so well I'm almost scared to put it in this book, in case managers read it and become immune.

well be a very short meeting with only the two of you present, but you need to make it clear to your manager that you need some time with them to discuss a particular topic.

When you do succeed in getting your manager's attention, *quickly*:

1 Introduce what you want to talk about,

2 Talk through the options as you see them (see the `>skills box` **THE THREE OUT OF FOUR TRICK** above), and

3 Ask for a decision.

Try to keep the discussion focused around what you want to present and don't get pulled off in other directions. But don't press too hard – do not *demand* that something be done, as you will most likely annoy your boss. Bosses like making decisions but they hate being told what they should decide.

▶ There are three likely outcomes from the meeting:

1 'I'll think about it.' This usually means 'I'll forget about it' or 'I'll think of a reason to say no'. If possible, try not to leave a meeting if this is the outcome, but press on and go over the issues again until you get one of the other outcomes.

2 No, your boss does not give you permission to act. Accept your boss's decision; it is a manager's job to make the decision and you have to live with it. Don't get bitter, don't keep revisiting the decision at every opportunity. Even if you don't like the decision it is still your job to do your best to make things work as well as possible.

3 Yes, you have permission to act. *Do not be at all surprised if your boss immediately hands you the job of implementing the decision.* After all, if you're so keen, you're the obvious choice. This may of course involve you in doing hard work, and if other people are going to resist the idea then it is you that is going to feel the heat, although as you will be acting with your boss's full permission this should be fairly easy to overcome.

A less likely but possible outcome is that your boss will ask you to make a more formal presentation about the issue to a group of people. This is something to be pleased about. See SECTION 7 : HOW DO I MAKE A PRESENTATION.

Most bosses do want the best for their departments and their people, as well as their customers. But they also may have priorities and problems you are not aware of, so even apparently sensible options may be rejected by apparently sensible bosses. You can only do your best to persuade your boss, and usually you should only do it the once. Make a good job of making a case, and even if you get turned down, there is a good chance you will not only trigger an eventual improvement to things but also enhance your own reputation.

30

MY BOSS IS USELESS // HOW CAN I PUT UP WITH THIS?

If you are lucky enough to have a brilliant boss who really knows how to manage a software department, you can skip this section.

Still with me? I thought you might be!

The software industry seems to suffer from a real problem with poor management, and there are several reasons for this:

▶ Software engineering is difficult. Managing people is difficult. It's not surprising that there are few people to be found who are both able and willing to do both of them at once.

Software managers are expected to be able to manage people, organize a department, and make strategic decisions concerning choices of technologies and architectures of products. It's not surprising that many software managers can't cope.

Perhaps a way will be found to split these responsibilities somewhat. The software industry is still immature and new job titles are being invented all the time. The 'mentoring' role sometimes found in bigger organizations may become more common and more permanent, perhaps becoming a sort of software coaching role.

▶ Software moves very fast. If your boss has been managing long enough to be an experienced manager, they must have stopped being a programmer several years ago, and unless they have made a conscious effort their technical skills will be out of date. While it may not matter that they can't program any more, managers tend to get out of touch and make stupid decisions that are based on press hype or on people feeding them rubbish. In other words, their judgement becomes less reliable.

▶ Some software managers love coding so much that they don't stop. As a result, their management jobs don't get done.

▶ Engineers often get promoted to management because they are good engineers. They may be lousy managers.

▶ Engineers often get promoted to management with no training in management at all. Perhaps they get a three-day training course. If it takes several years to learn how to do software engineering, what makes organizations think that people can learn the skills of management in three days? Or do they think that there is nothing to be taught, people just have to pick it up somehow, whilst in the meantime, their employees must suffer?

▶ Software managers are often recruited by more senior managers who are themselves not familiar with software engineering. Often, no technical people are involved in the recruitment at all. The result is that bullshit-merchants get hired, who are very good at making themselves look good but at little else.

In many organizations a good MBA is now a prerequisite for a management position. Sometimes, an exception is made to this rule for software managers. In my opinion this is a huge mistake, as it is bound to diminish the software manager in the eyes of the rest of the management team.

My reason for including this list is to point out that before you leave your current job because of your boss, you should be aware how likely you are to meet another poor boss somewhere else. It's not surprising that even a well-meaning and capable person can become a poor software manager. Things are even worse if the person has an autocratic or hopelessly spineless personality.

So what should you do about it? Firstly, you should not defy your boss nor actively undermine his or her position. You can quite rightly be sacked for this. If you are given clear instructions by your boss then you should try your best to implement your boss's instructions and to make them work, even if you disagree with them. Your boss has the authority to make decisions and you must recognize that authority. Equally, it is not a good idea to try to play politics or to get devious to show your boss up – these things usually backfire. Do your job to the best of your ability but don't get yourself into trouble just because your boss is useless – you might find yourself being made into a scapegoat. You should act honestly and treat your boss with the same respect you would treat anyone else, if you expect to be trusted and respected in return.

Fortunately, poor bosses usually have an inkling of their own incompetence. They often cover up their inability to make good decisions, by not making any decisions at all. If you have such a 'passively incompetent' boss this is not too bad because you and your colleagues will be able to take the decisions instead. This will involve you in doing work that your boss should be doing, but it's usually preferable to take on that work, rather than not have it done at all.

There are two levels to this taking-on of work: you can either **get your boss to delegate**, or you can simply **act anyway**. Let's take an example. Suppose that the office layout needs changing – the desks need moving because some people are too cramped. It might well be that if you ask your boss to sort something out, nothing will happen. But if you ask if *you* could arrange it, you might be allowed. Of course your boss may want to approve your decisions before you implement them, especially if money needs to be spent, but your boss's involvement might be reduced to giving you the go-ahead. That is the delegation approach.

If you take the act-anyway approach, you and your colleagues would simply rearrange the desks without reference to your boss at all. The approach to be taken depends on your boss and on the issue, but the delegation option is certainly less likely to get you into trouble.

One common characteristic of poor bosses is that they never come out of their offices. This can work to your advantage as they may not notice if you move the furniture around, work from home for a day or two, or emigrate on full pay.

Let's have a look at some of the things that a software manager is supposed to do, and see if you and your colleagues could help a 'passively incompetent' boss to get some of them done if they are not happening. Let's see which you can help out with:

▶ Recruitment: *Yes*

Talk directly to Human Resources about individual candidates and about the recruitment process as a whole.

Get CVs sent to you and your colleagues instead of your boss for filtering.

Get involved in the interview process.

▶ Procedures: *Yes*

Work out improvements between yourselves and send them, piecemeal, to your boss for approval.

▶ Allocating people to projects: *No*

It will be very hard for you to judge the conflicting priorities of the organization and its different customers. You should not unilaterally decide where the organization's priorities lie, so you must appeal to your boss for decisions. If you don't get them then you can only carry on as instructed. Don't try to appeal to your boss's boss, as 'going over the boss's head' is likely to get your boss all upset.

▶ Encouraging open communication within the department and between departments: *Yes*

If you have a 'passively incompetent' boss it will be down to you and your colleagues to make sure that you know what is going on by talking to each other, and by talking to other people in the organization. If communications are especially poor, you might like to call some regular meetings (not too regular!), to discuss what is going on in different areas.

Don't underestimate the power of informal communications. If the problem is one of a lack of trust and understanding, a trip to the pub can be a far more effective way to get people talking than locking them up in a meeting. Plus you can arrange a visit to the pub without feeling compelled to invite your boss.

▶ Resolving personnel issues: *No*

If one of your colleagues is a pain to work with, or is lazy and incompetent, you can have a quiet word with your boss. If nothing happens about it then it will be very hard for you to act further. This is one of the major reasons why poor bosses destroy departments. People who should be disciplined or sacked are allowed to get away with murder, while good people get stressed out and leave.

Of course if one of your colleagues is doing something totally intolerable, like bullying or harassing you, then you should take more formal action, by following your organization's grievance procedures. But most personnel problems are not so extreme and are very hard to prove.

There is usually little point in going to the Human Resources department, as their first, and possibly only, action will be to talk to your boss, which just makes you look like a trouble-causer.

▶ Monitoring the budget: *No*

There is no incentive for you to try to get involved here. If you need some resources that will cost money, it will have to be saved elsewhere. You can try to agree this with those affected but you are not likely to have much success. Resources are tight in most organizations and people don't give them up unless forced to.

▶ Strategic planning: *No, except...*

Strategic planning means stepping back from the details and making the larger, riskier, more creative and longer-term decisions that a business needs to make if it is to keep alive. You can't do this because you don't have access to the other strategic policies such as the crucial marketing strategy, but you can provide the organization with some 'technological push'.

Many profit-making organizations are dominated by 'market pull', where they allow the market to dominate what they do, and by and large this is a very healthy way to run a business. But there is also a need for some 'technological push', where the organization's direction is steered to make best use of new technical possibilities. There is nothing to stop you providing this input directly to other parts of the organization, such as marketing.

▶ Training and developing staff: *Yes*

If you or someone on your team needs a training course, you should be able to get it by justifying how much time it will save you and what that person will be able to do that they could not do before. It will help if you choose a course and find out all about it, and present this to your boss for approval.

However, 'development' means more than going on courses, it means taking on more responsibility and growing as an individual. A 'passively incompetent' boss may actually help here, as you may find yourself doing things that your boss would normally do, although unfortunately you will not have the job title or authority to go with it – nor the salary.

▶ Representing the department: *No*

Most bosses realize that if they don't turn up for management meetings they will soon be out of a job and so this is one area where they may work very hard. Many managers are very good at making themselves look good and won't want any help in this direction.

The above assumes that you have a boss who realizes that they are out of their depth and so tries to keep their head down. But there are some bosses (thankfully much fewer) who are much more *actively* incompetent. The sins of such people include:

▶ Adopting an autocratic style, shouting and threatening.

▶ Not delegating any responsibility, centralizing all decisions.

▶ Surrounding themselves by cliques of cronies and yes-men.

► Appalling judgement, based on political and personal considerations, or out of an ignorance combined with arrogance that prevents them asking for advice.

► Nepotism (recruiting, or making business deals with, friends and relations).

► Politicking and war-mongering, encouraging rivalries and win–lose battles.

► Interfering in people's jobs at a level of detail that they should not get involved in.

► Closing down communications. Telling people not to communicate with other departments, or with each other.

Such people should be sacked. If you are of a serene and philosophical disposition you might like to take a balanced view, judging the problems caused by your boss against the positive aspects of your job, which are in fact all too easy to take for granted. You might decide that on balance you can put up with the problems. If you are of a less serene and philosophical disposition then you might be forced to look for a new job as the stress could become intolerable.

At the worst extreme there are managers who are bullies or who subject people to sexual harassment, discrimination or other forms of mental abuse. Nobody should have to tolerate being treated like dirt at work. Take legal advice and act on it.

31

I FEEL I'M NOT GETTING THE SUPPORT I NEED FROM MANAGEMENT // WHAT CAN I DO ABOUT IT?

Software engineers and team leaders sometimes feel as if they are having to deliver software *despite* their management, instead of with their management's help. Typical issues include:

1 Having to use old or under-powered computers. Having to use poor tools.

2 Not being trusted to have control over your own computer.

3 Working for an internal customer who keeps 'moving the goalposts' but still expects you to deliver on time. Having your time estimates 'trimmed'. Being expected to deliver on time but not being given the resources you need.

4 Not being believed when you explain why problems have occurred. Always being blamed even when the fault lies elsewhere.

5 Not being respected. The boss listening to certain cronies or external consultants, treating everyone else as 'resource'.

This is a section about dissatisfaction with the organization and what to do about it. Often, people just get dissatisfied because of 'lack of management support', but as a leader you should never accept such a simplistic and unqualified description. What exactly does 'lack of support' mean? How is it manifested? Why is it happening? What can you do about it?

Let's take each of these in turn, as examples of typical problems and how you might look deeper into them.

1. HAVING TO USE OLD OR UNDER-POWERED COMPUTERS. HAVING TO USE POOR TOOLS.

The most important thing to realize here is that *managers often don't appreciate the extent of the problem*. Why should a development manager realize that the version-control system is useless, if they never use it and nobody has asked them to change it? (If you *can* get them to use it, all the better – see the `>skills box` MAKE THEM EXPERIENCE YOUR SUFFERING.)

'But we've been moaning about it for ages' you may say, and that may be true, which leads me to the second thing you need to realize: *managers hear an awful lot of moaning and they learn to filter most of it out and ignore it.* Most managers are overloaded with work and are under intense pressure from above. They have priorities given to them by their bosses and those are the ones they will address. They won't do something about an issue that people keep moaning about, but that seems to be working anyway.

If you want to get something done, you need to get your manager's attention and persuade them to do something. Getting their attention usually means calling a meeting. It doesn't have to be a long or formal meeting, but it has to be an occasion where you have your manager's full attention to direct at the issue you are raising. See SECTION 29: GETTING MANAGEMENT SUPPORT, about persuading management.

If nothing seems to be happening, *keep nagging* your boss until something does happen.

2. NOT BEING TRUSTED TO HAVE CONTROL OVER YOUR OWN COMPUTER.

A computer is a software engineer's 'tool of the trade'. Yet there are organizations who insist on treating engineers like the dumbest of users, by restricting their control of their computers, not letting them use floppy drives and CD-ROMs, restricting internet access, and not allowing the super-user level of login access to the machine that is necessary to do the low-level fiddling often needed.

Of course, some policies need to be in place. You don't want people putting illegal material on their work computers or running programs that might cause damage. But these are policies that can be enforced through instructions and by disciplinary action against offenders; there is no need to treat everyone as if they can't be trusted to use a computer.

> skills box

MAKE THEM EXPERIENCE YOUR SUFFERING

A really effective way to get managers to understand that a computer or a tool is rubbish is to get them to use it. It's not always possible of course, but it works really well if you can manage it.

For instance, suppose you're designing web pages, and the tool you are using is useless. You want to get a better tool but you don't think your boss will approve the cost, considering the money already spent on the tool you're using. Why not see if you can get the boss to use the current tool? For instance, ask your boss to review a website you've created. When the boss raises some issues, say you don't really understand what to change – why doesn't your boss do it? If they would just borrow your computer for 10 minutes they could do it themselves... Your boss will use the tool and realize how poor it is. When, next day, you walk in and say that you can't stand it any more and can you buy something better, your boss is quite likely to be sympathetic.

To me, this sort of situation is unforgivable. There is no excuse for treating a software engineer as anything other than an expert computer user. You could try to persuade management to change it – although really you shouldn't need to try, because if your boss is responsible for software development, he or she should be trying to change it anyway.

I have known people who have left jobs because of this issue. While I wouldn't recommend walking out of a job unless you find something that is definitely a better opportunity, I can fully understand why people would start looking.

3. WORKING FOR AN INTERNAL CUSTOMER WHO KEEPS 'MOVING THE GOALPOSTS' BUT STILL EXPECTS YOU TO DELIVER ON TIME. HAVING YOUR TIME ESTIMATES 'TRIMMED'. BEING EXPECTED TO DELIVER ON TIME BUT NOT BEING GIVEN THE RESOURCES YOU NEED.

This little section summarizes the advice in SECTION 25: WHAT IS MEANT BY 'REQUIREMENTS CAPTURE' and SECTION 26: THE CUSTOMER KEEPS ASKING FOR CHANGES AND IMPROVEMENTS.

'Feature-creep' is much harder to deal with when it comes from an internal customer such as the sales or marketing department, than when it comes from an external, paying customer. With an external customer, significant 'feature-creep' can be met by refusing to do work that has not been paid for, and your management should be on your side.

Firstly, you should try to *achieve the same level of formality and detail* of requirements capture with an internal customer as you would with an external one. Do a thorough job of capturing all of the requirements, and get your management to approve them.

Secondly, you need to be quite careful about how you react when the goalposts appear to be moved. Never just accept it quietly, but don't get all upset either. Just point out the extra time and cost that will be incurred, and make sure that whoever has to approve this overspend does so – often the sales and marketing people ask for things, but there's no agreement from anyone else to pay for them. If you're told that time-scales cannot slip, then reply with the amount of extra resources you will need – or if it simply cannot be done then you will have to say so. You can't achieve the impossible. If you keep quiet it will simply be assumed that the changes were easy for you and you can do them with no impact. If you really can't put any more resource on the project because it's got as much as it can have, or if there is no more available, then you need to get your managers together to resolve the issue. Something's got to give – some features will have to be dropped, some serious overtime done, or the delivery must be delayed.

Don't be shy in asking for the extra time or resource that a requirements change brings. Even if it involves an extra week's work in a year-long project, still get it approved. A week will seem like a long time when the release date approaches. You need to get the extra time or resource sorted out soon, while there's time to plan the changes and when the reasons for the change are still apparent, not as a panic reaction near the end of the project.

Moving requirements are *NOT* a sign of lack of management support, they are a sign of an organization that is trying to provide the best it can to its customers. Do not respond to requirements changes as if the whole idea is crazy, nor as if changes are being made just to annoy you.

4. NOT BEING BELIEVED WHEN YOU EXPLAIN WHY PROBLEMS HAVE OCCURRED. ALWAYS BEING BLAMED EVEN WHEN THE FAULT LIES ELSEWHERE.

In some organizations it seems that engineers are always the 'bad guys'.

Such distrust usually has a history to it. It could be that managers have been promised things in the past and have then been let down. Since many senior managers don't understand what software developers do, once distrust sets in it is hard to reverse. It's easy to lose someone's trust but hard to win it back again. This distrust may have been caused by people who have long since left, but it tends to linger on and be self-fulfilling.

All you can really do is to make sure that *on your project*, you keep your promises as much as you possibly can. You need to show your management that things have changed.

It also helps if you *keep management informed about positive progress* on your project. If all they hear is bad news, they will think of your project as a problem. It doesn't take a second to write an e-mail such as 'Good news from project Z! The new morphing features are working really well, here's a sample...' You may feel a bit of a creep doing this but if there has been genuine progress it's well worth doing. You might be surprised at how high up the organization these messages get forwarded, as your boss may well be very pleased to have some good news to give his or her boss, and so on up the ladder.

If there is a history of distrust between management and engineers, try to take a long-term view of it and not take it personally. It's depressing when people don't trust you, but if they don't trust anyone in engineering at least you know it's not just you. If you can demonstrate that you are doing your best and acting in good faith, the trust is likely to return, over time.

5. NOT BEING RESPECTED. THE BOSS LISTENING TO CERTAIN CRONIES OR EXTERNAL CONSULTANTS, TREATING EVERYONE ELSE AS 'RESOURCE'.

In the previous little section I was referring to distrust of engineers by other departments. This section is referring to distrust of engineers by the people who are directly leading and managing those engineers.

This is a sign of *very* poor management. Firstly, it indicates managers who don't have the necessary knowledge or understanding of the things they are supposed to be managing and so must rely on second-hand opinions. Secondly, it shows a contempt for people within the organization.

When you join an organization, you expect that your opinions will be heard, at least to the extent that your experience and seniority merit. Managers that ignore their own employees and depend on a small clique of friends are greatly reducing the chances of good decisions being made. Similarly, if managers don't trust the opinions of their own staff and so bring in consultants as a matter of routine, it makes you wonder why they employ those staff at all.

There is very little that you can do about this situation. If you try to fight it you are likely to get pushed out even further. You can either decide to put up with it, if other aspects of the job compensate for it, or you can leave. Once again I wouldn't recommend leaving a job unless you find something that is definitely a better opportunity, but I can understand why people would look.

This has been rather a hotchpotch section because some types of management support can and should be lobbied for, some have to be earned over a long term, and some can be legitimately expected as your right. Your own situation may be a combination of several factors similar to the examples I've chosen, and you will have to decide how to react to each of them. The important thing is to get into the habit of analysing problems and looking for solutions, rather than reacting emotionally to issues. A situation may be bad enough to make you want to get another job, but that sort of decision should be made objectively after considering the situation, not out of anger.

When you ask for management support, make sure that you are asking for support to attack the real problem, not trying to find excuses. For example, if people are being held back by poor tools, then you need better ones – they used to say 'a workman is only as good as his tools', and this applies as much in software as in anything else. But beware. Poor tools may not be the real problem – maybe the tools are actually adequate, and people aren't using them properly. It could be a training issue, or it could be a problem with motivation. In this situation, if you get management to buy you new tools it's likely that nothing will change, and next time you ask for support, management will be much less likely to believe your promises of improvements to be made. Just because people on your team are moaning about the tools, it doesn't mean that this is the real problem – you should make up your own mind about what the problem is, not just pass on the moans to your boss.

It is also said that 'a fool with a tool is still a fool'!

As a leader, you should be able to evaluate problems dispassionately, analyse the root causes and see through the emotions, and decide what actions to take. As a leader you don't have the luxury of just blowing off steam every now and again and hoping that someone else will make something happen. You have a responsibility for making things happen, which may involve the hard job of persuading management to support and to trust your team.

>> MAKING DECISIONS

32

I CONSTANTLY HAVE TO MAKE DECISIONS ON THE PROJECT, OFTEN WITH LITTLE TIME FOR CONSIDERATION // HOW CAN I BE CONFIDENT THAT I'M GETTING THE DECISIONS RIGHT?

As an engineer you will be used to making decisions, including ones that affect other people (such as users of your products). The decisions to be made as team leader are not fundamentally any different from the detailed decisions that a senior developer is expected to make. However, because leadership decisions are made for other people, in public as it were, you may feel exposed and tense about the process.

As team leader you will have to make decisions that are bigger, more far reaching than those made by other engineers – you may be considering scrapping the approach your team has taken and starting again, for instance. Taking this sort of decision takes courage but if you do some preparation, you can increase the confidence you and everyone else has in the validity of your decisions.

Decision making is one of the few software activities that can benefit from following a defined process. I don't mean it has to be a formal or time-consuming thing, but if you follow the steps set out below, rather than relying on 'gut instinct', you are likely to end up with a better (and, believe it or not, a quicker) decision.

1   **Make sure that you have a good understanding of the issues**. This is especially important if you have one or two 'experts' who are trying to lobby for their preferred outcomes. It is essential that you can maintain credibility during the discussions.

This is not to say that you need to become an expert in every field; you have better things to do with your time, and you might be seen to be trying to 'score points' if you tried. And you should certainly not pretend to have more knowledge than you really have. But if a decision is becoming contentious, you should delay it until you've had a chance to find out a little about the issues by your own independent means.

Of course, for many day-to-day decisions you will be very close to the issues and have all the information you need anyway, and there will be nothing to do for this step.

2 **Decide how to decide**. Some decisions are best made in a group, others are best made by you alone. Some decisions must be made with your close involvement, others can be completely delegated to someone else.

Deciding in a group will increase the commitment of the people who must carry out the decision, and often produces a better outcome since 'many heads are better than one'. A group decision is especially appropriate for large or contentious issues. It gives everyone an opportunity to air their views, and can produce more creative ideas than any other way.

There are, however, a few problems with getting a whole group of people together to make a decision:

▶ It can cost more person-hours than it is worth.

▶ It can fail to produce a decisions at all.

▶ If there are senior people present, everyone else may feel intimidated.

▶ Quiet people may not speak, even though they would have useful things to say if they did.

▶ By sheer weight of numbers, people who should not have great influence on the decision can outweigh those who are truly knowledgeable and involved.

Making a decision on your own is rather autocratic, but there are times when it is appropriate:

▶ In an emergency, when speed is essential.

▶ When it involves personnel issues that should not be discussed with others.

▶ When you can be certain you have all the information you need to make the decision, can make it with confidence, and are sure that the rest of the team either wish you to make it alone, or at least will tolerate you making it alone.

A good compromise between a group decision and an autocratic one is to *consult* a few people, individually, about the problem, *and then decide yourself.* This gives you lots of input, but leaves the decision under your control. However, there are some drawbacks with the consult-then-decide approach:

▶ It is time-consuming and costly. You have to explain the problem several times over, and you probably will have to go round all the people several times to talk about issues that arise.

▶ If you do not involve everyone, you may be accused of favouritism. In the extreme, some people might feel that there is a clique, from which they are being excluded.

Many decisions can be *delegated* to others. Delegating a decision is no different from allocating any other task to a person:

▶ Make it clear what is to be decided, and when by.

▶ Set out any constraints or preferences you have on how the decision should be made.

▶ Make sure you review the decision later so you and others can learn about it.

Delegation can be a powerful motivation tool. It demonstrates trust and develops responsibility. But you should only delegate if you really mean it. If you tell someone that you will let them decide, then let them decide, and support their decision. If you don't have sufficient confidence in a person to delegate a decision to them, then don't do it, as you will have to live with the decision. *You can only delegate the authority to act; you cannot delegate responsibility for the consequences*, which always stays with you.

It is for you to decide how a decision is to be made. For most day-to-day decisions, you will probably decide on your own after a little discussion with others. The best way to make sure that your decisions are sound, fair and consistent is to base them on *defining principles* that you have previously worked out for your project.

For example, you may have decided that you will not use any new technologies on the project, so when someone suggests there is a new way to do something, unless its benefits are overwhelming you can quickly reject the idea. Of course, the defining principles have to be appropriate to the project or all the decisions you make will be wrong! These principles usually appear in the early stages of a project, when the requirements are becoming clearer and the team is assembling and starting to work together and to argue (see SECTION 28: ARGUMENTS). There is little you can do to make them appear, except to try to extract some general principles from all the individual decisions that are made on the project, and to mentally judge the emerging principles for correctness.

One of the best ways to judge your principles is to consider what a user of your product might think of them. What would they think about your choice to stick to old technology? Would they welcome it as being tried and tested, or reject it as inefficient? The answer depends on what sort of users you have, and for this reason it is a good way to generate appropriate principles.

Having clear principles and priorities is what enables you to make decisions that are both fast and good. You may have heard that senior people often make 'snap decisions', and it seems to be true. This is not because they have super-fast brains, nor because they decide rapidly without careful thought. It is because they are already very clear about the principles they believe will allow them to achieve their aims, and when a decision is brought to them they can quickly test the options against those principles to make a choice.

3 Generate criteria and weightings

▶ What must a given solution deliver, otherwise it is no solution at all? For example, 'we cannot choose any option that ties us to a single supplier'.

▶ What other desirable features would a given feature have, and how important are they relative to each other? For example, 'low cost is desirable, but quality is the most important factor'.

Ideally, decide these criteria and their relative importance, *before* coming up with any options, and revisit them later if necessary. One reason for doing it this way round is that sometimes when you investigate the options you find that a particular option has unexpected benefits, and you can convince yourself that these are essential, when in fact you could easily live without them but have got seduced by the possibilities.

For example, if I'm looking for ways to access data from a database, I may find that one of the options would let me execute Java code written on the database server, which I could use to do some complex and clever processing in the future. Whilst this might be true, if I don't need it in any situation I can foresee at present, this cool idea should not be given any importance and should not be made a criterion for judging options, otherwise we might reject an option that is actually more appropriate to the things we really need to do.

Deciding on the criteria *before* looking for options tends to make the process more objective.

4 **Generate and investigate options.** Now someone needs to investigate what options there are. This might take some time (for instance, finding possible vendors of third-party solutions), or the options may be fairly obvious.

Each option needs to be understood well enough to be scored against each of the criteria. Another advantage of choosing the criteria first is that if you have to investigate some complex options, you can concentrate and focus on those issues that have been identified as important. For example, if you are looking for a cross-platform tool and you know it has to work on Solaris, you can flick through the brochures and very quickly reject all options that don't work on Solaris. This sort of filtering is enabled by selecting the criteria first, and can save hours of time.

If you have a particularly 'fuzzy' problem where you think there may be many creative options that could be discovered, you might like to try 'brainstorming'; see the >skills box **BRAINSTORMING** opposite.

5 **Choose an option based on the criteria**. Reject any options that don't meet the basic 'essential' criteria. Then decide how well each remaining option meets the other criteria. It's important to stick to the criteria and not be swayed by other matters. Use the relative importance of the criteria to decide which option is the best overall.

For important, complex or contentious issues, you might find it hard to decide or to agree which option best meets the criteria. See the >skills box **DECISION MATRICES** for a way to approach such decisions.

A decision must be clearly made and committed to. Often there is no ideal answer and no solution that will satisfy everyone. But one option must be chosen and the consequences of that decision must be emphatically pursued.

6 **Communicate and implement the decision**. You need to make sure that everyone affected by the decision is made aware of it.

> skills box

BRAINSTORMING

Brainstorming is one of those techniques that are described in trendy management books, and people have made money describing in enormous detail various procedures and methods for doing it, to the point that many people have got put off the idea completely. This is a shame because the basic concept is quite sound and it works perfectly well.

The idea is very simple: get a group of people together to generate as many ideas as possible *without evaluating or criticizing them*, and then evaluate them later. By deliberately encouraging people to bring up crazy ideas in the knowledge that they will not be criticized, more creative thinking can be encouraged and more ideas will be generated. Later, these ideas are taken away and some sensible options can be distilled from the chaos of the brainstorming meeting.

A brainstorming meeting will only be successful if everyone there really wants to make it work. You can't have people who are there because they have been told to be there. You can't have someone senior shouting at people 'come on, I want more ideas, get on with it'! You can't have people who want to score points and put others down. So the make-up of the group in a brainstorming meeting is vitally important and worth considering carefully.

It is very hard for people (especially engineers, I suspect) to stop evaluating ideas. But people must at least be made to do it silently. If you have a group of people who want to brainstorm then they will police this themselves, and there is no real need to have someone running the process except to make sure that all the ideas get written down.

In the second stage, the more sensible ideas are sifted out. So are the more outrageous ones – often, a crazy idea can form the core of some genuine option. For example, I once attended a brainstorming session where we were asked how to measure water flowing down an existing water pipe without cutting the pipe, so that the water could be metered. Someone shouted out 'you could listen to the gurgling sound!'. This crazy idea was taken away and thought about, and eventually the concept of using ultrasound was investigated as a serious contender.

Brainstorming is worth a try if you're convinced there must be lots of options, but just can't see what they all might be.

Just communicating the decision may be sufficient to get the decision implemented, or you may have to take further actions and make more decisions as part of the process of getting it to happen.

If your decision will affect the way people will do their jobs, do not under-estimate people's resistance to change. People can continue to do things a familiar way, long after they have been told of a decision to change direction. The best way to reduce this resistance is to involve the people

infobar // **WHEN A DECISION IS REJECTED**

Frequently, a decision gets made, either by the leader or by the team as a whole, but one or more team members resist its implementation.

This is perfectly normal human behaviour. People always resist change. It's an emotional response that we all have. Normally, people need to be reminded and put under a little pressure to change, and eventually they will do so and the new situation will be accepted as the 'normal' rather than the 'new' state of affairs.

But sometimes a decision is actively rejected or undermined in a sustained way by one or more of the affected people. In this situation, you have the following options:

- *Try to bring people round*. Encourage, persuade and cajole, until you get your way. *This is often the best way to make a decision stick*. On the other hand it may take a long time to achieve results, or it may fail altogether. This should be your first approach unless the decision is very important and there is little time.

- *Change your mind*. Maybe the decision really was wrong. It needs to be considered. But don't change your mind just because of the resistance; this would set an unwelcome precedent.

- *Get tough and drive through the resistance*. You could use your own authority (or call on your boss's authority) to coerce people into complying. You could throw people off the team if they won't conform, or even threaten disciplinary action. These actions are only appropriate if the matter is sufficiently important, and time is short. This approach will only work if you have unquestionable authority or you have significant management support. And you'd better be right.

- *Get sneaky, or play politics*. I would never recommend this in any circumstances. Keep things open and honest. If you find yourself thinking in terms of battle lines and allegiances, there is something seriously amiss about the way you are approaching the problem.

- *Appeal to arbitration or to higher authority*. If the situation becomes highly emotionally charged and you find yourself having endless circular arguments, you might like to involve either your boss or some independent arbitrator whose decision will be accepted.

Choose the option, or combination of options, that is best for the situation and the people involved.

affected by the decision in the decision making itself, so that they feel they 'own' the decision. Even then, with a decision that is communicated and accepted, resistance and resentment can prevent decisions from sticking. This, unfortunately, is normal human behaviour. In the extreme, it may require a whole plan of action of its own, just to implement a decision against the forces of resistance to change.

7   **Monitor and review**. Keep an eye on the implementation of the decision and make sure it has really 'stuck'. Some decisions that seem right can turn out wrong and need reversing, because the information you had when you made the decision was poor, or because risk factors came into play and upset your assumptions. So be ready to revisit the decision if necessary, and don't be afraid to admit you were wrong if that is the case. See the   infobar //   WHEN A DECISION IS REJECTED opposite.

Experience has shown that this seven-step process produces decisions that are high quality, and it produces them quickly. Don't be tempted to short-cut the process in the belief that the depth of your knowledge and experience allows you to rely on 'gut instinct'. *The way to use that knowledge and experience is to apply them to the individual steps in the process set out above.*

I am not recommending some complex and laborious process here. I haven't said that you must document every step, hold meetings or circulate options – though you can do these things if they are necessary and appropriate for a given decision. For small, everyday decisions, you will probably know the issues, involve a few people informally, talk about the criteria and options, and make a decision on the spot. The whole sequence often takes a minute or less. But it is still worth being aware of the process above and following it. If you get into the habit you will soon work this way naturally.

Although decisions can often be reversed later, the ideal decision-point – the moment at which you have the opportunity to get *it right first time –* never comes back and, if wasted, is lost forever.

> skills box

DECISION MATRICES

For large, complex or contentious decisions, a thorough way of analysing a decision is to draw out a *decision matrix*. I'll go through an example (concerning options for communicating with a database, but that is not what is important – it is the concept of the table that matters here). Here is an example table, which is explained below:

		ADO	DAO	RDO	DB Vendor library
Efficiency	5				
Simple to program	2				
Future-proof	3				
Can call stored procedures	E				
Simple client installation	2				
Database independent	8				

The options are along the top and the criteria at the side. In this example, there are four options being considered (ADO etc.). There are six criteria that have been identified as being pertinent to the decision.

To the right of each criteria is a *weight*. If something is essential it has an E in the weight. Otherwise it has a number from 0 to 10 indicating its relative importance. So for instance in the example, we can see that the chosen option must meet the criterion 'Can call stored procedures' – it is essential. We can also see that the criterion 'Database independent' is considered four times more important than the criterion 'Simple client installation'. Remember, this is just an example; the numbers in my example don't matter, it's just the process that we're interested in here.

This table can be created by you individually (or by the person to whom you have delegated the decision), or it can be created in a group session, depending how you decided to decide. Hopefully a consensus will emerge and let you fill in numbers that everyone can agree with. Failing that, you will have to put in *your* numbers. If you are responsible for the decision then that is your prerogative. It is also your threat if agreement seems unlikely.

Ideally, you decide on the criteria before you select the options or investigate them in detail. You then find out what options there are and investigate them in detail to see how well they each meet the important criteria.

At this point you need to go back to the table, which may mean calling another meeting if all of this is being done as a group process, to fill in the scoring of each option against the criteria. Even if you are the only one who has investigated the options, others may have different interpretations to put on the facts that you have discovered, and there will be some discussion. Hopefully again a consensus should emerge regarding the scoring, but failing that you will have to impose your own scoring.

The scores are put into the table, each option being scored out of 10. Note: you don't score from 0 up to the weighting, but always from 0 to 10.

For each option, firstly it must fulfil the essential criteria, or it is a non-starter. If it does that, then *each score is multiplied by its criteria weight* and the total sum is recorded. For example:

		ADO	DAO	RDO	DB Vendor library
Efficiency	5	3	2?	1	10
Simple to call from C++	2	0	5?	5	6
Future-proof	3	7	8	8	4
Can call stored procedures	E	Yes	Yes	No	Yes
Simple client installation	2	10	0	10	10
Database independent	8	9	8	8	0
		128	108	NO	94

The option that meets all the essential criteria and has the highest score should be chosen.

In practice, the scores will probably be quite close (because if the decision was easy, you would not be using the matrix approach), so some more discussion and fiddling is likely to occur. At the end of the day however, the option with the highest score must always be chosen.

Quite often, not all of the values will be known and some will have to be guesstimated. These can be marked with question-marks as above. If one of these unknowns might potentially swing the decision another way, you may have to decide to defer the decision, pending a more thorough investigation. In the above example, if someone contends that the DAO option is extremely efficient and should score 9 against this criteria, this needs to be investigated before the decision can be made, as this would swing the decision decidedly in favour of DAO.

33

I HAVE TO TAKE A DECISION, AND IT INVOLVES TAKING A SIGNIFICANT RISK // HOW CAN I DECIDE WHETHER TO TAKE THE RISK?

Many organizations have adopted a policy of reducing the number of layers of management they have, and of pushing decisions down to the lowest level at which they can be made. Often this means that ordinary employees, rather than managers, have to make decisions of a sort they've not had to make before – bigger, more commercially sensitive, and riskier. In general, if not taken too far, this is a good thing, as decisions get made by the people 'on the spot' who really understand the issues, and people gain new control over their own working lives. This all sounds quite grand and empowering, but the everyday reality is that people end up having to make scary decisions without much support, because there is nobody else to make them.

Of course, you as a team leader should not have to make decisions that affect your whole department or your whole organization, at least not without significant support from other people, including management. But you may have to take risky decisions on your own project, and there may be nobody else to turn to.

I'm going to present to you a simple technique for making risky decisions. The idea is to provide you with a method you can actually follow in real life when a risky decision needs to be made. As well as coming up with a good decision, it provides a simple record of the decision-making process, which you can use to justify your decision to those who review it, and to defend yourself later if risks do happen and things turn out bad – more on this later.

Before starting to follow the process, you need to decide who will be involved. Who should make the decision? Who should be consulted?

Who will review it? Will you or someone else decide alone, or will it be a group decision? If a decision is risky, it's important to involve the right people, people who really understand the implications of the decision. The more people that are involved the better, as long as those people are knowledgeable about the decision. People who have a more peripheral interest in the process should be consulted and should be kept informed, but should not be allowed to influence the actual outcome by sheer weight of numbers, nor to slow it down by pointless discussions.

Let's do this by following through an example. Suppose you are working on a project where you've subcontracted some work out to another company, but you're unhappy with the results and you want to decide whether to bring the development work in-house. If you continue to subcontract then there is a risk that the results will be poor and need reworking, but if you bring the work in-house you will have to hire temporary staff to get the work done and this itself has risks as well as costs.

We start by drawing a diagram showing the possible options (two in this case). Note that there are always at least two options because there is always the 'do nothing, continue as before' option. For each option we can list the consequences of the decision going that way – both the certain consequences, and the risks that arise. Each risk has a cost and a likelihood (probability). For example:

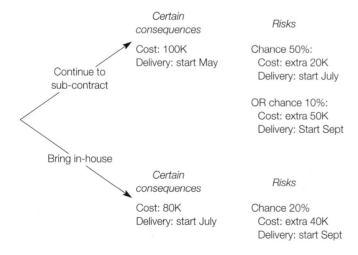

Certain consequences

Risks

Continue to sub-contract

Cost: 100K
Delivery: start May

Chance 50%:
  Cost: extra 20K
  Delivery: start July

OR chance 10%:
  Cost: extra 50K
  Delivery: Start Sept

Bring in-house

Certain consequences

Risks

Cost: 80K
Delivery: start July

Chance 20%
  Cost: extra 40K
  Delivery: start Sept

This diagram shows what is estimated to happen for each option. Of course, these are just 'guesstimates', made either by one person or by consensus of the people involved in the decision. For example, whoever made these estimates reckoned that if the work was brought in-house the cost would be 80K for sure, and the work could not be finished before July, with a 20% chance of it costing another 40K and not ending until September. These costs are mostly related to the delay, because they are costs of wages and overheads.

According to the textbooks, to make a balanced assessment of each choice, you now multiply each of the outcomes by their probabilities, and add up the result, thus giving you an 'expected' outcome. This is easy with money, but how do you do it with dates? Easy, you just work in terms of delays instead of dates. So a delivery in July is a 2 month delay from one in May, and if the chance of this is 10% then the 'expected' delay is 0.2 months.

Working this through for our example:

Continue to subcontract

Chance	Delay after start May	Cost		Expected delay	Expected cost
100%	0	100K		0	100K
50%	2 months	20K	➡	1 month	10K
10%	4 months	50K		0.4 months	5K
			Expected outcome:	1.4 months	115K

Bring in-house

Chance	Delay after start May	Cost		Expected delay	Expected cost
100%	2 months	80K	➡	2 months	80K
20%	4 months	40K		0.8 month	8K
			Expected outcome:	2.8 months	88K

We can show this as a revised version of the diagram:

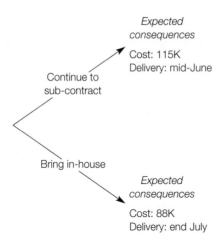

Expected consequences
Cost: 115K
Delivery: mid-June

Continue to sub-contract

Bring in-house

Expected consequences
Cost: 88K
Delivery: end July

Note that *whichever decision we make, we are not expecting to deliver at the start of May*. It would be foolish to make any promise to deliver in May. Even if we go for the quickest option, our expected delivery date is in June – and there is considerable uncertainty about it. This is the message you should give to your customers, not a promise to deliver at the start of May, which can only be achieved 'if everything goes right'. If you chose to continue to subcontract, you should quote Mid-June, and point out that there are risks involved – this is the balanced and mature way to deal with the risks.

It may be that you can make your decision from the information we have so far. There might be compelling reasons to choose the cheapest option, or, more frequently in our industry, the quickest option, or perhaps the lowest risk option. Or senior managers may decide that the decision must be made in the light of some corporate policy, such as 'we will reduce the amount of subcontracting we do as much as possible'.

If there is no such obvious way to decide, then the way to make the choice is to *convert the time element into money*, and make a purely finan-cial decision. The extra costs quoted in the example so far include wages for the in-house example, but that is far from being the whole story. To see why, let's take our example further. I'll throw in some extra facts (which relate time to money) and then we can see how to handle them:

1 We have already paid 20K to a third party to analyse our software and determine who best to subcontract it to. If we bring the work in-house, this money will have been wasted.

2 If we bring the work in-house then people will not be working on other projects. Typically, we would expect each person to contribute to about 10K of profit each month by working on profitable projects.

3 If we fail to deliver by Start August, we will lose a future contract from our customer that is worth 60K.

How should we handle these facts?

Item 1 should be *completely ignored*! The money was spent in the past and the *cost will not change no matter what we decide*. Concepts such as 'don't throw good money after bad' or conversely 'get value for what you have already spent' have no place in a balanced decision – make your estimates, add up the numbers, and use them. This sort of money, which has already been spent, is called a 'sunk cost', and is ignored.

Item 2 is an 'opportunity cost'. It represents the fact that if we make a decision to do more work, we close the door on other opportunities and so we lose the profit from them. Since many organizations are limited by the number of people they have, you need to include this factor otherwise you might take what seems to be a good decision if taken in isolation, but in fact ignores the fact that there are better things that people could be getting on with. **Opportunity costs are often large and any decision that excludes them will be very questionable.**

Item 3 is another opportunity cost, and we need to add it to the analysis.

Putting it all together:

Continue to subcontract:

Chance	Cost		Expected cost
100%	100K		100K
50%	20K		10K
10%	50K + 60K lost business		11K
		Total expected cost	121K

Bring in-house:

Chance	Cost	Expected cost
100%	80K + 20K opportunity cost	100K
20%	40K + 40K opportunity cost + 60K lost business	28K
	Total expected cost	128K

Drawing this again as a diagram:

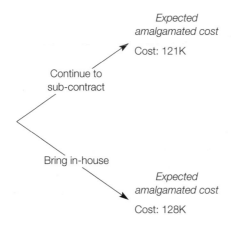

Expected
amalgamated cost
Cost: 121K

Continue to
sub-contract

Bring in-house

Expected
amalgamated cost
Cost: 128K

You may look at this and say 'whoa, that's too close to call!' and you might well be right. The fact is that these analyses usually do come out pretty close – because if the decision wasn't close and difficult, you wouldn't be doing the analysis at all. But what we have done is built up a profile of the choices in terms of time and money. Most people, given the above analysis, would feel quite comfortable in deciding to continue to subcontract – the expected cost is a smidgen lower (it's easy to forget that we're talking real money here – wouldn't you like another 7K in the bank one month?), and the expected delivery is sooner.

Of course, because things are so close you may be tempted to play with the figures, and in fact this is no bad thing – you might for example find that the outcome is very sensitive to one factor above all others. If you present this analysis to a group of people, the underlying estimates will no doubt be called into question at this point if not before. If it's your job to do the estimates, then stick to your guns and allow no changes to the figures at all unless you are genuinely persuaded that you made a mistake – do not give in to pressure to change your numbers just to make the desired result appear. If it's a case of gaining a consensus from the group for each of the estimates of costs, delays and probabilities, then accept the consensus and recalculate the numbers – and accept whatever result the analysis produces.

If you have converted time to money and included all opportunity costs, if one option has noticeably lower expected cost (or higher expected profit) than the other, then that option must be chosen.

If the result is still close, I would usually choose the option that produces a *quality result*, not a dirty fix, *in the least time*. Usually, time is more impor-tant than money in software – when things take longer, other projects get impacted, customers get upset, staff get demotivated – better to spend the money and get on with something else worth doing. This assumes of course that you have something else for people to do. If not, then the opportunity costs and the wages leave the equation, and the decision would be made in favour of the option with the lowest payments to third parties – in the example, if we had no other work to do, then we should decide to bring the work in-house and so save the money given to subcontractors.

Suppose you decide to continue to subcontract the work, and you tell people that the 'expected' delivery is in mid June – but the software is not finished until September. The costs escalate, you lose the extra order you were expecting, customers are upset. Does that mean that you made the wrong decision, and should have brought the work in-house? Almost certainly you will be told that you got it wrong – probably by someone quite senior. This is RUBBISH – if you made a decision to continue to subcontract, based on the above facts, which were the best available to you at the time, *then you made the right decision*, even if it turned out bad. The right decision can turn out bad, but that doesn't mean it was the wrong decision. It doesn't even mean it was the wrong decision made for the right reasons. It was the right decision. Risks may or may not happen, and nobody knows what would have happened if you chose to bring the work in-house.

'But,' you will be told by someone senior, 'you said the chance of this happening was only 10%. But it did happen! You got it wrong, it wasn't 10%, it happened!' More RUBBISH! Ten per cent chances happen – they happen one time in ten in fact. You made a balanced decision, fully including the possibility of the software being delayed until September – you did it right. In this circumstance, do not accept fault or blame, but defend yourself robustly, because you have nothing to be ashamed of.

As with any analysis, the benefits of doing the analysis are not in the paper that results – although that is useful in allowing others to understand and review your work and enabling you to defend it later – but in the fact that *it makes you think*. With difficult decisions it is far better to find some way of analysing them, rather than having all the issues going around in your head and then trying to make some judgement by gut feeling. Analysing the situation, letting others review your analysis, and making a balanced choice, results in a better quality decision and much less personal stress.

“In this world nothing can be said to be certain, except death and taxes.”

Benjamin Franklin

“Shit happens”

Anon

>> ANALYSIS AND DESIGN

34

IS 'ANALYSIS' REALLY NECESSARY, OR CAN I GO STRAIGHT INTO DESIGN?

Analysis is the work done to *understand what a system must do*. This is different from design, which is work done to decide *how to make a system that will achieve its purpose.*

Although analysis and design are often written about together, they are in fact very different processes. Analysis is part of understanding the requirements of a project – indeed, you may do analysis before requirements capture, or as part of your requirements capture process (see SECTION 25: 'REQUIREMENTS CAPTURE'). You may need to do analysis very early in the life of your project – sometimes before a bid can be made for the work – in order to understand exactly what you are required to do. But you shouldn't start design work until the requirements are well understood. Analysis is a process of gathering and collating information; design is a creative process of inventing solutions.

The key points to remember when performing analysis are as follows:

▶ **Identify the boundary of the work to be done**. For example, suppose you are going to automate some of the functions performed by clerks in a lending library. The paper-card system for tracking books is to be replaced by a computerized system. But where will that new system start and end? Will there still be people involved, entering information, or is the whole thing to be automated? If a book is overdue, will the system collect fines automatically from the borrower's credit card?

Where a system already exists – especially if it already includes human beings – it can be very hard to draw the line that represents the boundary of the new system. You must clearly identify this boundary, otherwise you may waste a huge amount of time in defining detailed requirements for completely the wrong areas of work.

If the purpose and boundary of the system to be developed is quite ill-defined, then you must spend significant effort clarifying it. If the system is to replace an existing system (whether manual or automated) it makes sense to first analyse that existing system, creating a model of how it works. It is essential that you then *draw a line through the system* to represent those parts which will be replaced or automated, and those that will not. You should not decide on the boundary on purely technical grounds, because the decision of what to replace or automate can have far-reaching financial implications and a very significant impact on the jobs of people who use the system. You must thoroughly consult users, and their managers, as part of the process of replacing any existing system.

Knowing the boundary of your project is absolutely fundamental. Do not start any detailed design work or sign any contracts until you know the limits of the work you are being asked to do.

▶ **Do as much analysis as the project requires**. Some projects should start with an extensive analysis phase. An example would be where a complex, business-critical, paper-based system is being replaced by an IT solution. Here it is essential to understand what the existing system does, where it works well and where not so well, and why it is to be automated. This will typically require a *thorough analysis of the system from the points of view of several different classes of user*. More on the importance of the users' perspective below.

At the other end of the scale, there are projects that require very little analysis. An example might be where a piece of embedded controller code is being ported from one processor platform to another or even from one language to another. In this case, although there may be stringent requirements to be met, there is no need to review afresh what the whole system does or how the embedded component fits into that system. A component is being replaced, it has a defined interface, and you can skip analysis completely and start at the design stage.

Of course, these are extreme examples and most projects fall somewhere along a continuum defined by these extremes. It is up to you to decide where your project falls on the continuum. *You need to do enough analysis to be sure that you understand the boundary and the scope of the system to be created*, so that you can identify the detailed requirements for it.

Of course, you should choose to use a tool or a method, or not to use it, on the basis of some knowledge and understanding of the options. Deciding that formal analysis methods are inappropriate for your project is one thing, deciding not to use them because you don't understand them, and have not tried to, is quite another. You need to keep up to date with the available options so that you can make a sound decision.

As well as benefits, there are drawbacks to using a predefined methodology.

▪ It will place constraints on the way your team works and affect the way people work together. These constraints are an intentional part of a methodology, which is intended to guide you and prevent bad practice. There are times when the constraints should be relaxed, but they may not be relaxed because the methodology prevents or discourages it.

▪ It will tend to make you look at issues from a certain point of view, which may not always be the appropriate point of view.

▪ Methodologies tend to attract a few purist devotees who will insist that the chosen method is the only one and true way to solve every problem. Such zealots are not helpful people on most practical engineering projects.

Use a methodology by all means, but don't let it use you.

Most projects suffer because of a mad dash to the coding stage, and analysis is one of the principal victims. Never believe there is insufficient time to do analysis – *make the time to do the level of analysis that needs to be done.*

To start into the design or code of a project without having done the level of analysis that is necessary is like starting out on a journey with no idea of where you are going.

▶ **Do the analysis in any appropriate way.** As long as the objective of analysis – understanding what the system must do – is achieved, it does not matter what techniques you use. Of course, some techniques are more appropriate in certain cases, and some tools can speed up the process. In the skills box below, I have given a very brief introduction to Use Cases, which are a powerful and useful tool for analysis. But don't let me or anyone else tell you that you *must* use Use Cases or any other method – as long as you succeed in understanding what your system must do then you are doing the job of analysis.

Talking to customers, talking to marketing and sales, creating mock-ups, explaining things on the whiteboard: these can all be components of an effective analysis process. You don't *have* to use any special tools or any defined methodology.

Defined methodologies such as Use Cases and other parts of UML (see APPENDIX 2: BRIEF INTRODUCTION TO UML) provide a common language and a guiding process to follow, which helps efficiency and communication and raises confidence. These are positive benefits, but there is nothing to prevent you from doing analysis without using a standard methodology if you so desire or if circumstances dictate.

▶ **Analysis should be based on a user's perspective.** Analysis takes a problem-domain view of a system, whereas design is based on a solution-domain view.

One problem with skipping analysis and going straight into design is that you miss out the user's perspective. It is all too easy to implement something that is quick to develop but not pleasant for the user to use. For example, suppose that we are going to write the software that controls a conveyor belt in a factory production line. The conveyor will go as fast as the factory process will allow. The operator will be given a user interface showing the speed of the conveyor, which will have colour coding to aid identification of the current situation (for example, a warning red colour if the conveyor is going very slowly). The mapping from speed to colour coding is to be user-configurable. In discussions with another supplier it has been decided that the colour coding for each conveyor will be stored in a database table. This is all quite tightly defined – the database already exists – and we might be tempted to go straight into design. If we do, most likely we will end up with a user interface design that shows a table of speed ranges for the conveyor, and lets the operator assign a colour to each – this matches very nicely with the database storage.

But suppose instead that we do some analysis, from the user's point of view. We ask ourselves 'what does the user want to achieve?'. The operator really isn't interested in assigning colours to speed ranges. What the operator wants to do is to achieve functions such as 'if the conveyor slows down because of a problem I know about, I want to be able to quickly set the warning level down just below the current speed, so it doesn't keep warning me about a problem I'm already dealing with'. This would lead us to give the operator quite a different user interface. It might, for instance, have a button specifically to implement the above function, setting the colour settings according to the current speed. This might be less convenient from a design point of view, but is far more appropriate to the way the system is to be used. Thinking from the user's point of view doesn't actually take much time, and it's amazing what a difference it can make to the solutions you come up with.

It is important to understand what each class of user needs, which involves understanding those aspects of their jobs that interact with the system. Spend time with users, talk to them wherever possible, rather than relying on second-hand opinions and marketing input.

Typically there is more than one class of user of a system. For example, an e-commerce system for selling goods over the internet might have customers accessing the website, purchasing staff who manage the stock of the company, financial staff who need reports of activity, and so on. There might even be significant sub-classes, for instance first-time customers versus existing customers. Each of these classes of user have different needs, skills and interests, which you must take into account when designing the software systems that will power the website.

Some 'users' of the system may themselves be other software components rather than people. Of course these 'users' will not be upset by an interface that is difficult to use, but it is still essential to analyse from the user's point of view. It still makes perfect sense to consider the services and facilities your users expect, and the nature of the interfaces they will need, even if those users are machines.

See also the infobar // ANALYSIS FROM A USER'S PERSPECTIVE IN OO.

The user's perspective is the most important when analysing a system, but other viewpoints should also be considered, especially when thinking about the boundary and scope of the project:

■ Your customer may not want the same as the end users. You have to satisfy your customer. Even if your customer is an internal one, you cannot ignore their stated requirements even if you believe it would be in the interests of end users.

■ There are times when you should be quite selfish and ask what is best to do from your own organization's point of view. Most organizations do not exist to satisfy end users, they exist to make money.

■ In a public-sector project, you should consider what is best from the taxpayers' point of view.

The user's view is so important because quality of a product is often defined as its 'fitness for purpose' – meaning the user's purpose.

Actually the product also has a purpose for the people who sell it, and so quality can be looked at in another way altogether – the fitness for the vendor's purpose of making money.

infobar // ANALYSIS FROM A USER'S PERSPECTIVE IN OO

If you're adopting an object oriented approach (see APPENDIX 1: INTRODUCTION TO OBJECT-ORIENTED CONCEPTS), part of the job of analysis is to *identify classes of objects and their interactions, in the problem domain*. Problem-domain items will become candidates for solution-domain items when you move into design.

An easy way to transition from requirements, to analysis, and then to design in an OO project is to make an OO model representing the problem domain. Identify classes, and their responsibilities, interactions and attributes, in the problem domain. These may not make sense in the final design, but if they help to explain how the problem is structured, they will help to guide good design.

Wherever possible, objects in code should represent real-world objects in the problem domain, including their state and behaviour. The real world is full of objects and using software objects to represent them is an ideal use of OO technology. Usually, a design built around classes of objects in the problem domain will be much more appropriate than one made of classes thought up with the intention of making the design or coding easy.

If your users or your requirements documents keep using particular nouns, these are good candidates for problem domain classes. For instance, in a lending library system we might be told that 'when an item has been on loan beyond its return date, a fine will become due'. From this we can spot the nouns 'item' and 'fine', and these are worth considering for classes. 'Item' might have a 'return date' attribute, and there is even the hint of a possible state model operating as the item becomes overdue. These may or may not be directly converted into the solution domain when you come to design, but they are still worth capturing as classes of an analysis that represents the problem domain.

▶ **Use analysis to make more money**. Analysis often overlaps to a very large extent with requirements capture. Taking the example of the conveyor system above, it could be that your customer has listed the requirements of the operator user interface, and there seems to be little analysis needed. However, many customers are not experienced in specifying computer systems, and if you do some analysis and consider the situation:

■ You might come up with some useful ideas to present to your customer. These may turn into new requirements, for which you can charge more money and make more profit.

- You may impress the customer that you're really thinking about what you're doing. This may lead to more orders, and hence more profit, in future.

- At the very least the customer may give you some reason why your analysis is flawed, in which case you will have learnt something more about the job in hand. Learning about the requirements is vital in avoiding costly mistakes, and leads to a cleaner product and more profitable outcome.

Analysis is not a pure overhead, non-productive task, it is part of doing efficient and profitable software development.

▶ **Move between analysis and design as appropriate.** Some textbooks tell you not to start the design until the whole analysis and the requirements process is entirely complete and signed off. It never happens that way in practice.

Certainly, you should not proceed with the design until you understand what it is that you are trying to design. But analysis is a process of elucidation, of seeing the way ahead. There comes a time when you have done enough analysis and requirements capture to be clear enough about the overall purpose of the project, and at this stage there is no harm in doing some top-level design. Indeed I think it a very good idea. The architectural design often clarifies the issues, identifying new problems or issues to be addressed in the analysis.

Crucially, doing the top-level design will enable you to start thinking about the roles of the people on your team, which will probably be organized around the top-level structure of the design.

When you do the top-level design you may spot fundamental issues left to be resolved in the analysis. For instance, interfaces and interactions with external systems may seem clear until you try to put together a system to integrate with all those systems. It pays to identify such problems early on, and this can safely continue in parallel with more detailed analysis and requirements capture.

Good working practices are often iterative – you do a little analysis, then a little design, then loop back to fill in some gaps in the analysis. This is not an excuse for chaos. When you are designing you should know that you are designing, and you should know how much analysis still needs to be done, but each activity provides insight into the other.

Sometimes there are contractual pressures to get the analysis completed and approved before design starts. In practice the only way to proceed is to iterate, as set out in this section, performing some design as part of the process of elucidating the requirements.

See SECTION 35: ARCHITECTURE AND DESIGN

▶ **Use analysis to help testing**. Analysis at the start of a project can improve the quality of testing at the end, and also speed up the process, by providing good tests almost ready-made.

Both design and testing benefit from analysis, but testing, like analysis, is in the solution domain. If you think about testing as you do analysis you will not get dragged into the problem domain, as you might if you think about design.

▶ **Prototypes are often a good way to do analysis**. If your project is heavily centred around a user interface, then creating a mock-up and letting users or marketing people play with it is a great way of getting to understand more about what they want.

If you take a fairly structured approach to this, the benefits can be especially large. What I mean by 'structured' in this case is that you don't just let the user 'play' with the user interface (although there should be some time for this as well). Instead, make the user think about how they would use the software to do real jobs.

Try to take a 'this is how you do this job...' approach, rather than 'this is what this feature does...'. Try to get the user into their normal working mind-set and get them to walk through the jobs – all of the jobs – that they really want to do. For example, users don't have needs such as 'moving text to the right' – they have needs such as 'writing a letter'.

Get the user to talk to you about what they are trying to do and how, and take notes of things they cannot do, mistakes they make or confusions that arise. If the user gets confused by the interface, try to resist the temptation of blaming the user, and instead think how you could make it more obvious in future.

It is worth mentioning a few dangers about a prototype-driven approach, however. Firstly, there are still plenty of users and managers around who think that software is not much deeper than the user interface, and so if they see a nearly finished interface, they think the project is nearly done. I even had this happen on a body-scanner project, where a manager saw a mock-up user interface and thought the project was nearly done, even though nobody had created the actual body-scanning machine yet! You need to beware of giving such people a false expectation of progress. One way to do this is to create several small prototypes for different parts of the system, to make the point that you are still putting things together.

Secondly, engineers often get carried away about making a lovely user interface, and spend far too much time on it. But the whole idea of the prototyping exercise is that you want the interface to get changed – you want to find out how to make it better. Spending ages on an early version makes no sense as the effort may be thrown away. Even though they know this, most engineers can't resist finishing off the interesting parts, making pretty icons and so on. One way to stop this is to put a strict deadline on the prototype work if there is not one already, and get the best done that can be done within a certain time.

Lastly, and perhaps most importantly, is the fact that almost no code that is written as a 'temporary throw-away' actually gets thrown away. It usually gets used in the product in one way or another. This is a real problem because prototype code is often thrown together with little regard for the rules of good design, commenting, error checking and so on, and often without proper reviews. There is nothing wrong with building prototypes this way – the code is temporary after all, and likely to be frequently changed and only run by developers, so you don't need to make it bullet-proof. But again you need to beware of creating false expectations in managers, and you need to build in a very definite 'tidy-up' phase into your project to convert the prototype code into production quality code. In particular, in a prototype you will not have worried about structure and interfaces. The first thing you need to do with a prototype when it starts to become real code is to put in place the correct structure and interfaces, as the later this is left the harder it gets.

One advantage of doing prototypes is that it keeps hands-on developers busy. In a team of people, *it usually does not make sense for everyone to be analysing*, then all stop and everyone starts designing – this would not make good use of the mix of skills and aptitudes found in most teams, and it would suppress a good flow of ideas from one stage of the project to another. Some developers have no aptitude for analysis or requirements capture and only want to code, and throwing together prototypes is a good use for such people in the early stages of a project.

▶ **Beware of getting stuck**. A few projects suffer from an excess of analysis, known as 'paralysis by analysis', forever going back over the requirements and the architecture, reconsidering the same issues again and again (rather than merely elucidating finer levels of detail). This is a sign that something is very seriously wrong. If you find yourself in this situation, take a good step back and see if you can find some fundamental problems either with the inputs the project team is being given, or with the make-up of the team.

It is quite common for non-technical managers to get confused between demos, samples, test benches and prototypes, and to assume that one piece of code can do all four jobs. Before you make one of these things, be certain which category it falls into, as they are largely self-exclusive. The options are:

■ Demos – designed to look good and show off fancy features, but may have very little useful function. The code does not have to be brilliantly structured or commented but it must be robust.

■ Samples – designed to be provided to other programmers, to help them understand how to use components that you supply. The code must be very neat and well commented, with a bare minimum of functionality in order to reduce complexity.

■ Test benches – designed to check that code under development is working, by exercising it through many conditions, including error conditions. May have a very simple and dull user interface, and the code may be very repetitive and not necessarily very well structured or commented.

■ Prototypes – designed to answer questions about user interfaces or technical feasibility. The design and the code can justifiably be truly awful, as long as the question is properly answered.

Not every project needs lots of analysis, but most do benefit from it. It puts the project on a firm footing and gets you in the habit of looking at things from the user's point of view, right from the start. Methodologies such as Use Cases (see below) can help communication and can make the process more thorough, but are not essential. All that matters in the end is that you achieve the aim of finding out exactly what the system you are going to design needs to do.

> skills box

USE CASES

If you have not used Use Cases, they are well worth getting to know. This is a very brief introduction to them. Here I show a textual way of doing Use Cases, although there are also diagramming methods that can be used – see the Object Oriented Analysis and Design section of the bibliography (SECTION 42) for some suitable further reading. Use Cases are part of UML (see APPENDIX 2: BRIEF INTRODUCTION TO UML), although actually there is very little that is object-oriented about them.

Use Cases are a powerful way of elucidating the interfaces between a system and other systems or its users. One Use Case describes *one use of the system* – one specific interaction with it, not a general pattern of interaction. Error scenarios and alternative paths can be spelled out in the use case, or might be put into separate use cases.

Here is a very simple example of one Use Case for a bank teller (ATM) machine. In real life this would be one of a set of use cases for different interactions with the machine. The full set of use cases would include use by customers, by bank staff, and by other computer systems communicating with the machine.

Title/brief description

Customer obtains cash from their account.

Main flow

1 User approaches machine and observes that it is in service. Machine prompts user to insert card.

2 User inserts card. Either way up/either way round.

3 Machine prompts user for PIN.

4 User enters PIN.

5 Machine checks account and PIN details and finds them correct (see Error 1 below if the PIN is wrong). Machine displays list of cash values (quick list plus option to enter own amount).

6 User selects one cash value.

7 Machine returns card.

8 User takes card. See Alternate 1 if they fail to take it.

9 Machine vends cash. Any legal combination of notes is allowed.

10 User takes cash.

11 Machine prints receipt.

12 User takes receipt.

13 Machine returns to state of waiting for next customer.

cont >>

\>\>

Alternate flows

Alternate 1 – User fails to take card back

At point 8 above, if the user fails to take back their card, after 30 seconds the machine will withdraw it and place it in its secure card bin. No cash will be issued. The user's account will not be debited. The account will not be marked as invalid.

Error flows

Error 1 – User enters illegal PIN

The user will be given three attempts to get the PIN right. At any stage, they may give up and withdraw the card. The count of attempts is held globally so it applies to any machine. It is not reset to zero until the next day. If they fail on the third attempt, the card is withdrawn and the user's account is marked as invalid.

Whilst doing this analysis, you come across all sorts of issues that might otherwise crop up much later and cause major design headaches. For instance, what happens if the user does not take their receipt? Does the machine have to suck it back in after some time and dispose of it? If so, this implies more hardware, and a bin to store the paper. It may be that receipt printers cannot be purchased with this facility, and another mechanical unit will be needed to suck the paper back in – which will have a direct impact on the top-level structure of your design.

Also, by thinking from the user's point of view, a bit of psychology can come in. Is it really best to give the receipt last – won't some people walk away without waiting for it to appear? Why not dispense the cash last, as they're not likely to walk away without that?

Use cases are great for generating test cases. As you can see from the above example, it is very easy to turn a use case into one or more useful tests.

Whilst purists will tell you that you must complete the entire set of use cases for a system before starting design, I consider this to be unrealistic and excessive. *You need to do sufficient analysis that you don't stumble across problems in the design and so waste work.* Stop analysing when you judge this criterion to be met – it could take five Use Cases, it could take five hundred. For example, I see no need to do a Use Case for entering the PIN number, complete with details of correcting mistakes etc. This sort of detail can be left to the detailed design stage as it does not impact the architecture of the design.

Use cases are a powerful tool, but they are not without problems. They can take a long time to generate. It is difficult to avoid duplication. And they are very function-oriented, making them hard to use for non-functional issues such as performance, robustness, 'touch and feel' or marketing acceptance. Nevertheless they are a great tool to have in your tool-box and well worth using to a greater or lesser extent on almost every project.

35

HOW DO I DECIDE ON THE BEST ARCHITECTURE AND DESIGN FOR MY PROJECT?

When you're faced with a whole system to design, it can be overwhelming. There is often so much freedom of choice, so many possible options, that it's hard to get anywhere without changing your mind. Breaking the problem down into a collection of smaller problems makes it easier to tackle. As one guru observed, 'How do you eat an elephant? One bite at a time.'

Design is the most creative aspect of software development. There is no simple routine that will convert a set of requirements into a solution. There are usually many possible solutions, and good designers learn to consider several options in succession and pursue the most promising.

The most top-level view of your design is called the architecture. The architecture is the block diagram of packages or components that are responsible for major parts of the system. In a distributed system, the top-level blocks might be separate executables, plus shared libraries that will be used in several executables. Typical examples of top-level blocks are user interface, database, business logic, machine control, but it can be anything that makes sense to your project. Breaking the problem down in this way makes it more manageable.

There really is no difference between designing an architecture and doing the detailed design. Architecture simply refers to the most top-level design view.

Whether you and your team have to design a whole system, or just a small part of a bigger system into which you must integrate, makes no difference. There will be a top level of design that is fundamentally intended to fulfil your requirements, and below this there will be levels of detailed design. Quite often there is little freedom over the architecture as much of it may have been specified or assumed for you, whilst you will have more discretion in the details. Even so, you should always analyse the architecture you've been given and verify to your own satisfaction that it is suitable for the job.

Design is best done by a group of people, rather than just one. Different people have different experiences and skills to bring to the process, and so when more people are involved there is more scope for a creative solution. Invite anyone to attend who can make a contribution. Invite junior engineers who can learn something from it or who will contribute (if only by asking sensible questions). Don't invite non-technical managers – if they need to be involved, do this by allowing them to review the results later.

Unfortunately, along with their useful skills, people also bring strong preferences and preconceptions to the design process, and so quite often there will be disagreements that tend to polarize into 'his design versus mine'. When two or more competing approaches are proposed, people will often look to the leader to decide between them. Usually this is not an easy thing to do, as each design may have its good and bad points. It is usually not a good thing to do either. Rather than deciding between the proposed designs, it is often better to act as a mentor and sounding-board. Bring people together for design discussions, and play your part by identifying the good and bad points of each design and encouraging the whole team to look for a new design, one that incorporates as many of the good points as possible whilst removing the bad points. Act more as a facilitator than a decision maker, encouraging people to make creative and constructive contributions, and to accept valid criticism of their designs and opinions.

When one of the designs is yours, defend it as you would expect anyone else to do, but don't try to give it precedence over the other options.

Help people to take an outward-looking view, evaluating how appropriate the designs are from the viewpoint of the system architecture or even from the user's view; discourage people from favouring options on the basis of what is easiest to develop in the short term.

Usually, a consensus will emerge as the design options improve and converge. Your job is to guide and enable this process of design change. Engineers get emotionally attached to their designs, and there is often a need to propose some creative compromises in order to get people out of an entrenched position of 'defending their design'.

It also happens that people can become so eager to avoid further disagreement that they accept a poor design, just to avoid friction. If you see people starting to agree on a design that is simply not good enough then say so, and make sure a new round of discussion is started and a new consensus approached.

Arguments in design discussions are not uncommon, nor necessarily unhealthy, as mentioned in SECTION 28: ARGUMENTS. Allow constructive argument, as it leads to consensus. Only if a consensus fails to emerge and discussions are getting nowhere should you start to make decisions in favour of one design and against another. If you do get to this stage, this is indicative of serious problems with the make-up of your team or with one or more individuals on your team. A team that can't agree on a design is unlikely to work properly together at all. See SECTION 22: SOME-ONE WHO'S A REAL PROBLEM for more about problem people.

Although there is no fixed procedure to produce the best design, there are certain guiding principles that should be followed in order to produce a design that will be easy to implement, test and maintain, and will get the most from the people on the team. Here are my 'general design golden rules' to help you produce good designs and judge the designs of others:

1   **A good design consists of a simple framework, beneath which the details are hidden.** When you look at the details, you again find a simple framework, with further details hidden. At every level of detail, you find a self-contained system, one that does not rely on the detailed design of other systems.

The way to produce such a design is to build the design *top-down*. Later, you do the coding *outside-in*. Let me explain that!

By doing the design 'top-down', I don't mean that you start at the top of the page and work down! What I mean is that you draw the big picture first, breaking the problem down into a few architectural blocks. Think about what these blocks are for, what their interfaces will look like, and how they will be used.

Then step into each of these blocks, and again break them down into smaller units. In some cases, you may have only one level of block diagrams, with each of the blocks being made up of modules or classes. In larger designs, blocks may contain blocks for a few levels until you get to the level of detail where individual modules or classes appear.

Having done the design 'top-down', you should then do the coding 'outside-in'. What I mean by this is: code the interfaces first, then step into the implementation.

Create the top-level architecture code, write the interfaces in detail, fill the implementation with dummy stubs, and get the components all present and compiled.

See also SECTION 36: OBJECT-ORIENTED DESIGN, which contains some more design rules specifically tailored to object-oriented designs.

Another phrase for the 'top-down' approach is 'divide and conquer'. This is very memorable and graphic but unfortunately open to misinterpretation by some people, who take the phrase to mean that you should divide and conquer the other people on your team!

Then write the test code that will drive the production code, through its interfaces. Writing the test code before the code under test helps to 'sanity-check' the interfaces from an external point of view, before any real implementation is done, and it enables unit testing to start straight away.

The job of writing the actual implementation then becomes one of filling in the gaps, implementing already defined interfaces. As you write the implementation you can start testing it immediately, using the test benches already created.

Whilst design is often an iterative process, the higher the level in the design, the less iteration there should be. It is essential that the top-level architecture is agreed and stable early in the design process, and that the interfaces between the components are clean, simple and very well specified. These interfaces specify what each component does and how it responds to inputs. At the architectural level every aspect of the interfaces should be considered, to explicitly state the expected pre-conditions, post-conditions, error conditions and exceptional events that could arise.

At lower levels of the design, the same degree of *up-front* specification and rigidity is not necessary and indeed often not healthy. At the lowest level of modules and classes, the interfaces should be well defined in the end (possibly only as well-commented code), but this can come as the result of a few levels of iteration around design, code and test. The interfaces of a module or class must be designed before coding, but the exact details can be allowed to change as the implementation reveals possible small improvements in the original design.

It is not acceptable to be so relaxed about iteration at the architectural level, as small changes here may imply large changes to the detailed design and code, which would be very costly. Iterate around the architectural design as you consider it and review it, but don't step into the details until you're sure that the architecture will meet all your needs and is going to be very stable from now on.

2   **In a good design, components do as they are told and know as little as possible about who is telling them, or about the structure of the system in which they operate.** At the top level, good designs often have a *layered approach*, where higher-level packages know about lower-level packages, whilst lower-level packages are 'slaves' that do as they are told and know nothing about the package that is using them.

This approach of top-down design, followed by outside-in coding, is especially effective in OO projects, see SECTION 36: OBJECT-ORIENTED DESIGN.

At the top level of a design, every component should be sufficiently independent that it can be tested through its interfaces. For example, a database system should be testable through a test-bench that feeds it data and queries – including erroneous ones – without relying on the presence of a real front-end system. Of course, a component may be built on top of libraries and packages that must be present in order for it to work, but it should not make any assumptions about how it will itself be used or what will drive it, except that its interface must be adhered to.

At the lowest level of detail, this isolation and purity may not be so complete. Modules or classes need to work closely together to get the job done, so they will have to know about each other and understand something about the system in which they are operating. Nevertheless it remains a solid principle that things should do as they are told, and make the minimum number of assumptions about who is telling them or about the structure or behaviour of the system in which they are used. Certainly, any assumptions that a module or class does make about the rest of the design must be strictly limited to its local neighbourhood of collaborating modules or classes.

3 **Consider both the static structure and the dynamic operation at each level of detail.** Static diagrams are like the designs for the construction of a machine, but dynamic diagrams are more like a video of the machine in operation. Both views are very useful in designing a system that will work properly, and in explaining its operation.

Sequence diagrams, as defined in UML (see APPENDIX 2: BRIEF INTRODUCTION TO UML), are especially good for capturing the details of interfaces, as well as the way a system operates in response to external events. They can be used whether the design is object oriented or not.

A good way to generate the dynamic diagrams is to write Use Cases (see SECTION 34: IS 'ANALYSIS' NECESSARY?) to determine exactly what the system must do, and then draw one or more sequence diagrams for each use case.

The infobar // EXAMPLE DESIGN, illustrates these first three points further.

4 **The logical organization of the design should be reflected in the physical organization of the code, and also in the organization of the people on the project.** The packages in your design represent logical sets of work at design time. When you come to implement the code, create physical objects – executables, libraries, or whatever – that match the logical

Together, points 1 and 2 are intended to encourage designs that have *strong encapsulation*, where packages and modules expose well-defined interfaces for the caller to use, and hide all information about how they work. I find poor encapsulation to be easy to see in code but hard to spot in a design, and so I have presented the issue as these two points that are easier to see in a design. A design that adheres to the principles in these points should have good encapsulation, as well as other beneficial design properties.

design, one-to-one. This should be done right at the start, when your code is just a framework shell.

Organize the people on the team so that each person is primarily involved with one package, or one part of one package. Delegate work and responsibility to people on the basis of the design, so that each person has a cohesive lump of work that is their own responsibility. This works much better than allocating work on the basis of functionality.

Sometimes there are different architectural options that have little to choose between them technically, but if you consider how to organize the people on the project you immediately see that one option is much more appropriate with the people available. Keep people in mind even when making purely technical decisions.

5 **Efficiency doesn't matter.** Never be influenced by the efficiency of implementation when considering a design, when this is of no practical relevance.

For example, in order to obtain a clean design it is sometimes necessary to 'wrap' or hide lower-level libraries, writing calls that do nothing except call another package to do the work. Typically this happens when a simple interface has to be created out of a subset of several other interfaces. In a typical situation, the loss of efficiency caused by adding these do-nothing delegation calls will add up to a few nanoseconds every second, and will be totally inconsequential in any way. Despite this, some developers will be adamant that this reduced efficiency proves, categorically, that the design without the wrapping interface is better.

They are wrong. Efficiency proves nothing one way or the other. The design with the wrapper is better if it simplifies the design overall (improving maintainability and flexibility), it is worse if it adds unnecessary complexity for little benefit. Efficiency just doesn't come into it.

Of course there are times when efficiency does matter, but these are precious few compared to the number of times when design matters (which is all the time). If in doubt, go for the cleaner design, and add some means to improve efficiency later if necessary.

If you know for certain that certain efficiency measures will be needed – caching of huge files from a slow server, for example – then of course this should be designed in from the start, but otherwise efficiency should be ignored during design.

If an executable or library is sufficiently complex that the individual modules or classes within it need to be organized into groups of related items, it is often better to make these groups into sub-libraries and build the final component from these libraries. This enforces encapsulation, enables detailed unit testing, and speeds compilation.

You should always allow some time in your plan for optimization. Often it is best to leave this to the end of the project, when the final system is being integrated, rather than investigating the speed of individual units using test benches. It is often only when the final system is running that you find the real bottlenecks, and these are the ones where your optimization effort should be concentrated. Experience shows that it is often hard to predict where efficiency problems will appear, and it is better to wait for the facts (and have time to act on them) than to try to second-guess all the problems before they occur.

6 **Keep the design up to date.** As people start coding they will find minor things they want to change in the design. When this happens, make sure they don't let the design get out of date, or it will quickly become unusable. When someone finds a design problem, even a minor one, they must stop coding (close the compiler), and start designing. Only when they have found a design solution should they start implementing again. If someone tells you that they had to change the design, make sure they did it to the design, not to the code.

Note that the more design you do up-front, the smaller the changes that can be made during coding, without looping back to design. This is one reason why it is not *always* sensible to do the maximum amount of design that is possible before starting to code (see SECTION 18: THEY JUST WANT TO CODE).

These points encourage designs that facilitate easy coding and testing, and have flexibility to cope with requirement and design changes, resulting in a smooth-running and successful implementation.

infobar // **EXAMPLE DESIGN**

Here are some example diagrams that illustrate the first three design rules. These diagrams show various views of a system that monitors a production line in a factory.

The following diagram shows the top-level architectural design, showing physical computers, platforms, executables and databases. In this particular example, the packages that make up some of the executables have also been shown. Some of these packages are used in only one executable, some are libraries used by several executables on the project, and although this is not explicitly indicated the Comms library is in fact part of a company-wide framework of libraries used across multiple projects:

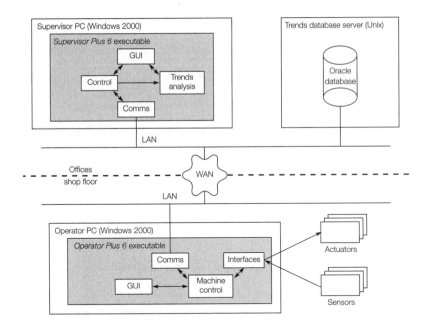

The above diagram is very much a physical view of the system, which will be especially useful to system administrators and service personnel. The following diagram represents a more logical view of the system, which will allow us to more clearly identify the interfaces:

cont >>

>>

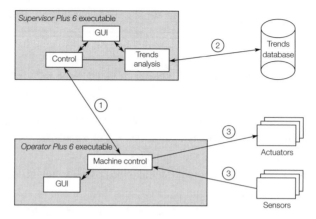

Interfaces

1 Supervisor 4 protocol (see document sup4prt01.doc) over LAN/WAN using standards Comms library

2 SQL over ODBC

3 IEE488 using standard Interfaces library

As we step into the detailed design of the GUI package of Operator Plus 6, we see the components that make up that package. In this example this next level of detail goes straight down to the level of individual classes (this example is an object-oriented design drawn with UML; see the appendices if these concepts or notations are unfamiliar to you). We can see the classes and their relationships, and the names of the most important method calls of some of the classes.

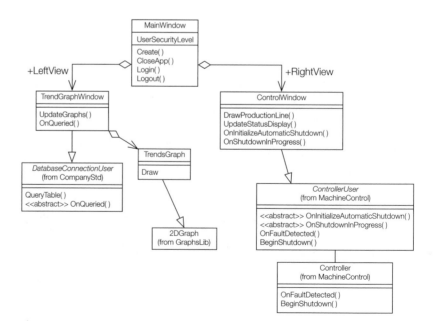

In addition to this picture, there would need to be some description of the responsibilities of each class – this text might be stored in the design tool if one were used to draw the diagram, or maybe in a document that accompanies the diagrams.

Here is an example sequence diagram for the top level of the system. This sequence shows the way the components work together to shut down the production line in the event of a sensor detecting that a component of the production line has failed, which would result in all production being defective (Sequence diagrams like these flow easily from Use Cases, see SECTION 34: ANALYSIS).

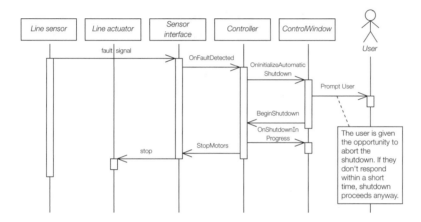

(This diagram includes some objects that are not in the software packages shown so far – for example, the sensor and actuator are real objects sending messages electrically, not software components.)

As well as documenting how the system works, these sequence diagrams are part of the specification of the interfaces between the components of the system. For example, this diagram shows that the controller part of the supervisor system can be sent a message 'begin shutdown', and it shows how the controller will respond.

You can see that this design conforms to the first three rules in the main text:

1 Simple at each level of detail, with further details hidden. The detailed design is not apparent in the architectural design, nor is it necessary in order to understand the architecture. Nothing is lost from the understanding of the architecture by hiding the details.

cont >>

>>

2 Layering and master–slave relationships. An example of this is the Comms library, which is being used by other packages. The library can know nothing about what is driving it, which allows it to be easily and flexibly reused.

Also, in the detailed design we can see that the Controller has been implemented using an abstract interface (see APPENDIX 3: A COUPLE OF USEFUL OO TECHNIQUES), meaning that the Controller knows nothing about its user except that it is a ControllerUser.

We can see that the classes in the package shown in the detailed design do not rely on the contents or structure of other packages, and so there should be a high degree of encapsulation. The sequence diagram tends to support this, showing a simple interface for example between the sensor interface and the controller. There is a more complex, detailed interaction between Controller and ControllerWindow, but these classes are in the same package and closely interacting so this is appropriate.

3 Both static views and dynamic views have been shown, and you can see how each provides an insight into the other.

36

WE HAVE ADOPTED AN OBJECT-ORIENTED APPROACH, BUT EVERYONE ON THE TEAM SEEMS TO HAVE A DIFFERENT IDEA ABOUT HOW BEST TO USE IT // HOW SHOULD AN OBJECT-ORIENTED APPROACH BE USED?

This section is intended for someone who is familiar with OO technology as a developer, but not necessarily as a team leader. If you are not confident of the basics of OO, for instance if words like 'inheritance' and 'polymorphism' are not totally familiar to you, then please see APPENDIX 1: INTRODUCTION TO OBJECT-ORIENTED CONCEPTS, before returning to this section.

As well as these specific rules, it is also worth emphasizing the importance of the general design golden rule number 3, 'Consider both the static structure and the dynamic operation at each level of detail', in an object-oriented context. An object-oriented design is not complete unless both aspects have been considered. In OO, much behaviour emerges from the interaction of objects, and so this interaction must be designed.

For some reason, there seem to be more design disagreements when OO is used than when a structured design approach is adopted. I don't know why this should be, but in general it seems to be a healthy thing. Provided that people are willing to listen to each other, a better design will usually emerge as the result of such disagreements. Design discussions not only improve the design, they also give people a sense of ownership over it, and help to build team spirit.

You should make sure that design meetings are held for the larger design issues, and let individual engineers fill in the detailed design. *Make sure that all designs are reviewed before they are coded.* I believe it is essential in an OO project to hold design reviews for the detailed design. Two heads are better than one and it is worth the time and the slight discomfort of a review to improve the quality of the design. Junior engineers should have their design work reviewed by someone more senior, whereas senior people with good design skills can be left to organize peer reviews between themselves. Design reviews appear to be more important, and also more effective, when OO is used. See SECTION 4: WHEN SHOULD I REVIEW OTHER PEOPLE'S WORK? concerning reviews.

The following points are my 'OO design golden rules', which should be taken conjunction with the 'general design golden rules' listed in SECTION 35: ARCHITECTURE AND DESIGN. The following points have value in any design but are especially important in an OO context, which places special emphasis on clarity of concepts.

1   **Keep it conceptually clean.** For example, never allow an inheritance relationship between classes where it is not 100% clear that the derived

class 'is a' specialized type of the base class. Conceptual mess leads to messy code which leads to slower development, bugs and maintenance nightmares.

If you come across a conceptual design flaw, stop and put it right. Unless you're extremely close to the end of your project – like nearing final test – it will be well worth the disruption and delay.

This sort of problem is much less likely to happen if you have done some analysis before you do design – see SECTION 34: ANALYSIS, especially the infobar // ANALYSIS FROM A USER'S PERSPECTIVE IN OO.

Classes, attributes and interactions in the solution should be based on real-world classes of objects in the problem domain. Almost always, basing your design around classes of objects familiar to a user of the system will produce a comprehensible and straightforward design, whereas thinking purely in terms of what is easy to develop will actually produce the opposite, a design that is hard to understand and to develop. For example, suppose we are making an application to edit 'build trees' (these are used in industry to define the structure of components to be manufactured – component A is assembled from sub-components C and D etc., forming a tree structure). If we take a problem-domain approach we will have classes such as Component, and each Component would have a list of 'child' Components that it is assembled from. But if we take a solution-domain approach we might base the design around the table structure of a relational database where the data is stored, and so the Component would not have a list of sub-components, instead most likely each Component would know the identity of its parent, and would know nothing about its children, because that's the way tree structures traditionally have to be stored in a relational database. This may seem to make things easier, as the data structure in the code will match that in the database, but you won't get far into the design before you realize that everything the user wants to do relies on quickly finding the children of components, propagating changes down recursively to all children, moving and deleting sub-trees and so on – things that would be much easier with the problem-domain-based design.

In a few places this guiding principle of modelling the problem domain has to be broken because software doesn't work like the real world. For example, the real world doesn't have problems with passing ownership of objects around, and parallel processing is not an issue either. If solution-domain issues like these matter in your program, it is far better to invent a solution-domain manager class to handle them, than to try to spread the necessary smart behaviour around every object in the system.

2   **Think about the responsibilities of the packages and classes in the design.** That word 'responsibilities' really sums up what a class or package is about. What is it for? What is it in charge of doing? Concentrating on this word 'responsibility' can help you to avoid all sorts of design flaws.

That's not to say that every class must be responsible for a significant amount of behaviour. Some classes are just data structures, responsible for holding data, nothing more, and that's fine.

For example, one place where I find this word to be very useful is when people are arguing about how clever an object should be. In a 'paint' program, for example, people might disagree on how clever the Image class containing an image should be. Should it, for example, have methods such as Blur to blur the image, or should this be done by a method of some other class, acting on an image?

The answer depends on what an Image means in a paint program. Conceptually, is an image something that blurs itself, or is an image something that is blurred? Is it the *responsibility* of an Image to blur itself, or does it fit better within the responsibility of some other class to blur images?

Whilst many developers would instinctively add behaviour to the Image class, on the basis that smart classes are better than dumb ones, I believe that it is quite often a mistake. The word 'responsibility' often helps me decide what is conceptually appropriate.

3   **Keep the interfaces clean, and keep them one-to-one.** For example, if you have some classes that are calling each other as shown below:

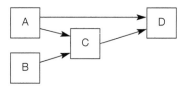

then it may be better to give D a one-to-one interface:

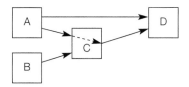

The dotted path through C will just be a simple delegation: A calls C and C makes a call straight to D.

People not used to OO may claim that having lots of do-nothing calls is a sign of stupid design, but in fact it is usually the opposite. In the example above, we have now made C uniquely *responsible* for D. Ownership and control have been clarified. In the future, if we want to make the system smarter, we have a place inside C where extra smarts can be added for controlling D more precisely. Or D could be removed or replaced completely, without affecting A or B.

It will also be much easier to test C now, because nothing is 'going round its back' to D and confusing the situation.

This is just an example, and it would not always make sense to remove direct associations between classes if they are working closely together. The point is that you should consider this option, and if it simplifies the design and the interfaces of the classes then you should clean up the design, even if you know that this will result in a little tedious programming when you come to code.

4   **Names matter**. The name of a package, class, relationship or whatever is important. It should succinctly describe what the thing does, what it is responsible for, but not how it does it.

The name of a class should encompass all of its responsibilities. If something is called 'Truck' then it ought to encapsulate the state and behaviour of a truck. It should not have any connection to speed limits, nor should it be able to choose the best route from one place to another!

If someone cannot find a good name for a thing, there is probably something wrong. If the most descriptive name they can find for something is 'Truck Route Speed Connection Interface Adapter', the design is probably getting a bit knotty! The responsibilities of a design element should be quite apparent and obvious from its name.

Some people are not very good at explaining their designs, but strangely these same people are usually good at thinking up names. If someone is having trouble explaining an idea, try asking them to draw it out and add names for the classes, relationships and maybe methods.

Larger OO projects often benefit from imposing naming strategies. For instance, you could prefix names with package identifiers (e.g. all classes in the GUI package would be prefixed with GUI, for example 'GUI_MainScreen'). This can help people to understand what is going on more quickly, and to find things in the design and the code.

The reason I've not used UML for the diagrams in this section is that if I did so, they would not be clear to every reader, as not everyone knows UML. Instead I made up my own drawings that, with a few explanatory words, are intended to make sense to anyone.

5   **Use a standard graphical notation.** There are many advantages to adopting a stable, universally understood notation, rather than trying to make up your own. UML is the obvious choice, as it is rapidly becoming the industry-standard notation – see APPENDIX 2: BRIEF INTRODUCTION TO UML if you have not come across it.

However, even if you use a standard notation such as UML you should not feel constrained to use all of it. Certainly you should not use parts that you are not confident of, or which you find confusing. For instance, if you feel that a textual note attached to a diagram can state what you're trying to show more clearly than the notation can, then use the text note. The diagrams are only worth drawing if they are going to be useful, and what matters is how well the diagrams will be understood *by the people who will use them*, not how elegantly you have used the notation.

6   **If you use a design tool, use it for maximum effect.** Make sure that the design is captured into the tool, with all the level of detail that is appropriate. As the design iterates, detail will be added, but at each stage the design in the tool should represent the current situation.

That is *not* to say that *every detail of the code* has to be in the design tool. Implementation details can be left out of the tool if they add nothing to the clarity of the design. For example, with the current generation of tools, it is usually not appropriate to put every data attribute into the design tool, instead only add those that are needed in order to understand the design, not those that are implementation details. Adding unnecessary detail actually makes the design pictures harder to understand, and it is much faster to add implementation details into the code than to go through the design tool.

Similarly, I would only add parameters of methods where these are useful as part of understanding the design. For example, in the 'paint' drawing example mentioned above, if a method `Blur()` acts on images, then it is important that the parameter is shown in the design, for example as `Blur(Image)`. But we don't need to see all the other parameters of the call if these are implementation details, and we don't need to see any parameters at all for many calls (e.g. of a standard window resize handler).

An exception to this advice is when you are creating an interface or API that will be used by other groups of developers, and providing a design model to go with it. In this case all the accessible calls should be totally described in the tool, although inaccessible calls and hidden data attributes can still be left out. The rule is: if it's useful to people when designing then it must be captured in the design tool, but if it's only of interest when coding then it should only be in the code.

Many people look forward to a time when we will have 'compilable diagrams' in software, where all the code will be written for us by the design tool. I think that will be fantastic, but in the meantime it is not possible. At present, maintaining every detail of the code in the design just causes delay, version control problems, and duplication. For now, coding details should stay in the code, and the design should be kept clean and intelligible.

7 **Get people the help they need.** At present, design is not very well taught in most universities, so if you have newly trained engineers on your team, try to get them some training and encourage them to read a book on the subject, and be willing to act as a coach and mentor whenever this is needed.

More experienced designers may benefit from reading one of the excellent 'design pattern' books (see the bibliography [SECTION 42]). But I wouldn't recommend pattern books for beginners. There is a very common tendency to use the book to justify an otherwise dubious approach, or to try to use every pattern whether appropriate or not.

If your whole team is new to OO, it is essential to gain lots of access to someone who can help and mentor you. Ideally this should be an experienced OO designer from inside your organization. If nobody is available internally, an external consultant must be brought in. This is expensive, and you will need to make a very strong argument to management in order to secure it. That argument is simple: 'if we don't get in such a person, then the project will probably fail', as first OO projects often do unless the team gets the help it needs.

Quite often, management choose a mentor and for various reasons they do not contribute much. Make sure that you make full use of any sources of help you can get, and keep them on-line all the way through the project, from the architecture stage until well into the coding. If you become dissatisfied with the help you are getting, make management aware and try to get a new mentor, don't just let it drop and try to soldier on alone.

The phrase 'middle-out' is often used to describe the way OO design and code should be done. You have to know what you have to do, the top. Now you have to know what you are going to use, such as lower-level classes or operating system calls. Now you have to match these up. Thus middle-out design. The difference between my concept of 'outside-in' and that of 'middle-out' is not very great, it's merely a matter of emphasis. I want to emphasize the importance of defining the interface first, and implementing afterwards. But I only apply the concept of 'outside-in' to the *coding* stage. I believe that *design should be done top-down*, in proper engineering fashion, and not 'outside-in' or 'middle-out'.

See also APPENDIX 3: A COUPLE OF USEFUL OO TECHNIQUES.

The outside-in approach, as described in SECTION 35: ARCHITECTURE AND DESIGN, works especially well with object-oriented projects. Code the architecture first, especially the interfaces which should be completely defined. Then add all the classes into their expected libraries and executables, implementing the basic inheritance and ownership relationships, and get the whole thing to compile. Add the detailed methods, initially stubbed-out.

Before starting to write the implementation code, write the test benches that will test the code through its interfaces. Finish the test benches before starting on the implementation of the production code.

Then as you start to implement real code, you will start to call methods (initially stubbed out) in other classes. So the job of implementation becomes one of filling in the mechanisms inside a framework of interfaces that has been put in place at the start.

The object-oriented approach relies heavily on careful design. That's not to say that a certain amount of iteration between design and coding is unhealthy, but in each iteration the coding should not start until the static architecture, the responsibilities, the interfaces and the dynamic interactions are all sufficiently well defined that the code can be written and tested without repeatedly   stumbling over design flaws.

37

SEVERAL OF MY TEAM MEMBERS WANT TO ADOPT A NEW TECHNOLOGY ON THE PROJECT // SHOULD WE USE THE NEW TECHNOLOGY OR DO IT 'THE OLD WAY'?

In any industry nowadays it is essential to keep moving forward by adopting new technology. This is true both for people and for organizations. If you stand still you get left behind. But there is also a need to adopt the *right* technologies, not to jump on every bandwagon, because many of them end up in technological dead-ends. If you commit yourself or your organization to a technology that doesn't take off, you can leave the organization with legacy systems that give it no lasting benefit but which it can't afford to rewrite, and provide yourself and your team with skills that nobody wants.

It makes much more sense to consider adopting a new technology if you are at the start of your project, or at the start of some major phase of the project, than if you're some way through it.

Sometimes a new technology is used to try to rescue a project that is well under way but is in trouble. My experience is that this very rarely works, because if the project is in trouble then it needs clarity and stability – throwing a new unknown into the mix is likely to cause chaos.

The key word for deciding whether to adopt a new technology (or rather, whether to evaluate it), is 'appropriate'. Is the new technology being supported because it is appropriate to the project's work, or because people have used it before and feel comfortable with it, or because they want it on their CV? These possibilities are not necessarily mutually exclusive of course, but you need to decide where the forces for change are coming from, in order to decide how to respond to them.

It is crucial whether the 'new' technology is really leading-edge, or is actually a fairly mainstream technology that would be new to the organization. The difference lies in the ease and speed with which problems can be ironed out. If you're *forging a new frontier* you may be the first to hit a problem, whereas if you're *joining the mainstream* there will probably be help instantly available should you run into difficulties. Being on the leading edge is always risky, but if you choose to adopt the right technology it can give you a huge leap over the competition.

Even if a technology has become mainstream, that does not mean it is bound to be appropriate for what you do. For instance, distributed object technology is probably quite appropriate if you work in internet banking, but it probably isn't very appropriate if you work in embedded motor control. Don't be persuaded to adopt a new technology just because 'everyone's using it'.

If you are being nagged to adopt a new technology, and feel like a real stick-in-the-mud for not responding positively, you should spend a little time finding out about the technology for yourself. You don't want to get bogged down in the detail, all you want to know is:

▶ *What is it for*? Often it's claimed that you can do all sorts of things with a new technology, but usually the only thing it does really well is the thing it was first invented for.

▶ *Is this a technology or a product*? Is this something you buy or is this a new concept that you can adopt? Often suppliers try to sell you a product when you actually just need an idea.

▶ *Is there a second source*? If it's a product, are there competing suppliers, or would you be bound to one supplier?

▶ *How mature is it*? Is it standardized? Is it stable?

▶ *What will it cost to adopt it*? Not just the cost of products but also training costs and the costs of the 'learning curve'.

Sometimes, it is quite clear that the technology is not appropriate. Other times, you can see that it might offer real benefits, so great that any costs involved will have been repaid by the end of the project. In these cases you should be able to make a decision quite simply. But quite often, you can see that a new technology would be worth evaluating as it might be beneficial to the organization in the longer term, but you also feel that it can't be evaluated *on your project* without producing unacceptable delays

I think that object-oriented methodologies are appropriate in nearly all circumstances. If you're still using structured coding and data flows, it is definitely time to consider OO. See APPENDIX 1: INTRODUCTION TO OBJECT-ORIENTED CONCEPTS if you're unfamiliar with OO.

and costs. You have to be quite ruthless in this situation. Your team has objectives to accomplish, which must take priority over your desire to develop people with the latest skills, and it's not your team's job to damage its own work in order to help the organization at large to go forward. It's not really being selfish, it's about achieving what you've set out to achieve for your customers. Having briefly investigated a technology and recognized that it might have value for the organization, you should bring this to the attention of management, and actively encourage them to start a small project to evaluate it. But you should try to avoid having the burden of evaluating a new technology placed onto your project, unless there is a very clear acceptance from your management and from your customers that this will be done, with all the attendant increases in cost, time, resources and risk that this implies.

If you want to go ahead and look at the technology in more detail then you need to evaluate it. You need to try it out on a fairly small sub-project or prototype that is completely self-contained and isolated from the rest of the project. Make sure that the trial addresses some real need that your organization or your project has, don't just go through a tutorial exercise. Make it clear to everyone that this is just an evaluation; if it doesn't go well, the work will be scrapped and will be re-done 'the old way'.

Keep a close eye on the evaluation, but *don't be surprised if things start slowly*; there is a learning curve to get over. After some time, probably a few weeks, you should be able to review progress on the evaluation and decide whether to adopt the new technology on the rest of the project, or to drop it. **You either adopt the technology or you don't. There is no halfway house.** There is no fallback position if you decide to adopt the new technology. If it turns out bad you will either have to limp ahead using it, or you'll have to scrap what you did so far and start again. It's a high-risk decision. In reaching your decision, take a balanced view of the likely benefits of the technology, and also the risks and costs involved (see SECTION 33: TAKING A RISK).

Always make sure that *you make a conscious decision* to adopt or not adopt a technology, never be swayed by sheer pressure of nagging alone, and never let the evaluation spread and merge with the rest of the project so that the decision to adopt the technology is made for you.

If you decide to go ahead and use a new technology, there are some things you can do to improve the chances of success:

▶ **Always evaluate a technology** before you finally decide to go ahead, as described above. Never commit to the new technology until the evaluation is complete. Never pay any money for an expensive product until you've tried it out on a limited basis.

▶ **Give the right people the right training.** Give everybody training in the basics, preferably sending everyone on the same course at the same time, as this results in people having a similar understanding of the technology, and reduces the rivalry that can occur when people try to set themselves up as 'the expert' on the team. Books and computer-based training have a role as well, but where practical skills are involved a hands-on course wins hands-down.

Get more advanced training when people are ready for it and are using the basic skills they've learnt.

Don't think that you can skimp on training by getting one person trained and then getting that person to teach the others – this never works.

▶ **Get access to an expert** that people can call up or get in to help them. This could be a guru from elsewhere in the organization, an outside consultant, or a helpful supplier.

▶ **Use only the basic features of the new technology at first**, don't try to get too advanced too soon. Only do things that you fully understand, even if you end up reinventing the wheel a little.

▶ **Be extremely careful when mixing technologies**, especially when they must work intimately together. Mixing languages, platforms and technologies in one project is becoming more common with the use of component technology and with multi-tiered approaches, but there are dangers if some basic rules are not adhered to:

- The interfaces between the technologies must be clean, clear, well designed and well documented. This is true whether it's a COM interface, a http request protocol or any other form of connection. It's likely that the two sides of the interface will be implemented by people with different skills and backgrounds, and it is essential that the interface is understood the same way by both sides. Document the dynamics of the interface – how it should be used, the expected sequences of operations – not just the static operations. Consider error handling very carefully.

In principle I'm sure this would work, if the person trained was themselves good at teaching, and sufficient time was allocated for the other people to be trained (without interruptions), and if the original trainer was available for consultation should there be any difficult questions from the new trainees. It's just that I've never known these conditions to be met.

- Test the lower-level or back-end technologies independently of the higher-level or front-end parts that use them, using independent test methods. When a problem is found, you want to be able to work out very quickly which component has the fault, as simultaneously debugging multiple languages or technologies is a nightmare.

- If possible, move all the complexity into one of the technologies and keep the rest simple. For instance, on a complex website either have very smart client-side web pages or very smart server technology, but avoid having both.

If using multiple languages, make one a wrapper or interface adapter if possible, and avoid having complex logic in multiple languages. For example, suppose you are making a web browser plug-in and you decide you need some native C++ code to do some low-level work, and that you must also have some Java for the front-end. You could either have a thin layer of C++ to do the few tricky bits, with the rest in Java; or you could have significant functionality in both languages; or you could have all the functionality in C++ with Java as a thin wrapper. These options could be drawn as follows:

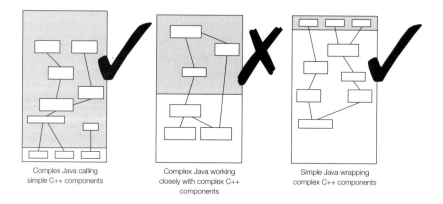

Complex Java calling
simple C++ components

Complex Java working
closely with complex C++
components

Simple Java wrapping
complex C++ components

There are very few circumstances where the middle option is actually necessary, as usually you can put all the complexity into one language or the other, but on large projects this kind of solution tends to happen 'by default', due to the preferences and backgrounds of different groups of people. This should not be allowed to simply happen; the top-level architecture should be carefully designed, with the intention of reducing complexity if possible. If your organization already has significant code you can reuse in one of the languages but not the other, it should be obvious which choice is most appropriate.

▶ **Adapt the technology to your needs**, don't slavishly follow the advice you're given and the books you've read. Do what seems appropriate to your needs, not what a purist might demand. But, don't stray too far from the well-trodden path or your chances of getting help will be greatly reduced.

As an example, suppose a company dealing with safety-critical software decides to adopt a graphical design methodology for the first time. They decide that they strongly desire a way of distinguishing those parts of the design that are safety-critical from those that are not. They may decide for instance to use a standard methodology, but to adapt the drawings by giving all safety-critical modules a red fill colour, and other modules a white colour. This is a perfectly sensible adaptation of the methodology, making a small change to add a new aspect to the drawings that the methodology otherwise couldn't clearly indicate.

But if this organization, right from the start of using the new methodology, decided that it must adapt it by using a completely different set of visual symbols and relationships from the standard, to the point that they are using the methodology in a very different way from other people, it's likely to be a mistake. Confusion is likely, and there will be ongoing costs (such as in training) to maintaining the in-house methodology. Save the tuning and the power-features until people have mastered the basics and gained experience.

Make sure that if you do adopt a new technology, you do it carefully, after consideration of the costs and risks and evaluation of the actual benefits. Everyone needs to move forward, but technology can be a minefield and you need to proceed with extreme caution.

38

THE DESIGN OF MY PROJECT IS IN A MESS // THE ARCHITECTURE NEEDS RESTRUCTURING, BUT THERE'S NO TIME TO DO IT // WHAT SHOULD I DO?

I suspect we've all been in this situation. It happens to some extent with most projects, because no matter how thoroughly you try to think ahead, you still learn things as the project progresses. Of course, the situation can get quite dire if the requirements were never properly understood, or if the original design was rushed, or if you've been forced to cut corners due to heavy time pressures.

A poor architecture reduces the efficiency of development quite significantly. Features that should be easy to implement turn out to be difficult because the architecture gets in the way, bugs that should be easy to fix turn out to be duplicated or distributed around the code, and compilation and testing often take much longer than they should. Everyone gets frustrated because they can't work out how the thing works and they keep hitting obstacles that are not of their making. People want to leave the team.

It usually works out that it *is* worth some effort to sort out an architecture that's in a mess, even though people will *tell you* that it's not possible. The time you spend will almost certainly be saved back over a fairly short interval, and everyone's morale will be given a boost.

Don't be put off by the doom-merchants who tell you everything will grind to a halt for months if you try to change the architecture. Trust your own estimates of how long it will take and how much time will be saved in the long run by the improvements.

You need to buy yourself the time to do the restructuring work, which may require you to slip deliveries in the short term, and to move things around in the plan.

If the architecture really is in such a mess that the code can't be rearranged at all without it all falling apart, this is an indication of an urgent need to do something about it, not an excuse for leaving things as they are.

Often, restructuring doesn't happen because of management pressure to keep coding. But a good team leader does not always bow to management pressure! *Decisions should be made by the people who are best placed to make them*, and for your project that means that the decision whether or not to restructure should be made by you, as the person on the spot, not by your boss. If you're confident that what you want to do is entirely within your responsibility as team leader, there may be no need to get permission from your management. You only need to involve your management if you need their support, for instance to renegotiate short-term deliveries with the customer, or to secure extra resources, or if the decision is especially risky. When you've made the decision, you should keep your management informed, but make this a low-key affair otherwise they may get nervous and start interfering where this is not required. Managers often see restructuring as time-wasting, no-added-value effort, and are opposed to it on principle. To overcome this attitude, you must make a hard-nosed commercial justification for what you want to do – see the infobar // THE BUSINESS CASE FOR REDESIGN, below.

Quite often, a team leader wants to restructure the code but it never happens because nobody else wants to – not even the other team members. This is one time when strong leadership really does pay off. Usually, if the architecture is in a mess it should be tidied up, even if this disrupts the team's work for a while. The strong team leader will be confident of this and will make it happen. It's hard to believe that team morale will improve as a result of restructuring, when the rest of the team seem to be opposed to it, but if the work needs doing then be confident that this will in fact happen.

Of course, if the primary aim of your project is to provide reusable modules for other teams, or for external customers, then the need for a clean architecture becomes overwhelming. On the other hand, if a previous version of your reusable modules is already in use, you will have to be very careful about how and when any interface changes are made, to avoid disruption to your users.

> Most customers can accept a little disruption if they can see that it improves the quality of what they receive.

There are fundamentally three approaches to doing a redesign:

1 **Coarse-grained approach** This approach is most appropriate if the detailed design and code are of high quality, but the top-level infrastructure of the project needs reworking, perhaps because it can't cope with some major new feature that needs implementing. It consists of a thorough redesign, as a group effort, followed by a period where lots of code is moved around to implement the new design.

infobar // **THE BUSINESS CASE FOR REDESIGN**

I'm a strong believer in the idea that a clean architecture is a business asset. It's worth money. If your architecture is well modularized, it will be flexible and will cope with requirements changes easily. New features can be added quickly, and it's likely that parts of your design can be reused on other projects as fundamental building-blocks. All this means less coding and faster time-to-market, hence more profit.

On the other hand, if your code is in a mess it will probably *still* be used again, not by reuse as components but by some future team taking a copy of the code and hacking parts of it around for their own purposes. This propagates and duplicates the mess and the bugs, and is not a recipe for business excellence.

It can be quite hard to prove how worthwhile restructuring is going to be. It's easy to estimate how long the restructuring will take, but it can be hard to show how much time it will save.

Sometimes you can estimate the time to be saved implementing future features, or show how much code could be reused on a future project. But often, the best that can be done is to estimate that future development will be a certain amount faster – say, 10% faster. Naturally, the more time there is remaining before the project finishes, and the larger the project team, the more worthwhile the clean-up will be.

Don't claim that some enormous improvement in productivity will result from restructuring; be very conservative in your estimates. Many managers have been promised such things before and been disappointed, which partly explains their reluctance to agree to restructuring work. Ten per cent is quite a significant improvement in productivity, equivalent to every person on your team saving half a day per week – don't go overboard on what you promise.

First, get together a small group of people who understand the project and have a good aptitude for design, and in that group decide how the design should be changed. You must be pragmatic and avoid a total redesign based on what 'would have been nice'. You have to identify the changes that are essential, given the current situation.

Make a priority of reducing dependencies and complex interactions, by breaking the design into independent and encapsulated sections. Also, try to isolate any areas that you know to be quite poor, so they can be independently tested and reworked or even rewritten.

Then get this design implemented, ideally by one or two people, no more. It's hard for more people to be involved in moving code around without getting in each others' way. The emphasis of this approach is on implementing the new design, rather than on producing cleaner code, so try to avoid the temptation to rework code as you move it, just concentrate on moving the existing code into the new architecture.

The ideal time to implement this strategy is at the start of a large phase of work, such as just after a release has been accepted, or when major new features are about to be implemented. This gives you some time to breathe, and a stable baseline to work with (and to fall back on if the restructuring is a total failure). Another suitable opportunity is if the team is reduced to just one or two people for some time; this gives you the opportunity of moving code around without having to worry about merging in changes made by other people who are trying to add functionality or fix bugs.

2 **Fine-grained approach** This approach is most appropriate where the design consists of a large number of small independent modules, or where the overall architecture is sound but the detailed design and code in some areas are poor.

The approach is to allocate a certain amount of the team's time to cleaning up and improving the design and code. For instance, you could allocate every Monday morning to it.

This approach is good if you have a boss that just wants you to keep coding or fixing bugs and doesn't care about the quality of the design, provided that the problems are in the detail and are amenable to the fine-grained approach.

Alternatively, you could decide that every time a module is to be worked on, some time is spent redesigning and cleaning it up first. This works well if your software consists of many independent units (for instance, if you have many drivers for different peripherals or hardware). The modules that get worked on the most then get the most clean-up effort.

Spend the allocated time going through the design and code, making small changes, tidying up, commenting, adding encapsulation and robustness and simplifying, to improve the details.

Remember, though, that *some people are simply not good at design*. There is no point telling someone to redesign something if they are going to add as much mess in the redesign as they remove. For this reason, it may make sense to start off each clean-up session with a design review, so that you or some other designer can help decide what is to be done.

3 **Code-centred approach** If the basic problem is that you didn't have a software architecture at all, and now everything is one tangled web, then you need to put an architecture in place. Typically, if you never did a top-level architecture, you will have:

▶ a team that concentrates entirely on code, because there seems to be 'no need' to design;

▶ lots of cut-and-pasted code;

▶ spaghetti code where everything knows about everything else and nothing can be isolated;

▶ fat modules, thousands of lines long, that do all the work (and which everyone needs to work on simultaneously);

▶ complex rules and logic that nobody is entirely confident of, implementing logic that tries to solve implementation problems and is nothing to do with the application domain;

▶ code full of special cases and 'temporary' hacks;

▶ functionality that is repeated or implemented twice, because developers didn't realize that it had already been done, or couldn't understand what was there;

▶ software that is tested only through its user interface, and with real data rather than test data, because unit testing and simulation is not possible.

A common way that projects end up like this is if they start off as a prototype, and this prototype is allowed to turn into the final code without anyone stopping to consider how it should be restructured for 'production' use.

If you find yourself in this mess, you will need to isolate functionality as much as possible and move it into modules, each with a unit test bench.

This should be done 'bottom-up', isolating fundamental low-level code first, and then restructuring the top level to use the newly modularized units. Do this stage by stage, rebuilding and re-testing as you go. At each stage, you should still have a complete, working, system. But don't use the complete system for testing, until you've thoroughly tested your new modules using test benches.

If the project has taken a code-centred approach, then the restructuring probably has to be more about encapsulating and tidying blocks of code than about design. Just try to get well-structured code in the first instance, rather than trying to switch development to a design-driven approach, which probably can't be achieved in the short term.

This does take significant time and so you will have to prioritize. Which code seems to be in the biggest mess and full of the most bugs? Try to isolate the worst parts and test them independently.

The rest of the design and code may have to stay rather more messy than you would like. Restructuring is not a job for a perfectionist, as the job is usually one of finding the worst parts and making them acceptably good, no more.

Seeing the need for restructuring and making sure that it happens is one of the ways that a team benefits from a strong and capable team leader. I once worked for an organization where the quality of code on the main product was simply dire, and this was acknowledged by everyone, including the team leader. His argument was that he had inherited the problem and there was never enough time to stop bug-fixing to put it right. To me this shows appalling leadership – the problem may not have been of his making, but as leader he was responsible for solving it. His team did nothing but fix bugs for four years (the software was later completely rewritten, after he left). Be a strong leader, not an excuse for a leader!

If you really cannot afford the time to restructure right now, at least make some notes about what you would like to do. If you know what the bigger picture should look like, then if an opportunity comes along you will be able to make some small changes that are consistent with the master plan.

People will always tell you that there isn't time to change the design. My experience is that it pays to *make the time*. You need to target particular design issues and not try to redesign from scratch, and you need to choose the right moment to act. The improvements in quality, productivity and morale can be quite dramatic.

>> TESTING AND PROJECT RELEASE

39

SHOULD I CONCENTRATE ON UNIT TESTING OR FINAL TESTING OF MY PROJECT IN ORDER TO CATCH THE MOST BUGS IN THE LEAST TIME?

FINAL TEST AND UNIT TEST

▶ In *final testing*, the aim is to use the finished product and try to identify features that are missing or not working. Final testing should take place in an environment as similar as possible to that in which the product will be used. Although test data might well be used, and sometimes other systems might be simulated, the aim is to try to break the software by using it *as a user might*. Final testing is 'black box' testing – you can't see what's in the box, only exercise it from outside.

▶ In *unit testing*, the aim is to use what you know about the design and the code to try to break it. Unit testing may be possible via the normal user interface, but more usually test beds are used, which can drive units of code directly at their calling interfaces. Often, a unit is tested in isolation, by *simulating* the effects of other units or of external systems. Frequently, sets of test data are prepared that allow the unit to be placed into a known state and then acted upon. Unit testing is 'white box' testing – you can see inside what you're testing and use debugging and other tools to watch it operating.

The following diagram is intended to illustrate the difference between the way the two types of testing are performed. The complete system is shown being tested through its user interface on the left, whereas on the right the component parts are under test using unit test benches. In this particular example, two test benches have been used to test the three units in the system – it was felt that adequate testing could be achieved this way. While units B and C are tested, a dummy piece of code simulates unit A.

Note that in both cases, both 'real' realistic data, and special test data intended to probe the limits of operation and to simulate errors, are used. Frequently, unit testing requires sets of smaller, lower-level data to test low-level code in great detail, whereas final testing often requires several examples of different types of full data sets in order to exercise the system fully and with a realistic load.

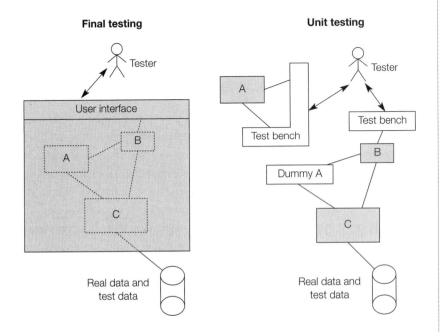

▶ *Final testing* should be based on the original requirements specification of the product. The tests should aim to simulate real use of the product. Tests that instruct the tester to follow procedures in the user manual are especially appropriate, as these test the manual as well as the software. Final test should force or simulate errors (from the user and from the operating system and external systems) as well as normal operation.

The products of analysis, such as Use Cases, are also a useful source of test scripts, see SECTION 34: ANALYSIS.

Unit tests should be based on the detailed design of the code. If the unit has a detailed specification then that should be used, otherwise the unit's coded interface should be used. Unit tests should drive the unit through both normal and abnormal conditions. The unit under test may be totally isolated from the normal system, or may still be connected to some other units, as appropriate, but the more isolated the unit is the better, since you are trying to find faults in the unit itself, not in other units or in the system integration.

The errors and abnormal conditions you should include in testing, for both final and unit testing, are those that *should* be handled by the software failing gracefully. There is no point in forcing errors that the software is not even expected to tolerate.

▶ *Final testing* should include testing by 'naïve users', who know something about the application domain but are not expert users of the software. Such people tend to use the system more as a real user might, including making the same mistakes and getting into the same confusions. They are also likely to understand (or misunderstand) the user manual in the same way as a real user. Detecting confusions and misunderstandings, both of the software and of the manual, is a valuable outcome of final testing, which can only be achieved by using a tester who has *not* been closely involved with the software development. That is not to denigrate the importance of expert users and automated tools in final test, but a naïve user should also be included, and they should be encouraged to perform some 'monkey testing' (unstructured testing, playing with the system) as well as formal testing.

Unit testing should be done by engineers. *Independent testing is much better than allowing a developer to test their own code.* One way that works well is if engineer A writes the unit test bench while engineer B implements the unit, and then engineer A comes back and does the testing when the unit is complete. This makes the unit test bench available from the start and so usable during development as well as testing, while keeping all the testing independent.

▶ Engineers will do most of the unit testing on their own machines, whereas final test is best done 'from scratch', installing the operating system and the software afresh on a machine that is representative of the user's machine. The different environments, including differences in the operating system and installed programs, plus the speed, memory capacity, screen size and so on of the hardware, tend to expose assumptions made during development that apply on engineers' machines but not on users', as well as exposing speed-related and other obscure bugs.

WHICH SORT OF TESTING TO DO

Both types of test are useful and are more than worth the time they take. You can use the differences between them to advantage, to get the most from your testing and avoid testing the same thing twice. Some projects naturally lend themselves more to one type of testing than another, but it is a sign of a well-designed project that both unit tests and final tests can be used to advantage. If a project has a good architecture then both unit testing and final testing should be straightforward, and you should do both. The two types of test discover different types of fault, at different stages of the development. See the infobar // HORROR STORIES, for examples of what can happen if you miss out either unit testing or final testing.

It's instructive to consider a couple of examples of what can go wrong if you skip either unit testing or final testing.

An example of a product that was extensively unit tested but had no final test is the Hubble Space Telescope. This machine was completely reliable – nothing broke – it just didn't work! Final testing discovers problems in use – if you don't do final test then you don't know that the product will be usable. 'Usability problems' sums up what happens when you don't do final testing, although this seems a pretty weak phrase to describe the disappointment of the astronomers when they started receiving pictures that looked like someone had smeared jam on the camera lens.

An example of a project that skipped unit testing and tried to final-test its way to success was the British High Speed Train in the 1980s. The whole train was designed and assembled, and even though there were many new technologies involved, none were thoroughly tested as component assemblies, only as part of a completed train. An example of one of the many problems was when someone noticed that all the brake units were falling apart, because the new magnesium alloy they were made of was dissolving in the special oil inside them. This was confirmed by putting some bits of metal in a bucket and shaking them around – something that might sensibly have been done before building a train on top of them. The project stayed in final test for about two years before being scrapped, and many people were fired. 'Reliability problems and constantly discovered faults' sums up what happens when you don't do unit testing.

Automated test tools save an enormous amount of time and tedium, especially for final-test. They also increase quality as they make it easier for testing to be used all the way through development, rather than as a separate activity at the end. See the infobar // **AUTOMATED TOOLS**, below.

HOW MUCH TESTING TO DO

With all tests, your approach should be to *try to break it*. Hopefully you will fail. Don't write tests that comfortably test the things you know work, and shy away from testing the limits of operation or probing things you're worried about, just to get the tests passed and 'show' that the software is good. Never take the approach 'it seems to be OK in normal use' – that isn't good enough, it has got to be *definitely* good in *all* situations of

infobar // AUTOMATED TESTING

Automated testing got a bad name years ago because the early tools available were a nightmare to use, and just couldn't cope with real, complex products that were not 100% finished and stable. But automated test tools have become pretty sophisticated in recent times and can now cope well with almost all types of project, from the web-based database browser to the real-time machine controller or the 3D graphical game. Many can simulate network traffic, database responses, and other electronic inputs, as well as user input. And gone are the days when any minor change to the user interface meant that the tests had to be edited by hand – often, test software can recognize user interface layout changes automatically.

Using a test tool has many advantages:

- You don't have to write a detailed test document for the tests that are automated; the test document only has to list the tests to be run. Many tools allow you to write comments and placeholders into the test scripts, so you can write the outline of a script up-front, before the code to be tested is written. So if you want to make test notes or produce outline tests from a document, you can do this in the form of comments to be filled in later.

- Automated tests can be run much faster than manual ones, and can be run and rerun with none of the tedium of following a document step by step.

- Automated tests can be run overnight.

- Automated testing encourages people to test more thoroughly because it takes less time – so when you make a change in one part of the code you can quickly verify that nothing else has been broken.

- Many test tools can simulate more than one copy of the software at once, so you can test systems at peak capacity, or synchronize actions to test what happens if two users try to access the same data at the same time.

- Test tools can integrate into many source control and bug-logging systems if you want them to, recording what test was run and how it failed, saving manual entry of bugs.

Many projects can't be completely tested automatically, but many engineers greatly underestimate the usefulness of these tools. If you've rejected the idea of automated testing, perhaps because of an assumption that there will be no tools available that could cope with your specialized or extreme needs, I strongly recommend you go and take a look at what is available from the specialist test-tool providers.

normal use *and* fail gracefully in error conditions. Take the attitude that 'if it hasn't been tested, then it doesn't work'. You'd be amazed at how often this turns out to be true!

Tests that pass usually don't take long. Even writing a test bed doesn't take many hours if the architecture of the software is amenable to it. It's best to throw in tests even if you think they are 'bound to pass' – frequently these tests find bugs that nobody thought it worth testing for.

Most customers expect to receive thoroughly tested software with 'zero defects', and if they find a bug they get very upset. This is a perfectly reasonable attitude and is the attitude you should presume from your customer unless you know otherwise. But some customers, especially those who are themselves software developers, are more flexible and are willing to expend effort in testing your product for you. This can save you significant time and can actually improve the quality of the product because the customer will test your work in a very different, and probably more realistic, way than you would. But be very careful not to take advantage of such a customer and use them as your free test house to perform all your testing for you. If your customer constantly trips over obvious, stupid bugs they will rapidly become annoyed by testing and re-testing your work and the relationship will deteriorate. You always need to do adequate formal testing before releasing anything outside of your project team, but with a more flexible customer you may not have to spend too much effort trying to reproduce the exact conditions of final use, as the customer may do this for you.

Usually, the first time you throughly test some code, you find bugs. You should try to complete the test set, before doing any bug fixing. Then after the bugs are (believed to be) fixed you will have to repeat some of the testing. Usually it isn't possible to completely repeat the entire test set, due to time pressures (unless the testing is entirely automated and can run overnight), and so someone – you, as team leader – must decide which tests need to be repeated. This is always something of a trade-off between the risk of late delivery and the risk of bugs getting through, and all you can do is apply your judgement, based on the nature and extent of the changes made. Sometimes you know that the changes are very localised and can be completely tested very simply, perhaps just with a single unit test case. Other times you have to decide that so many changes have been made that the entire test set must be run all over again. You have to be firm in your own judgement on this kind of issue, as there will always be pressures on you to skimp on testing.

If you skimp on testing, all that will happen is that bugs will be found later, almost certainly at a much less convenient time. If you find a bug in the test phase then at least you will have a stable build to fix it in, whereas if the customer finds a bug some time later, you may have to stop future development in order to go back to a stable build that you can put the fix into. If the customer does not report the bug until long after you have 'finished' the project and gone on to something else, you will have to set up the project development and test environments all over again just to fix one bug. You will have to take extreme care not to include recent code changes that might introduce new bugs. Having fixed the bug you will have to do another lot of testing and another release. Not suprisingly, the later a bug is found, the more it costs to fix. **Test your software thoroughly, because software gets tested very thoroughly by use in the real world.**

TEST DOCUMENTATION

As well as being confident that your product is adequately tested, you often have to justify that confidence, either to your customer or to quality assurance people, by having adequate documentation showing that the testing covered all the right things and that the tests passed.

Frequently, test specifications are derived from source documents such as requirements documents or interface specifications. It makes sense to organize your documentation along the same lines as the source documents, perhaps numbering your tests to match the source requirements, or at least cross-referencing them.

But don't let this useful traceability obscure the need for adequate testing. If test documents follow requirements documents too slavishly they tend to test the obvious very throughly, and completely fail to test subtle features added by the engineers as part of the development. Take control of the testing and ensure that it is adequate and logical, don't let a purely mechanistic approach dictate what gets tested and how.

If you are using automated tools, you may have little written test documentation, but you should still have documentation, in the tool. Use comments in the tests to describe what each test covers, and if appropriate to record which requirement or specification it is derived from.

As with all project documents, the most painless way to create test documents is to *start them early*, and keep adding to them as you go along. Not only do you have something useful earlier on, it saves the horror of writing a tedious test document under heavy time pressure just before release.

Quite often during a project you say to yourself 'we mustn't forget to test x' – if you have a test document started, you can at least jot down a note in the document there and then, and turn it into a documented test later. If you use automated test tools the concept of starting early still applies – start some test scripts early in the project, and record 'to-do' notes in the automated test tool as you go along.

Always record the results of testing, even if this just involves scribbling on the test document by hand. As well as the results, include the version of software tested, the data and time, who tested what, what machine you used for testing, and any other information necessary to enable you to reproduce and repeat the testing later if necessary. This stuff can save all kinds of confusions when you hit an intermittent, hardware-related, apparently non-reproducible or confusing bug.

BUGS THAT SLIP THROUGH

If a low-level bug gets through unit test and is only found in final test then this points to a deficiency in the unit testing, which you should put right for next time.

If a bug is found in a released product then this shows that the final testing was not adequate, as the bug should not have slipped through, and so the testing needs to be improved. It is very helpful if support personnel, to whom bugs get reported, have access to test scripts and so can point out where they need improving, or can even edit the scripts themselves.

Sometimes, a bug is found that needs to be fixed urgently, and so a patch or service pack has to be released. Often this patch is a 'branched' version of some old code base, modified to fix just one bug, without including all the latest development changes to the code. If you make such a branched patch it is essential to add a 'regression test' to the latest development test scripts, to ensure that the bug fix has been merged into the main development and doesn't recur next time a release is made. A regression test is simply a test to ensure that a bug that slipped through before doesn't do so again.

If someone finds a bug in your code, or even if they report something that *seems to them* to be a bug but turns out not to be, always say thank-you. Never grumble at people who report faults in your work, because they are doing you a service in helping you to improve your product. If someone reports something as a bug when in fact it is expected behaviour, never moan at them to 'read the manual next time' – instead, ask yourself where their confusion came from and how you could make the product more obvious in future.

FINALLY

Testing is viewed by many engineers as one of the least glamorous aspects of software development work, which is a shame because good testing is actually very difficult, surprisingly creative, and requires the best people.

You cannot allow software to go untested simply because of this reluctance of engineers to get involved in testing. Getting testing done – done by the right people, and done well – is something that requires tactful but strong leadership. You must make sure that the people who designed and wrote the software take an active role in testing it, or at least in defining and reviewing the testing, whether they like it or not. **It is part of the job of a professional engineer to do formal testing.** If an engineer wants to be treated as a professional then they must be willing to contribute to both unit and final testing.

Cutting testing to get a product shipped is almost always a huge mistake. Failing to do unit testing will result in a nightmare situation towards the end of the project, with bugs appearing constantly and progress grinding to a halt as every fault needs to be traced through a whole complex system to find its cause. This is no fun when you're under heavy pressure to deliver.

Skimping on final testing is just as bad. If, as is likely, the product ships with bugs then you will lose time and money, not save them, because you will have to make more deliveries to fix those bugs. No organization can expect to retain a good reputation if it releases bug-ridden products, and once a reputation is lost, it is very hard to regain.

40

WE'RE ABOUT TO RELEASE OUR PRODUCT TO OUR CUSTOMER // HOW CAN I MAKE SURE IT GOES WELL?

When you've been up to your backside in alligators, it's easy to forget you were there to drain the swamp.

Making a delivery to your customer is a significant event, and it needs to be handled well. Care has to be taken because small problems become big problems if they occur during delivery, or even worse if they are not discovered until after delivery.

Some time before the release you should **go through the requirements documents and make sure nothing has been forgotten**. It's surprisingly easy to forget an entire set of new features that you intended to add, if you've been busy getting existing ones to work.

As a release approaches, you need to **decide which features will be in the release and which will not**. Ask yourself, 'Allowing plenty of time for final testing, for fixing bugs found, for making the release, and for doing paperwork, how much time is left for development?' What can be finished in the time available? 'Finished' means not just coded but thoroughly tested – don't be tempted to squeeze inadequately tested features into the product.

You may not have time to deliver everything you hoped, even if everyone does overtime, and you may have to either drop features or delay the release – in agreement with your customer. If you can see you are not going to be able to deliver what you promised, don't just press on in the hope that it will somehow happen. It's far better to own up to the problem early, and so make yourself the time to complete features properly rather than fill the release with half-complete or barely tested features. If everything goes better than expected, you might be able to fit in more than you expected. This is far preferable to promising everything and then not delivering, or delivering a half-finished product. Talk to your customer because the sooner they know the bad news the better, and they will be able to advise you which issues are highest priority.

Those features that are not going to be complete and working for the release should be disabled and no work should be done on them. Let people work on something that *will* be in the release. *Features should either be finished and tested or should be removed.* Normally, customers would prefer not to see features that are not completely finished and tested. It's better to release something solid and reliable than something that has more features, but which you're scared of letting people use.

As you approach a release, the development process must become more formal. Hold a meeting of the team and make sure everyone knows what they've got to do for the release. Also make it clear that, from this point on, all bugs, concerns and issues must be formally recorded, and make sure people know how to do this. Bugs should be recorded in the bug-reporting system that you use (if you haven't got one, invent one). Other concerns and things-to-do should be recorded in some central place, where everyone can see and update them, or you could use the bug-reporting system for these items as well if it's set up for this. *Raise an item for every issue: bugs, documentation errors, things not to forget to do, everything.* Having a central 'to-do' document works well for small projects, but for larger projects some sort of database is more useful.

As the remaining features get finished, people will become free for final testing and for updating documentation and manuals. *Final testing should be quite formal,* using test documents or automated scripts based on the original requirements and on any other useful inputs (see SECTION 39: UNIT TESTING OR FINAL TESTING?). The version of the product being tested should be reproducible – it needs to be a known build that you can get back from the version-control system. Equally, the test data needs to be reproducible, as do the tests to be performed.

All problems that are found must be recorded. Ideally, developers should only test features which they themselves did not help to develop.

During testing, developers should *not* investigate or fix the bugs they find. If a test fails, the failure should be recorded and the testing should move on. *Bugs should be fixed according to the project priorities, not according to the order in which they are found.*

You will need to *call regular progress meetings*, probably becoming more regular as the release approaches – they may need to be held daily or even

In some organizations, raising a bug is a significant and public thing, and you may get censured for having too many bugs open on your project. To me this is a ridiculous situation, probably stemming from a management that doesn't understand the nature of development, as people should be encouraged to record any bug, no matter how minor. If faced with this situation I would bypass the system, and would make up my own document or database for the minor stuff and for things-to-do, only entering customer-raised bugs into the official system. It's a shame to have to bypass systems like this, but I make no apology for bypassing systems that are stupid.

See the >skills box
PRIORITIZING REQUIREMENTS
in SECTION 25:
REQUIREMENTS CAPTURE
for ideas on prioritization. One
way that works well is to rate a
bug by its *intrinsic severity*
(high, medium or low), and also
use the MoSCoW prioritization
(see Section 25) to decide how
important it is for the bug to be
fixed *in this release*.

It is quite possible for a bug to
be low significance but still
need to be fixed in this
release. For example, a
spelling mistake on the user
interface. Or bugs can be high
significance but consciously
won't be fixed in this release
(because there isn't time).

Separating the severity of the
bug itself from its importance
at this moment in time is
useful in clarifying decisions,
and it saves you from
constantly revisiting bugs that,
although important, have
already been decided to leave
unfixed in the present release.

more frequently just before the release. In these meetings you need to review newly found and other outstanding bugs and decide whether they must be fixed in this release. For those that must be fixed, prioritize them and allocate them to people to be fixed. You also need to decide how much testing needs to be repeated, to ensure that previously tested functionality has not been damaged by recent fixes.

Developers should fix bugs that are allocated to them, and test them using unit test benches and by use of the product. Nothing should go back into version control until it has passed this level of testing. This should be true at all stages of development, but it is especially important to be rigorous as a release arrives. Otherwise there is a danger that a bug will creep into a function that has already been tested and will not be tested again before release. When a bug is fixed, the fixer should record the fix into the bug-tracking system.

At regular intervals, do a 'clean build' of the software by cleaning off all source code and compiled output from a machine and building the whole lot from scratch using a known build held in version control. Follow the build manual to achieve the build (any faults in the build manual need to be raised as issues just like everything else). This ensures that the build is reproducible.

Final testing should *not* be carried out on developers' machines. Keep one or more machines free for testing, ideally of a similar specification and configuration to those the customer has. Clean the machines and reinstall the software from scratch when you test a new build so that you can be sure exactly what is being tested.

Normally, even if you use automated test tools, you won't be able to rerun all possible tests completely on every build. Instead you will have to consider the impact of the code and configuration changes that have been made, and rerun only those tests that are appropriate. Deciding which tests to rerun when software has changed is a question of balancing risks – if you reduce the testing you run the risk of obscure bugs getting through, but if you try to repeat 100% testing after every change you risk the project never finishing. You need to use your knowledge of how the software works to decide which tests to rerun and which not, according to the areas of code that have been modified.

Throughout the build-up to the release, **keep your customer and your management informed of progress**, with realistic estimates of what the release will contain and when it will be ready. If you need formal approval for the release, try to get it done in advance as far as possible, so you don't get held up waiting for a signature at the last moment. If such a signature requires all the documentation to be up to date, then get it up to date as soon as possible. The person who should work on the release documentation is the person who knows the product best and yet is least involved in bug fixing – usually you.

Eventually, the stage will be reached where the product is ready to be released. At last, the deliverables can be collected together. Make sure you can reproduce everything that is in the released package – make sure everything is identifiable in version control or by release number and that the numbers and labels are recorded somewhere so you know exactly what was released. It's a good idea to make a copy on tape or CD as well, including the source code, design, documentation and test data as well as the deliverables.

The build-up to a software release often generates extra work, long hours and stress. After a release has gone, let everyone wind down a bit before expecting the hard work to resume. If all has gone fairly well and people have been trying hard, why not organize some small social occasion, to celebrate?

Keep in touch with your customer after the release, and be ready to put right any problems that they find. Be proactive about contacting your customer; this makes a much better impression than assuming that 'no news is good news'.

After the release, spend a little time tidying up and putting things straight, archiving stuff that has become obsolete, and making a clean baseline for the next phase of the project.

If last-minute shortcuts and hacks had to be made to get the release out, make a priority of cleaning them up. Just after a release, before everyone gets back into the work again, is also a good time to consider making any architectural changes the project needs, to enable future work to go smoothly (see SECTION 38: RESTRUCTURING).

After a successful release, you should be proud of what your team has achieved. Make sure you let the team know how you feel about the product. If you get good feedback from the customer or from your management, make sure the rest of the team hear about it. If your management are not very aware of what you've achieved, why not let them know about it?

Making a successful release is hard work. Often, the satisfaction of finishing the job gets lost in the stress and the hassle. Everyone has a right to be proud of themselves afterwards, and to receive some recognition of a job well done. Play your part in helping the team to feel good about what it has achieved.

41 CONCLUSIONS

If you're new to leadership, it can be hard to let go of the details and to trust people to make their own decisions and their own mistakes, and even to allow people to do a job a little worse than you think you might do it. But it's vital to learn to let go, so that you can concentrate on the tasks of leadership.

You may have to take difficult decisions with little support. You may make mistakes and have to be brave enough to admit them and correct them. You may even have to decide to throw someone off your team, and there may be nobody you can discuss these things with. Take advice where you can, but be confident of your own decisions and take the actions that are needed. As a leader you don't have the luxury of moaning about things and expecting someone to listen, you just have to get on and make things happen yourself.

Lead from within your team, not from on top of it. Use persuasion and cajoling, gentle criticism and gentle praise, lead gently – but lead. Expect high standards on your project, and use reviews to make sure they're achieved. Never accept poor work just to have a quiet life, always get it improved.

Take control of your project. Make sure it has a realistic plan. Master its requirements and oversee its architecture. Organize people and delegate as much responsibility as you can, without losing control. Review designs and code. Keep the project tidy and organized. Do all this gently but firmly, as one of the team.

As a software team leader you must be able both to understand the intimate details of design and coding, and also to see the bigger picture, to see the development in the light of your organization's priorities and especially of your customer's.

It is vital that you make excellent technical decisions, but those decisions should be based as much on the needs of the project and its customers as on the technical issues. Don't always aim for the best technical solution, because the ideal solution is often a balance between competing needs such as those of the technology, your customers, and the people on your project.

Leading a software team is a unique position, one that involves leading other people without letting go of the mastery of technology you have worked hard to achieve. It can be stressful, tiring, frustrating. Even lonely. Even when you're doing it well you may not seem to be appreciated. But once you get the feeling for it and you know you are personally giving a significant boost to the chances of your project succeeding, you will want to keep doing it again and again.

I hope you have found something in this book that has helped you to be a better leader, and to enjoy fulfilling that unique and important role.

If you have any comments to make on this book, please visit my website at www.richardwhitehead.com

42 BIBLIOGRAPHY

I have tried to identify just a few *really good* references in each category, rather than list all the thousands of books that are available.

REQUIREMENTS CAPTURE

Mastering the Requirements Process, S Robertson and J Robertson, Addison-Wesley, 2000, ISBN: 0201360462

Managing Software Requirements: A Unified Approach, D Leffingwell, D Widrig and E Yourdon, Addison-Wesley, 1999, ISBN: 0201615932

RISK AND HAZARD ANALYSIS

Managing Risk: Methods for Software Systems Development, E M Hall, Addison-Wesley, 1999, ISBN: 0201255928

MANAGING PEOPLE

Peopleware: Productive Projects and Teams, 2nd edn, T Demarco and T Lister, Dorset House, 1999, ISBN: 0425098478

The One Minute Manager, S Johnson and K H Blanchard, Berkley Publishing Group, 1993, ISBN: 0932633439

Organization: A Guide to Problems and Practice, 2nd edn, J Child, Chapman Publishing, 1987, ISBN: 1853960144

TIME MANAGEMENT

How to Get Control of Your Time and Your Life, A Lakein, New American Library, 1996, ISBN: 0451167724

PROJECT MANAGEMENT

The Complete Idiot's Guide to Project Management, S Baker and K Baker, MacMillan Distribution, 1998, ISBN: 0028617452

Getting A Project Done on Time: Managing People, Time and Results, PB Williams, AMACOM, 1996, ISBN: 0814402844

REDESIGN

Antipatterns: Refactoring Software, Architectures and Projects in Crisis, W J Brown et al., John Wiley & Sons, 1998, ISBN: 0471197130

Refactoring, M Fowler et al., Addison-Wesley, 2000, ISBN: 0201485672

CODING

General

Code Complete: A Practical Handbook of Software Construction, S McConnell, Microsoft Press, 1993, ISBN: 1556154844

Language-Specific

Writing Solid Code: Microsoft's Techniques for Developing Bug-Free C Programs, S Maguire, Microsoft Press, 1993, ISBN: 1556155514

Effective C++ CD: 85 Specific Ways to Improve Your Programs and Designs, Software CD-ROM edition, S Meyers, Addison-Wesley, 1999, ISBN: 0201310155

OBJECT-ORIENTED ANALYSIS AND DESIGN

Design Patterns, E Gamma et al., Addison-Wesley, 1995, ISBN: 0201633612

UML Distilled, Second Edition: A Brief Guide to the Standard Object Modeling Language, M Fowler, K Scott and G Booch, Addison-Wesley, 1999, ISBN: 020165783X

Applying Use Cases: A Practical Guide, G Schneider et al., Addison-Wesley, 1998, ISBN: 0201309815

PROCESSES AND PROCEDURES

(See also the web references on the   infobar//   in SECTION 14: A GOOD JOB
WHEN PROCEDURES ARE BAD?)

Solid Software, S L Pfleeger, L Hutton and C Howell, Prentice Hall, 2001, ISBN:
0130912980

Introduction to the Team Software Process, W S Humphrey, Addison-Wesley, 2000,
ISBN: 020147719X

MANAGING YOUR BOSS

*When Smart People Work for Dumb Bosses: How to Survive in a Crazy and Dysfunctional
Workplace*, W Lundin and K Lundin, McGraw-Hill, 1999, ISBN: 0071348085

How to Manage Your Boss, K Fritz and K Kennard, Career Press, 1994, ISBN: 156414139X

STRESS MANAGEMENT

*Don't Sweat the Small Stuff at Work: Simple Ways to Minimize Stress and Conflict While
Bringing Out the Best in Yourself and Others*, R Carlson, Hyperion Books, 1998, ISBN:
0786883367

>> **APPENDICES**

INTRODUCTION TO
OBJECT-ORIENTED CONCEPTS

This appendix is very much an *introductory overview* to object-oriented design and coding (not analysis, see SECTION 34: ANALYSIS for this). This section is for you if you're new to object-oriented methods and want a simple explanation of what it all means. If you're already comfortable with object-oriented concepts, you can safely ignore this appendix.

The object-oriented (OO) approach to software development is, in my opinion, the most significant advance in software in the past thirty years or so – it is as significant a step forward as the 'structured' approach to software introduced in the late 1960s.

Just like the structured approach, OO is mostly about enforcing rules on yourself and avoiding doing things that make the software hard to understand and hard to maintain. It's not about efficiency of execution. For instance, in the 1960s most branching and looping in software was done with 'goto' (jump) statements, and it was normal to have gotos jumping backwards and forwards all over the place without any obvious flow of control. The structured approach famously declared that 'goto statements are harmful', and should be replaced by subroutines, structured tests and short loops. Similarly, global data was frowned upon, with parameter passing considered to be much less prone to confusion and unexpected side-effects. This structured code might be a little less efficient than the unstructured code – accessing global data is very fast, passing parameters is slower – but that tiny loss of efficiency is immaterial compared to the huge increase in legibility, maintainability and robustness of the software.

OO is not an *option*, it is an *advance*. Most projects benefit from using OO, and for those few that don't benefit, it does no harm.

The OO approach takes this one step further and asks you to enforce other rules on yourself. The basic rule is **encapsulate** – at a given level of granularity, a program should consist of a set of calls to 'black box' objects, objects that present us with well-defined interfaces for us to use, but which hide their implementation details from us.

Object orientation lends itself to designs made with drawings, which can represent both the fixed structure of the design, and the way it operates dynamically through time. These diagrams tend to correspond much more closely with the way people actually work when they design and code, and so tend to be more useful than the diagrams (such as data flow diagrams) that are available for structured design. One popular drawing notation for OO is UML, which is introduced in APPENDIX 2.

Object-oriented languages help you to use the compiler to enforce encapsulation, and they make object-oriented code easier to write and to read, but the approach is a philosophical one, not a language one – with some effort you can write object-oriented code in FORTRAN, C or almost any other structured language.

Early compilers for the object-oriented language C++ initially produced output in the structured language C, which was then compiled using the standard C compiler.

The fundamental unit of an object-oriented program is the *class*, which is the thing that defines an interface and that contains (hides) data. **A class is made by collecting together closely related data, and all the code fragments that implement the behaviour of that data.** Together, the data and the code define a single 'meaningful thing' that can be manipulated as a single useful entity in the software. In OO-speak, the class defines:

▶ **Attributes** – data variables belonging to a class, which may be basic types such as integers, or might be other classes.

▶ **Methods** – procedure calls or functions, depending on the language you use.

For example, you might define a 'bank account' class to represent bank accounts. It might define attributes such as the current balance, and it might have methods that can be called, such as 'deposit' and 'withdraw'. The attribute data is hidden behind the interface – you can't just come along and modify the balance in a bank account, without using one of the methods.

An *object* is an '**instance**' (one concrete example) of a class. For example, your personal bank account might exist as an object, an instance of the bank-account class. My account might exist as another instance of the same class. The class is a template for creating objects of that type. At any one time there might be any number of objects of a given class type, or there might be none. Each object has its own instances of the attribute data (its own data, its own state, its own memory), but they share the same instruction code.

A fundamental concept of object-oriented programming is that of **inheritance**. Inheritance can be used when you define a class. If you *derive* class A from class B, then class A automatically inherits (gets) all of the attributes (data) and all of the behaviour (methods) of class B. Class B in this case is called a '**base class**' or 'parent class', and class A is a '**derived class**' or 'child class'. This is useful when there is some data or functionality that is needed in several classes, as it can be defined in a base class rather than being duplicated. The derived classes can then add specific data and behaviour of their own, effectively specializing the base class for their own purposes.

For example, if we need to handle bank accounts, which may be either Current Accounts or Savings Accounts, we might choose to define a Bank Account class, from which we would derive (inherit) the Current Account and Savings Account classes. Behaviour that is common to all bank accounts (such as, let's say, calculating interest payments) would be defined in the Bank Account base class. Behaviour specific to one type of account would be defined in that derived class, for example the Current Account class might deal with 'standing orders' (automated regular payments that can only be made from a current account).

There are only three important ways in which classes work together (or '**associate**'). These are:

1 'Is a' – the **inheritance** relationship. This is where one class inherits the behaviour and interfaces of another, and *specializes* it for a specific use, as described above. Derive A from B if you can say, hand on heart, that 'A is a B'. For example, 'truck is a vehicle'.

Do not use inheritance just because some class has some useful functionality that you would like to get at easily. Only use inheritance if it makes conceptual sense. If you need to use the services of another class you can do this with one of the other types of association.

2 'Has a' – the **containment** association relationship. This is where one class contains or owns another. For instance, 'truck has a headlamp'. This relationship implies that the *lifetimes* of the objects are linked – creating a truck causes its headlamps to be created, get rid of your truck and you also lose the headlamps.

3 'Knows about' – the general or **unspecified** association relationship. This is where one class uses the services of another in some way, but the lifetimes of the objects are not linked. For example, 'radio receiver knows about radio transmitter'. The receiver depends upon the services of the transmitter, but if the receiver is switched off, the transmitter does not self-destruct.

Use the relationship that is appropriate in each case. If you are not sure, go for the one lower down the list.

One common mistake that people new to OO make is to create tall trees of inheritance with many levels, each adding a specific functionality (such as vehicle – wheeled vehicle – wheeled container vehicle – truck). This is usually a mistake, as it can make the system very hard to understand, as well as hard to test and hard to maintain. Another common error is to use inheritance where a simple attribute variable would do – for instance, in a drawing program there is no need to define a Red Circle class and a Blue Circle class and derive them both from Circle – the behaviour of the classes is so similar that the colour can simply be remembered as an attribute variable. If in doubt, keep it simple, and split the class up into base and derived classes if it becomes apparent later in the design process that some specialization is appropriate.

Block diagrams are used to structure a design. In OO, a block is called a **package**, inside which there may be other packages and classes. Packages are logical collections of related items, and don't necessarily have to correspond with physical collections such as libraries, although it is often a good idea if they do.

Beginners often get confused by the concept of **polymorphism** (see the infobar // WHAT IS POLYMORPHISM? below). Polymorphism is a useful technique – when you find a place that needs it, you will be very glad for compiler support for polymorphism. But don't go looking for places to use polymorphism just for the sake of it, use it when a genuine need arises.

If you are new to OO, beware rushing in. It takes time to 'adjust your brain' from thinking in a structured way to an OO way; it does not happen just by reading a book or two. On your first OO project, just concentrate on packaging data and behaviour together into classes, and on encapsulation. Don't try to apply fancy tricks with the concept, or with the language, until you've mastered the basics. Remember, your code is going to have to be understood and supported by other people in future, so adopt the KISS principle: 'Keep It Simple, Socrates'.

infobar // **WHAT IS POLYMORPHISM?**

Don't be put off by the fancy name, polymorphism is actually quite a simple concept, and probably one of the most powerful features of the object-oriented approach.

Polymorphism is very easy to use in an object-oriented language, but quite hard work if you try to use a structured language such as C or FORTRAN in an OO way.

The easiest way to explain polymorphism is with a tried-and-tested example. Suppose you have a drawing program that can draw various shapes such as circles, rectangles and so on. You have a drawing, which contains a list of shapes that must be drawn.

If you use polymorphism, the main drawing code does not need to know how to draw the individual shapes; this is taken care of by the shapes themselves. The specific drawing code is put in the individual objects, completely isolating the details of the shapes from the rest of the program.

The idea is that you have a basic class such as Shape, that defines (but does not implement) the drawing of shapes – it might define a Draw() method. Then you derive different classes from this. Rectangle inherits from Shape, so does Circle, so does Ellipse and so on. Each of these classes *implements* the Draw() method, to draw their own specific shape.

Now for the clever part. Your drawing can contain a list of objects which it knows are Shapes, without knowing exactly what sort of shape each of them is. The drawing can go through its list and tell each shape to Draw() itself. But the Draw method that gets called in each case will be the specific, specialized Draw() for the specific type of object in the list. So if the list actually contains a circle and a square, two different Draw methods will be called, even though the list is just a list of two Shapes as far as the drawing is concerned.

When a Shape is added to the list, the actual type of the object (for instance, Rectangle) is remembered in the program, and when the shape's Draw method is called, the appropriate derived method gets called. Using an object-oriented language, the compiler implements polymorphism for you; there is nothing special that you have to do, except to indicate that a given method should work this way.

The code that draws the drawing doesn't need to know anything about the specialized classes, in fact a new one such as Hexagon could be added later, and the drawing code would not change at all – but it would suddenly be able to draw Hexagons. All the other code that handles shapes – copying them, saving them to file, deleting them, describing them – can similarly be made polymorphic, so that none of it will need modifying when a new shape is defined. To define a new shape, it is derived from the Shape class, and the specific code for drawing, copying, describing etc. is implemented in the new class – thus it is all collected together and encapsulated.

Polymorphism removes long if-else or 'switch' blocks, and it enables related code to be collected together rather than being spread around the program.

Because OO is about structure, **if you're taking an OO approach it is ESSEN-TIAL to do some design before you code.** I've tried not to make prescriptive statements like that in this book, preferring instead to point out the available options and help you decide which are appropriate in your circumstances. But on this point I am going to be totally firm: you must design before you code if you do OO. Coding without design in OO is always a mistake, from the one-man, one-week project to the monster project. It is true even for prototypes and test benches. To me, it doesn't matter what tools you use or what notation you adopt. What matters is that everyone in your team gets used to designing up-front, and designing in OO.

SECTION 36: OBJECT-ORIENTED DESIGN gives some hints and tips on how to decide between various design options. However, if you are new to OO then **before you can be an effective leader of an OO project you will need to learn more about the subject.** There are some excellent books available; see the bibliography (SECTION 42) for a selection. In the meantime, while you are learning, it would be wise to delegate design decisions to someone who has more experience of OO. On a project using OO, it is not possible to be an effective leader of the design process, nor to usefully review designs or code, without a firm grasp of the concept.

This appendix is intended to demystify the terminology a little and allow you to understand SECTION 36: OBJECT-ORIENTED DESIGN, but for a thorough grounding you must read one of the books dedicated to the subject.

BRIEF INTRODUCTION TO UML

This section is a brief overview of uml for those that have not come across it before. If you already know something about UML then you can safely skip this section, as it is very much an introduction.

One of the appeals of UML is that it has a rich variety of diagram types to choose from, which you can use to represent different aspects of your design.

UML also incudes State Diagrams, see APPENDIX 3: A COUPLE OF USEFUL OO TECHNIQUES, and a diagrammatic notation to assist with Use Cases (see SECTION 34: ANALYSIS).

UML (Unified Modeling Language) is rapidly becoming the industry standard notation for object-oriented design. The reason is that it combines the advantages of two or three earlier, well tried and tested, notations.

UML is quite a large topic, and there are many books on the subject, so I will not try to cover the whole thing here! UML can be taken all the way to a formally proven method that allows the diagrams to be checked for self-consistency and enables code to be generated automatically, or you can just use it as a way of drawing pictures to help you think through the design, it's up to you.

I'm going to cover just two of the many diagram types that UML defines, which are enough to get you started in using the techniques, and I'll do it by way of example. Remember though that if you like what you see here and intend to use it on a project, you should make sure your whole team is familiar with the whole notation, by getting everyone some training or buying them some books on the subject (such as one of the books in the bibliography [SECTION 42]), as this is just a brief and not at all complete introduction.

CLASS DIAGRAMS

Page 323 shows an example of a class diagram. This is a diagram for part of a reporting system that prints a historical report of what jobs a system has been doing, and for how long it did each job:

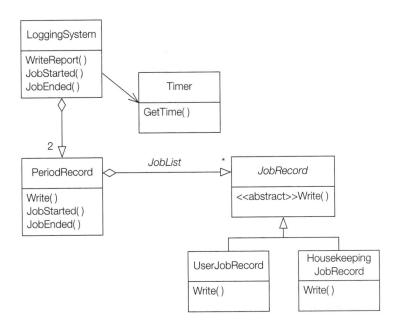

This diagram shows that there is a class called LoggingSystem, which has methods (functions, procedures) called WriteReport, JobStarted and JobEnded. LoggingSystem uses the Timer class. Each instance of the LoggingSystem *has* two instances of PeriodRecord (one of these is for recording the activity in the current period, the other remembers the activity in the busiest period so far). Each PeriodRecord *has* a list of JobRecord objects, to remember all the jobs done in that period (the asterisk next to the JobRecord class indicates 'any number', so the list could contain zero to any number of JobRecords).

The JobRecord class is a base-class for two derived classes, UserJobRecord and HousekeepingJobRecord, which *derive* from Job. The Write() method of JobRecord is abstract, and will be implemented in the derived classes. The fact that JobRecord is an abstract class is indicated by the italic font of the class name, whereas the fact that the Write() method is abstract has been shown by the *stereotype* '<>' (well, no notation's perfect). Stereotypes are used to identify when something is of a particular type or flavour that is beyond what the notation, or the tool supporting it, can represent.

The class diagram shows the relationships between classes. It is a static, structural, design-time view of the system – it does not show the state of a program at any given moment, nor the way object instances of the classes work together in time.

Sequence diagrams are still
often known by their previous
name of 'interaction
diagrams'.

SEQUENCE DIAGRAMS

This is an example of a sequence diagram:

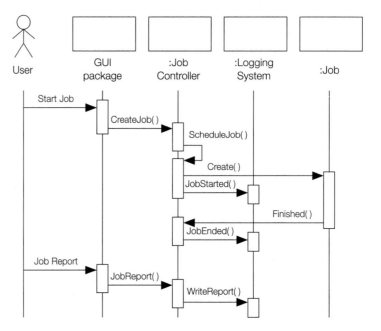

The things across the top of the diagram are objects, not classes. The User here represents a real live user of the system (sometimes called an 'actor'), whereas the other things are instances of classes with the given names (such as Job), or representations of modules that we want to consider in outline only (such as GUI).

The diagram shows the way in which these objects work together. This is a dynamic view of the system – time flows from the top to the bottom of the diagram. The arrows show one object calling another object, or in more general terms 'sending a message to' that object.

We can see that the user tells the GUI to 'Start Job', presumably by pressing a button or using a menu. The GUI tells a JobController object to CreateJob, which calls an internal routine 'ScheduleJob'. At this point the 'thread of control', represented by the vertical white rectangles, stops – the immediate processing of the user's action has finished and the CPU will be free to do other jobs.

Some time later the scheduled job starts, causing a Job to be created. When the job finishes, it tells the JobController. We can see that the JobController drives the logging system to record the starting and stopping of jobs.

When the user wants a report, he tells the GUI, which tells the JobController, which tells the reporting system. The indirect call, through JobController, is necessary to preserve the clean structure of the design. If the GUI were to call the reporting system directly, this would mess up the clean architecture that is apparent from the design – as it is drawn, we can see that the reporting system is only ever called from one place, JobController, and this means that there will be a clean and simple one-to-one class structure between the two classes. If we allowed the GUI to call the reporting system directly, we would have a more web-like structure, confusing the issues of ownership and control and making maintenance more difficult.

Sequence diagrams show the dynamics of how a system works and how its behaviour emerges from the sum of its parts. They are useful for explaining the operation of a system, and for clarifying interfaces.

These two simple diagram types are enough to get you a long way with OO design, defining both the static structure and dynamic behaviour of a system. I have avoided some of the bells and whistles, and of course there are other diagram types that are sometimes useful, but these two are enough to be getting on with. To probe further, read one of the many excellent OO books that are available (see the bibliography [SECTION 42]).

A COUPLE OF USEFUL
OO TECHNIQUES

This appendix describes two useful OO techniques that I think are suffi-ciently important that every team leader should know about them, and yet don't seem to be well described by many books or courses on OO.

1. STATE MACHINE DESIGN

This is only an introduction to state machines, so if you already know about them you can skip this section.

Whilst not as generally applicable as some other OO concepts, when used appropriately state machines can add enormously to the robustness and maintainability of a piece of software.

If you have code that is being driven by events that come from more than one source, for instance from the user and from peripherals or external systems, you can get into a mess where occasionally things go wrong due to events happening in an unfortunate order or interrupting each other in ways you had not considered.

One way to handle this is to create a controller object, into which the events feed. This controller should then have control over the rest of the system, instigating any actions that are required.

A good way to design such a controller (or event handler) is with a state machine. State machines are ideal where there are discrete events happen-ing which must be handled as they occur. State machines are very easy to transfer into code, and they produce solid, reliable code that does what the design says it will do. They help the designer consider every possible event and its correct response, in an accessible graphical way.

For example, here is a block diagram for part of a system producing web pages that display some real-time information. When new data arrives, the website must be regenerated to keep it up to date, but it is important that if data arrives very frequently, the website is not regenerated over and over again, overloading the machine – the website should not be regenerated more frequently than every two minutes. The Trigger System is the controller, responsible for deciding when to trigger the web generation:

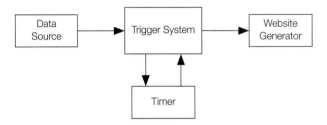

This controller has two sources of inputs (from the data source, and from the timer). These may take the form of method calls made on the Trigger System, or of messages sent to it. The controller has two outputs (to the timer and to the website generator). Again, these may take the form of method calls or of messages. In each case, each input and output could carry a variety of information – for example, the data source could inform the controller about new data arriving, about progress of downloading data, and about errors, probably as a number of different method calls or messages.

Here is an example of a state machine for the Trigger System in the above design. In this simple example, only one event from the data source, Data Arrived, has been handled:

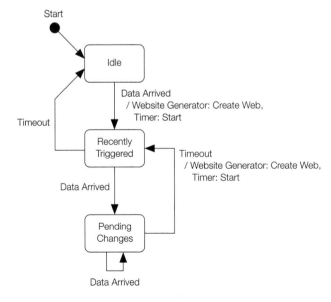

Each rectangle represents a state: it remembers the situation that the machine is currently in. Each arrow represents an event: something happening on the inputs, that may cause the machine to do something or move to another state. These are not objects, they are representations of different states of the Trigger System class. On each arrow is written the event name, followed after a slash (/) by any actions (outputs) that the machine makes as it handles the event.

The machine starts off in the Idle state, waiting for data to arrive. When data does arrive, the machine triggers creation of the new website, and also starts a timer. It goes into the Recently Triggered state.

If no more data arrives in the next two minutes, the timer will expire and the system will return to the idle state.

If data arrives within the timeout period, the website must not be regenerated straight away or the machine would be overloaded, but because the data has changed the site should be regenerated as soon as the timeout is over. The system changes state to Pending Changes to remember that it is waiting to regenerate the site when the timeout expires. When the timer expires, the system does not return to idle but instead regenerates the website as before.

The strength of state machine design comes from the way it prompts you to think through every possible event in every possible situation (every state). If an event is not shown as being handled in a given state, then it is illegal and should be trapped and handled as an error (for instance, we are not expecting the timer to time-out in the Idle state, so this would be an error). In the example above, data can arrive at any time, and so we must decide what to do if it arrives, for every state. For example, in the Pending Changes state, it simply does nothing. The ability to represent all situations and the need to handle them becomes very important in larger designs with more inputs and more states; adopting a state-machine approach forces you to consider all the possibilities, not just the most obvious ones.

Having completed the state design, it is quite trivial to convert it into code. A single variable (in our case, a variable in the Trigger System class) is set to a unique value specifying the current state. When any event happens, the state variable is tested to see what action to take, and if appropriate the state variable is changed to the new value.

As always, the implementation should be encapsulated. The state variable should be protected from being altered from outside the class. The variable should also be protected *from being read* from outside the class. The very existence of a state machine should not be assumed by external classes. In the above example, suppose that there is a user interface from which the user can explicitly cause the website to be regenerated, and let's suppose that this should not be allowed if the website was regenerated in the past two minutes – the button should be disabled. The button will of course send an event to the state machine, not control the website generator directly, but even so it is important for the user interface to reflect the current state of the system in order to provide a pleasant user experience.

In implementing this, it would be wrong for outside classes such as the user interface to find out explicitly what state the machine is in and have code such as 'if state = Idle...'. They should know nothing about the possible states, so if the state machine design is altered, nothing else is affected. What they should do is to query the system in a more generic way, for instance to ask 'HaveRecentlyRegenerated()'. Internally this method would just check the state variable, but the user interface shouldn't know that.

State machines should always be active things driving other systems, they are never passive repositories.

Make sure that all the events into your state machine interleave, i.e. don't let it be called into by multiple threads of execution, or if it must be multi-threaded then protect it to ensure that each event is completely handled and any state changes have completed, before another event can start being handled.

This has been only a brief introduction to state machines. The OO books in the bibliography (SECTION 42) cover state machines in more detail, and there are also specialized texts on the subject if you want to take a more thorough or rigorous approach.

2. SIMPLE INHERITANCE INTERFACES

This is a trick for making sure that a class is *independent of its user* (see 'general design golden rule' number 2 in SECTION 35: ARCHITECTURE AND DESIGN), *even when it must call its user back with asynchronous information.*

For example, suppose you are making a small tool for parsing a special type of file. You have a class whose job it is to get data from a disk file. While it's doing this, the user should be kept informed by a progress indicator that moves along the screen.

This section is concerned with using abstract classes to define bi-directional interfaces. If you are already familiar with this concept then you can safely skip this section.

The easiest way to code this would be to let your file reader class call the user interface class directly every time it has read some data. This is shown in the following diagram:

The arrows on this diagram represent instances of one class calling another.

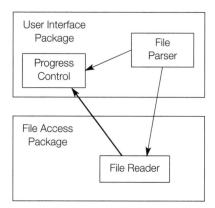

But surely it is not the responsibility of a File Reader to know anything about user interfaces? A File Reader should be responsible for reading files, no more and no less. It should not even know the class name 'Progress Control'. This is a poor design.

This is a bad design because the internal names and structure of the system *using* the file reader are assumed by the reader itself, which will make the design difficult to maintain and test. The File Reader should not know about who is using it, it should just do as it is told.

But the reader is an active class, needing to notify its user, in another package, about something it has done. How can it do this without knowing exactly whom it is supposed to notify? In a structured program we might 'register a callback function' – provide the address of some code that should be called to report progress – but this doesn't fit in well with an object-oriented approach – exactly which *object* is to be notified, and how do you guarantee that the object exists when the caller wants to call it?

There is a simple way round the problem, by splitting off the interface into its own class:

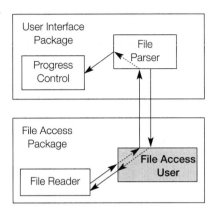

The file-reading class has been hidden inside the File Access package, hiding behind an interface called File Access User, which is all that can be seen from outside the module. This File Access User class is an *abstract interface class*, defined only so that it can be derived from.

The File Access User class does have a tiny bit of implementation code – calls to the File Access package (in this case, from the File Parser) are made on the File Access User class, and the implementation of these calls simply calls the File Reader.

This design has also been drawn in UML for those familiar with that notation; see the `infobar //` **ABSTRACT INTERFACES IN UML** below.

The File Reader class needs to tell someone about its progress, so it tells *whichever class is derived from* File Access User. It knows about the File Access User class as a name, but it doesn't know anything about the world outside the file access package. In the example above, File Parser has been derived from File Access User, and it is File Parser that will get called by File Reader.

Calls to the reader, and call-backs from it, are routed via the interface class, so the actual user (File Parser in this case) only sees the interface. The implementation could totally change in future, indeed the File Reader class might be designed out and be replaced by something else, but the caller will not be affected. This makes the design much easier to maintain. Equally, nothing in the File Access package knows anything about File Parser. The system is completely isolated, which adds robustness to the system design and enables flexibility to changes.

Testing of the File Access package has also been simplified. The package can be tested by deriving a test class from File Access User and calling the methods defined in its interface.

It is conceptually sound for the using class (File Parser in this case) to be derived from the interface class because it *is* a File Access User.

The solution presented here could also be called an 'object-oriented callback mechanism', since it provides a way for classes to call their owners asynchronously. However, I believe that this approach goes further than defining callbacks because the interface class defines the whole interface to a system, both calls and callbacks, and so I have used the term 'inheritance interface' rather than 'callback mechanism'.

infobar // **ABSTRACT INTERFACES IN UML**

For those used to UML, the example solution diagram is redrawn in UML notation here. First the two packages as an overview:

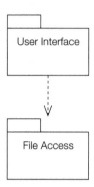

Now the details of the File Access package. I have added the method calls. ReadFile() is called to start the reading of a file, which will simply call Read() on the File Reader, and OnProgressUpdate() is the virtual method that is called back when progress is to be displayed:

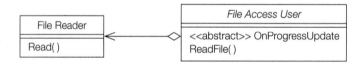

Finally the User Interface package, showing that the File Parser is inherited from File Access User and implements OnProgressUpdate:

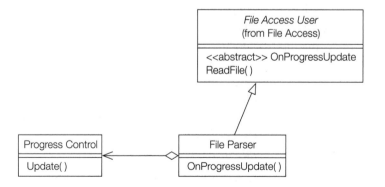

Using this trick has made the reader *independent* of its user, and has also solved the problem of poorly defined *responsibilities* in the design. The progress control is responsible for displaying progress to the user. The file parser is responsible for parsing files, for which it uses the file access package. The file access user defines an encapsulated interface for the file access package. The file reader is responsible for reading files. It's all clean and simple – and if you code it, you'll find that the code comes out clean and simple as well.

This trick is appropriate where you have an interface that you want to expose, which defines both calls and callbacks, and you want to keep the details of implementation entirely hidden. It is also very useful at points where you want to do unit testing. A typical example would be for the interface of a library package.

Component object technologies such as COM and CORBA take this process one stage further, allowing an object's interface to be queried at run-time. Such technologies are appropriate at the system level, where components expose interfaces intended to be used by any client that needs them (now or in the future), whereas the abstract interface described in this section is appropriate at a lower level in a design where it is acceptable for the system to be recompiled when the interface changes.

One problem with the interface style as presented here is that it is difficult to use more than one instance of each interface; for example it would be difficult for File Parser to use two File Readers. For advanced readers only, the solution to this is to make the interface class into a 'class factory', manufacturing worker objects as they are needed, each one calling back through the single interface.

INDEX